FREEDOM
JUSTICES
CHANGE
The Gospel

JAKO DEPO

ISBN 978-1-967362-32-5 (paperback)
ISBN 978-1-967362-33-2 (hardcover)
ISBN 978-1-967362-34-9 (digital)

This book is composed of two documents; the first book is called Freedom, Justice, Change, Challenge, & Peace. The main book is accompanied by bonus material, which is entitled Feelings & Opinions. Rather than debating about politics or threatening violence or insults against individuals, the book discusses the author's feelings, thoughts, and opinions about certain aspects of society. It draws upon the genuine life experience of the author, his acquaintances, and famous examples. Since we live in a democratic country, we have the freedom of speech and the right to express our opinions. Please keep in mind that, as the author, I am not trying to cause any disturbance with the government, police, or military of any country. Rather, I am only sharing my opinions with the public. My overall goal involves changing the world to make it into a better place for everyone. Everyone can make a small contribution by changing his/her own attitude and behavior. Accordingly, this book aims to educate people about the world and inspire people that they can make changes. We want people to stand up for themselves and realize their freedoms and articulate their rights. This way, everyone will be happy.

I want to acknowledge the contributions of my friend, and share his opinions, feelings, thoughts, and experiences about the various subjects discussed in this book. He provided examples from his own life experiences as well as those of his friends, family members and acquaintances. His contributions provided additional interest and inspiration for the creation of my book. Furthermore, my friend provided much of the material in the following chapters: Immigration Law, Police Force, Life Experience, Police Brutality and Afro Americans are Victims of the Police. These chapters represent my friend's opinions and life experiences in such matters. In addition, other friend shared his opinions in the chapter, Donation Organ, These other chapters Homage for Ms Marie Misamu, Resurrection for Ms Marie Misamu, represents my other friends, Message for RDC (Congo), Homage For A Friend and Why Congolese People are Silly represent my friend Government Member of the KKK and Race War and Plus Police Brutal represent another friend and the last Chapter New Ideas Dialog Technologic Represent another friend in my bonus book, Feelings & Opinions. Besides these six chapters, the rest of the chapters were written from my perspective. Without God's inspiration, I couldn't have written this book and published it for the entire world to read. God sent me to this Earth to speak the full truth about people's rights and freedoms. With God's help, this book is intended for the benefit and the full deliverance of all of mankind. This book will help people to change their lives and inspire them to success. As the creator of mankind, God is the Supreme Being over and above all of his creation, including mankind. God loves us and we should respect and honor Him by making Him a priority over everything else.

Anyone who wants to contact us and ask questions with respect, we will answer all people, including the Congolese citizens, Congolese journalists, the rest of all other nations' citizens and all other journalists in the whole world. Here is our email jakodepo10@gmail.com

Contents

Bonus Book (Feelings Opinion)

Dangerous Animals and Insects

Animals and insects occur everywhere in the world: deserts, water bodies, and forests. People encounter animals and insects during all human activities, including camping, national parks, swimming, and travelling by roads. People should be aware of the presence of animals in their local area or while travelling. If a place is safe for local people, then it should also be safe for travelers; however, if dangerous animals or insects are present, people should avoid that area. In many instances, these areas are illegal due to the presence of dangerous animals. Some of the dangerous animals include the following:

- Large cats, such as leopards, panthers, cougars, jaguars, tigers, and lions
- Simian species, such as monkeys, apes, baboons, gorillas, orangutans, and chimpanzees
- Reptiles, such as large snakes, crocodiles, alligators, and lizards
- Marine species, such as sharks, octopus, electric eels, yellow fish, starfish, and water snakes
- Other land animals, including coyotes and eagles
- Insects, such as ants, red ants, bed bugs, lice
- Disease-carrying rodents, such as rats, moles and mice
- Mammals such as bears and rattlesnakes

Most dangerous animals live in countries with warmer climates since they can survive more easily in these climates. Many animals and insects have lived in certain countries for a long time. When the Europeans explored and took over these places, the dangerous animals stayed in these places. If people don't want to remove these animals and insects, the government should make laws to protect people from these species. Also, people can build tall and strong gates of about 180 meters with electric protection to defend against the wild animals. These fences should be constructed throughout the entire country of Canada and the entire world, making it difficult for dangerous animals to jump or break the fences. Normally, harmful animals and insects don't live in cities, towns, and villages; however, some urban areas are close to forests and other places where wild species live. If animals are hungry, they will wander into urban areas and attack people. Since children are small and weak, animals generally target these individuals. People should be able to own registered weapons in order to protect themselves from wild animals; however, these weapons should not be used to commit crime, such as murder. In order to register a weapon, the government should ensure that the owner lives near dangerous animals or insects. People have a right to kill dangerous animals only if the animals threaten or attack them or another person. However, people should not kill innocent animals, and people that live in a safe place should not be allowed to own weapons.

In addition to erecting high electric fences, the government should also institute more security in public leisure areas such as water bodies, beaches, and camping grounds. Although people have varying opinions on the issue of animal control, most people agree on the importance of increased safety around dangerous species. While the cost of additional security may entail high expenditures, governments still need to follow through with this plan. Taxpayers fund government initiatives, so people should have a say in how the government spends their money. Most people consider safety and security as an important issue, so the government should use some of the tax money to protect people from wild animals and insects throughout the world. These measures will ensure that the animals won't threaten or attack people, which will make people safer and happier. Some animals are dangerous while others are safe; the government protection measures should only target dangerous animals and insects. These measures don't necessarily mean that people will intentionally bother or kill animals; they just protect people in cases that animals want to attack or harm them. The objective involves protecting people from attacks while leaving animals and insects alone. If the animals are stopped by the fences or by other security measures, hopefully they will leave people alone in the future. Furthermore, people shouldn't bother dangerous animals or insects because these creatures can harm people.

If people tell other people, such as their friends and family members, about implementing protective measures against these dangerous animals and insects, they may get offended because they believe that under no circumstances should people hurt animals. Another problem of warning people about dangerous animals involves the idea of frightening people, causing panic and stress about these creatures. However, people should realize that these protective measures are only for their own rights, freedoms, and safety against dangerous attacks, especially when travelling on roads or in foreign countries and engaging in leisure activities, such as camping. These protective measures help both human beings and animals; they protect humans from harm while ensuring that animals are still treated fairly. While these safety measures are meant for defense, they don't give people permission to treat animals or other human beings badly. All human beings, animals, and insects need to be provided with rights and given equal respect. For example, people shouldn't intentionally allow animals and pets to starve. Animals need food more desperately than humans; while humans can last a day or more without food and water, animals would die without these nourishments, and require daily care, which involves clean and disease-free food and water. If animals always have sufficient food, people won't need to worry about attacks because the animals and insects won't need to attack humans for food. Moreover, people can also spend more time with animals to ensure that they aren't bored, especially when people own pets. When animals are bored, they become destructive and may even attack humans. Although most people have very busy lives, they should still spend more of their free time with animals, including their pets, farm animals, and zoo animals. People need more training and education on how to interact with animals and how to ensure their own safety with different species. People who lack knowledge about animal behavior can get attacked or even die from a wild or domestic animal. If individuals understand how to interact with and treat animals while ensuring safety measures, animals will likely leave people alone and refrain from attacking them. Although wild animals can never live with humans because of different living requirements, improved safety and training will allow humans and animals to coexist in similar areas.

In Canada and other parts of the world, there are several animals that are prohibited as pets. A few examples are listed below:

- cougars
- leopards
- baboon
- panther
- jaguar
- gorilla
- crocodile
- tiger
- wolf
- monkey
- hippopotamus
- lion
- coyote
- chimpanzee
- rattlesnake
- jelly fish
- snakes
- bears
- lynx
- mice
- rats
- mosquitos
- ants
- lizards
- alligators
- sharks

These animals are all prohibited from use as pets because they are dangerous to people. Many apartments and condos ban these animals, and, even if a person owns their own house, national, state, or provincial laws can prevent them from owning dangerous animals. International laws also prohibit people from bringing dangerous animals and insects from one country to another nation. In particular, laws ban people from transporting from hot, tropical countries to Canada. When people own dangerous animals, the neighbors have a right to complain about this situation. In this case, the government should take their pets away and also take away their right to own any animals in the future. Also, people that own illegal animals may have to appear in court and potentially face a prison sentence. People that can't obey the law and rules should be held responsible and should go to jail for inappropriate and illegal behavior.

People shouldn't own dangerous animals and insects because these animals do not make appropriate pets. Some people see an animal and want to own that animal simply because of its appearance or other factors that make it desirable. While some people avoid large animals because they believe that bigger animals are dangerous, small animals can also represent a threat to safety. Individuals perceive animals as "babies" or children, especially in the case of smaller species. However, people misunderstand the nature of these animals, as many of them can be dangerous to both the owner and to other people. While some individuals argue that they have the right to own any animal, they don't have this right, as they are endangering the safety of other people. Furthermore, some people believe that dangerous animals are harmless as babies or young animals, as many of these breeds lack the desire or capability to kill. These individuals think that they can treat wild animals well and raise them as harmless, domestic animals. However, once wild animals grow into adults, they will kill or attack people because it is in their nature. Therefore, people need to realize that they can't use dangerous animals as pets. These animals can turn against their owner or hurt other people, which is why it is illegal to own these animals.

Many individuals have died as a result of wild animals. For instance, one Canadian man and woman were eaten by bears. Also, an American child was killed by a baboon, a woman was attacked by a gorilla, and an older person was attacked and killed by a chimpanzee. In Nova Scotia, two boys were killed by an African boa snake. The neighbor, an older lady, owned a pet store for wild animals. She was charged because her ownership of these pets was a criminal offense and she was responsible for the death of two boys and their mother, a young woman. Even if a person doesn't directly murder someone else, their possession of a wild animal that kills another person still makes them responsible for their deaths. The older lady had brought a snake into Canada and raised it from childhood, thinking that it was harmless. However, her decision was wrong and had major consequences. Regardless of a person's color or nationality, most individuals require more experience with wild and dangerous animals in order to avoid making the mistake or interacting with them, transporting them, or owning them.

There are some pets that people are allowed to own, such as dogs and cats. However, some of these animals are still dangerous. Unlike humans, animals lack the ability to distinguish between right and wrong. Owners are responsible for treating their pets well and raising them properly so that they are not dangerous with other animals or people. Pet owners should treat their animals with respect and provide them with the same rights as other human beings. Responsible pet owners need to provide their cats and dogs with sufficient food, water, and shelter while keeping them free of chemicals that can harm them. If pets are treated well, they will behave acceptably with other people and refrain from attacking those individuals. However, pet owners also need to ensure that they train their dogs not to attack other people, which is illegal. If people's pets attack someone else, the owner will go to jail and the pet will be put down. The owner will also have to pay the victim's medical bills and insurance costs.

In some countries, provinces, and states, housing and apartment laws prohibit people from owning certain breeds of dogs, such as the following:

- German Shepherd
- Husky
- Boxers
- Rottweiler
- Pit Bulls

These dogs are illegal in some areas and apartment complexes because they pose a threat to the neighbors. If people own these dogs, they will still have to face a penalty, such as a fine, a jail term, or the loss of the pet, even if the dogs haven't hurt anyone.

People can own dogs as long as they aren't considered dangerous. Many people have been attacked by dogs, especially in the United States. In particular, small children have been attacked by dogs, such as pit bulls, German Shepherds, and Rottweilers. Many people from other cultures outside of North America are afraid of dogs, especially dangerous breeds. They won't visit a person's house if a person owns a dog because they are afraid that they dog will attack them. People should be understanding of individuals from different cultures and refrain from taking offense if they don't want to visit a person with a dog. In addition, parents should protect their children from dogs and should never leave a child unattended with a dog, regardless of whether or not the animal is dangerous. Animals are not like humans and may attack a child or infant at any time, so dogs cannot necessarily be trusted alone. Similarly, parents shouldn't leave their young children or babies alone and unattended in a vehicle, especially with a pet. Parents need to take responsibility for their children and to avoid leaving young children unattended or unsupervised. When parents get old, their children will take care of them, so parents need to respect their children and provide them with good treatment and equal rights. In many cultures, people believe that their children are extremely valuable because children will care for their parents and bury them when they die. When children are adolescents, teenagers or adults, parents can leave them in the vehicle with pets because the pets are well-acquainted with these individuals and pets don't usually target adults. Additionally, parents are no longer legally responsible for their adult children, so parents can leave these individuals alone in the car with pets.

Conservation officers are individuals that protect national parks, forests, camps, deserts, beaches, rivers, oceans, and other parts of nature. These individuals enforce the rules in these areas, which involve booking appointments or asking permission to visit these areas before spending time in such parks. In some cases, individuals need to register with the government so that they can legally inhabit these areas on a short-term or long-term basis. However, when people encroach on these conservation areas and stay there without permission, they are committing an illegal action and may face a penalty. People need permission in order to engage in leisure activities, such as swimming, hiking, or camping, in conservation areas.

People should respect nature and avoid harming or vandalizing natural areas. For example, some people cut large plants or trees for their own use. These individuals destroy nature and harm the surrounding environment with their actions. In these cases, people may be charged because harming nature represents an illegal action. Conservation officers should respect people as long as individuals respect nature. Specifically, officers are allowed to shoot only if they feel as if they or another individual are seriously threatened by another person or animal. In that case, they can defend themselves or the other person in order to save their lives. However, if a person doesn't represent a serious threat, then the conservation officer shouldn't shoot at a person or animal. This action will cause them to lose their job due to the illegal nature of their actions. Conservation officers have been well-trained by the government in order to protect nature and people from threatening situations or direct attacks. Just as in the case of bad police officers, there are also bad conservation officers who will hurt a person when it is not justified.

Healthcare

Healthcare represents a positive aspect of society because it allows ill people to obtain medical treatment to cure their sickness or disease and improve their health. Countries have two types of healthcare: private healthcare and public health-care. Societies should have a combination of both types of health care. Public healthcare allows everyone to obtain basic medical treatment, including the poor people. Not everyone has enough money to pay for the dentist, doctor, hospital, and optometrist. Rich people can access private healthcare for extra treatments or services, but everyone should have access to basic care.

While wealthy people and doctors will complain about losing money to public healthcare, there are many other ways to make money. Regardless of financial status, everyone on this earth is a human being and we all need medical care. Some Republicans and wealthy individuals believe that soci-ety exists in a social hierarchy and that rich people are bet-ter than poor people and thus more deserving of basic needs such as healthcare. However, these people fail to recognize that all humans deserve equal rights and respect, and, despite their lesser means, lower income individuals still require healthcare.

Most people prefer public healthcare because people that are sick or injured and require the services of a physician need adequate treatment in a timely manner. People don't like to wait for a long time in emergency rooms, for specialist appointments, or for surgery. However, people with serious injuries from accidents, people with major diseases, or vulnerable populations such as pregnant women, children, and the elderly should be able to receive free medical treatment. In order to ensure that people receive adequate medical care, the government should hire more doctors and pay them well to ensure that they perform their jobs efficiently. The addition of more doctors will ensure that people don't wait too long to receive the appropriate care. When someone waits too long for treatment and their conditions worsens or they end up dying, they can sue the medical system because the inability to provide timely and effective medical care is against the law. Doctors and other healthcare professionals can't ignore people because they can't afford to pay for private healthcare. This will cause people to become very upset, especially friends and family members who lose a loved one because they can't afford medical care. Although doctors have some responsibility for this situation, the government is mostly responsible because they should ensure that medical practitioners and health care workers follow the law. Patients can also take care of their own situation by making sure to book appointments early and make sure that they deal with their condition as soon as it develops.

Many countries have a public healthcare system, including European nations, Australia, New Zealand, and Canada. This system allows everyone in the respective countries to see a doctor or to obtain medical treatment without incurring significant costs. Under this system, the government pays for healthcare treatments. While many aspects of public healthcare are free, such as physician visits and hospital care, patients still have to pay for their medications. In some countries, the government pays for medicine, but in other countries, patients have to pay for their own medication.

Other countries have a private healthcare system, including the United States. In these countries, individuals have to pay for their healthcare, including physician visits, hospital treatments, and medication. In fact, under privatized healthcare systems, patients have to pay more money for their medications than patients in public healthcare systems. Privatized healthcare systems prioritize monetary gain over people's health, whereas in countries in public healthcare, the government prioritizes people's health over financial benefits. Governments should consider all citizens as human beings and respect their health in the same way that they regard their own health. Tom Douglas, a Scottish-Canadian politician, first introduced the idea of universal health care to Canada. Prior to his proposal, Canada had implemented privatized healthcare like the United States. Canada initially balked at Douglas' proposal for public healthcare, leading to violent protests and demonstrations over healthcare in Canada. Doctors felt concerned that the introduction of public healthcare, or, as Douglas called it, Medicare, would cause a significant loss in their personal income. As a result, the Canadian government took several years to implement Douglas' suggestion of public healthcare. This implementation was delayed because of selfish government officials, doctors, and wealthy individuals that protested Medicare; these people were corrupt because they only cared about their own personal gain and didn't respect the wishes and needs of other individuals. Their mentality led to violent protests, war, and other problems due to their selfishness.

However, the Canadian government eventually realized that healthcare represented an essential basic need to which all Canadians were entitled. While the idea of public health-care originated in Saskatchewan, as Douglas had been the Premier of that province, the law applied to all of Canada. The government admitted that Tom Douglas was right and he won the election. Although many people believed that Canada would never offer public healthcare, Douglas' work enabled Canada to adopt public healthcare, which Canada still offers. Public healthcare provides Canada with a signif-icant advantage over other countries because healthcare rep-resents a major priority. As a result, Canada has an excellent healthcare system with many capable professionals, such as doctors, nurses, and other providers as well as many students taking medical courses in colleges and universities. Students that obtain a diploma, degree, or certificate in healthcare have access to an excellent job and a good life. Many gradu-ates of medical programs receive jobs and there are currently shortages in Canada for nurses and physicians.

In the United States, their healthcare system is privat-ized; however, the current President, Barack Obama, has won two elections in a row because of his proposal for bet-ter healthcare. He wants Americans to associate him with improved healthcare. While some people agree with his sug-gestions for improved healthcare, other people disagree with him; however, in some cases, people dislike him only because he is black. Most Americans have been brainwashed by the Republicans, who believe that healthcare is a privilege rather than a right, and they want to keep healthcare privatized and in the hands of the rich. North American nations, especially the United States, are among the wealthiest nations in the world, so they shouldn't make excuses about not having suf-ficient funds for healthcare. People pay taxes, which should go towards healthcare. Taxes provide the government with money, so the government should use the taxpayers' money wisely and on appropriate expenditures such as healthcare. Medical care represents one of the most important priorities, so the American government should allocate some of their tax money towards this area.

Employer Character

People can apply for jobs in a variety of ways, including in-person, mail, or online. Once people have applied for a position, they have to wait to see if they get an interview. Even when an individual obtains a job interview, they still may not get the job, because employers interview many different candidates for the position. Everybody hopes to obtain a position or career because jobs are necessary for survival. Job interviews cause many emotions for candidates, including stress, nervousness and fear. However, candidates should control their emotions during the interview process because the interviewer may perceive their emotional reactions in a negative way, resulting in their failure to obtain the desired position. In addition to controlling their emotions, job candidates should also dress appropriately. Men shouldn't dress like a rapper or a gang member and women should avoid wearing revealing clothing. For instance, women shouldn't wear shorts or very short skirts with high-heeled shoes. Rather, candidates should wear simple but professional attire without graphical designs in order to show respect for the potential employer. While interview dress codes depend upon the company and the industry, most employers prefer candidates to wear dress shirts, except in the case of trade positions, where simple attire is preferred. In addition to clothing, interviewees should also ensure that they have extra time when travelling to the interview so that they don't show up late. Candidates should also plan and practice for the interview by anticipating possible questions and researching or preparing answers to those questions. Although the process for obtaining a job is becoming increasingly difficulty, job search candidates should still make an effort to get the position.

While job candidates and employees should respect their employers or potential employers, employers should also show respect towards their employees. There are several laws regulating appropriate employer behavior. For instance, employers are not allowed to ask employees about their Facebook information, including their profile or their security code; however, employees should never lie to the employers and tell them that they don't have Facebook. Employers can check the Facebook profile of employees in order to check information about the employee. If the employer discovers something on the Facebook profile that they don't like, they will make an excuse not to hire that person. Other bad excuses that employers make not to hire someone may involve factors such as their skin color, nationality, gender, culture or religion. However, this discriminatory behavior is wrong and against the law.

In addition, employers are prohibited from asking candidates about their marital status unless the employee becomes hired. It's illegal to ask interviewees about their private life or to ask them confidential questions such as whether or not they have had sex. Most people don't want employers or other individuals to know about their private life during a job interview. Employers can ask candidates questions about the job or company and about the person's work experience and candidates can volunteer information about themselves. Another mistake that people make is that they assume they can shake hands with or hug a person only of the same gender. This behavior is sexist, resembling discriminatory behavior that treats people differently because of their color, nationality, race, religion, or age. For example, a man shouldn't care about the background or demographic status of a particular person; he should be able to hug or shake hands with another man or woman without worrying about getting into trouble or getting insulted. In Canada and in European nations, some people assume that because a man or woman talks to, hugs, or shakes hands with someone of the opposite sex that they have a romantic interest in that person. However, just because a man talks to or touches a woman in a non-sexual way, he doesn't necessarily have a romantic interest in her. This behavior doesn't indicate that the person initiating touch is demonstrating illegal behavior. As long as an individual respects the boundaries of another person, they are acting within the law. Gender shouldn't matter and neither should other aspects, such as race, religion, culture, or age. Also, a person's employment status or ranking shouldn't matter in this case; if an employer shakes a person's hand or hugs them, the candidate or employee should return the greeting. Some people may think that it's not appropriate for an employer to behave in this way and that they won't get hired if they return the greeting or fail to return the greeting; however, this shouldn't matter. Also, a person's gender shouldn't matter, as men and women should be treated equally and with equal respect. Employers and employees should respect people's genders, ages, culture, religion, and nationality by treating all individuals equally and by refraining from harassing or insulting other people.

When employees are working for a company, they need to respect the rules of the company and their superiors:

- Always show up at or before the scheduled start time. Do not show up late.
- Always work hard and get the job done as quickly and efficiently as possible without being lazy
- Take your time and do the job properly
- If you don't understand how to perform a job or task, ask someone rather than making assumptions and doing the job incorrectly
- In the beginning, jobs can be difficult depending on the position. However, you shouldn't give up because, over time, the job gets easier.
- The company should train their employees regardless of the amount of experience an employee has accumulated in that particular industry
- The company should focus on safety and train employees to work in safe ways that avoid dangerous situations. When employees receive serious injuries or incur accidents, the company is held responsible.
- All employees will make mistakes at times, but employees should learn from their mistakes and avoid repeating them. Employees should also make a serious effort to avoid mistakes by following proper procedures.
- Co-workers should respect each other. They should avoid insulting and fighting with one another. In these cases, someone may get suspended or lose their job. The person responsible for initiating the insulting and fighting should lose their jobs.

- The employer, supervisor, or manager should respect employees and employees should respect their superiors. However, the employees should respect their bosses because they have authority. Employers should refrain from arguing with, insulting, or disrespecting their bosses.
- The employer shouldn't treat the employee badly or differently because of their skin color, religion, race, nationality, sex, age, or ability level.
- The employer shouldn't abuse, harass or insult their employees by screaming at them, embarrassing them, or putting them down in any way. Regardless of the salary that the company pays, the employer should treat employees with respect.
- Employers should treat employees equally regardless of their employment status, whether the employee is full-time, part-time, temporary, or volunteer.

Employers can't fire an employee for no reason or treat an employee very badly over a small mistake. Employees do their best, and employers should respect their efforts and believe their employees' explanations. The employer can only fire an employee if they made a major mistake, refused to work, or did something illegal. When employees are sick, have an appointment, have an emergency or have to deal with a government issue, they should get a note for their employers to prove that they didn't intentionally miss work. If employers have proof for their absence, they shouldn't get in trouble with their boss. Most companies treat their employees fairly well, but some companies mistreat their workers. Occasionally, employers in public or private companies are criminals and will kill their employees.

In cases where employees feel as if an employer has mistreated them, they should respect the following rules:

- Do not complain or report the employer unless it is a serious offense. For example, employees shouldn't complain about their salaries or about minor things. The employer can lose their job, or, if they are the business owner, they can lose contracts or customers.
- Do not argue or fight with the employer because they have the ultimate authority. In some cases where employees try to attack or insult their employers, the employers may take a gun and shoot them.
- If employees don't feel comfortable in a job, they can quit the job and look for employment in another position or with another company. When employees leave a job, they should do so respectfully and nicely without insulting people or causing trouble.

During a job interview or during a temporary position, employees should work hard and respect their employers if they want to be hired permanently by the company. Even when workers are on probation during the first year, they should avoid asking the employer certain questions or they should avoid asking the employer to hire friends or family For instance:

- How much do you pay or how much are you going to pay me, my friend, or my family member?

- When are you going to hire me and/or my friend or family member?

People shouldn't ask these questions nor should they beg the employer for the job. This behavior is not appropriate and the employer may think that the candidate wants money more than they want the job. The employer realizes the people need jobs in order to pay for their expenses, such as rent, food, bill payments, debt repayment, and savings. When you apply for the job online or via job banks, some companies will show you the salaries and benefits. In other cases, employers will inform the employee about their compensation at the interview or during orientation.

Canada has many jobs, but some regions of Canada have more employment prospects than others. For example, Alberta has the best job market in Canada because of the oil industry. Many people come to Alberta from different parts of Canada in order to improve their job prospects. Other parts of Canada also have good prospects, including BC, Saskatchewan, and Manitoba. When people get their diploma, they can work any place in Canada to improve their job and their life.

Education

Education represents an extremely important aspect in society. Although some people will argue that individuals do not need high school diplomas, this diploma enables an individual to obtain a job and a good life. People that want to improve their career situation or even open their own business require a high school diploma with at least a grade twelve education. In order to increase their employment prospects and enhance their lifestyle, people should obtain college and university educations. While at any level of school, students need to work hard in order to achieve high marks, enabling their acceptance into higher education. School officials should implement rules and order into schools in order to remove barriers to student success. The curriculum should be assessed and possibly changed in order to ensure that students are learning the right material that relates to their future careers. When the school lacks rules and the curriculum is poor, students will drop out of school and become criminals. For their part, students need to respect school rules, teachers, and principals, especially in public schools, which are funded by taxpayers. School funding is important because it allows a wider variety of students to succeed despite their background or socioeconomic status. Governments shouldn't cancel funding because it allows students to attend school without having to work at the same time. Most students have difficulty balancing school and a part time job, even when students can obtain a job that can fund their education.

Students require high marks in order to obtain a high school diploma, which enables them to improve their career opportunities without failing and wasting valuable time trying to repeat grades or courses. Although some people argue that the public funding of education encourages students to waste time and money by neglecting to work hard in school, many students don't waste time and money; rather, government funding provides them with opportunities that they otherwise wouldn't afford. Some schools have advisors, who help students choose appropriate courses and provide them with resources. Most students are hard-working and try their best to complete their homework and assignments as soon as possible. Many people don't realize the difficulties that students face in completing their degrees.

In order to stay in school, students have to respect the laws and rules of their institution. They should avoid negative behavior, such as displaying a bad attitude, being late for classes, making excuses for poor work or attendance, fighting with other students, attacking teachers, and exhibiting disrespectful behavior to other students, teachers, or officials. If students display this behavior in their job, they would lose their job, so they should avoid these behaviors in school. Students should inform teachers or officials of real problems in their lives, such as illness, family emergencies, or legal troubles. They should phone or email school staff to let them know of these problems. Then, students should also obtain proof in the form of doctor notes or government documents informing teachers and staff of these issues. If students can provide adequate proof, they won't have any problems with their teacher or principal, which means that their grades or funding won't be negatively affected.

Teachers and students should foster mutual respect for one another. Students shouldn't cheat in school because they won't learn anything. Students came to school to learn and make progress without failing or being expelled from school. Cheating hurts this objective because students that are caught cheating get kicked out or fail their classes. Some students have more potential than others, which may motivate some students to cheat in order to gain an advantage. Students need to learn fairly in order to achieve understanding and respect in their academic careers as well as their future endeavors. Students should respect teachers because teachers were once students that had their own strengths and weaknesses. People that cheat risk losing their opportunities and ruining their entire life.

Some students complain that teachers make their lives difficult or have problems with them, and teachers experience difficulty with some students who have problems learning or exhibit disruptive behavior in class. In some cases, students are taking courses above their level of competence, which causes teachers to discriminate against them or become frustrated because they are difficult to teach. At the same time, students become frustrated because they lack the ability to master the course material. In this case, students should obtain help from academic resources such as tutoring or student counsellors. Teachers should refer problematic students to counseling in order to help the student understand their problems and provide them with resources that will help them. While some challenging students have learning disabilities or mental problems, other students simply require academic counselling or help with their subjects. Students shouldn't necessarily be sent to a psychologist or psychiatrist unless they have a proven problem. Some teachers can ruin a student's life by failing to provide that student with adequate resources that can genuinely help him/her. As a result, the student lacks the ability to progress in school and fails to obtain his/her diploma, which costs him/her the opportunity to obtain a good job and support a family.

In addition, some teachers can treat students with a lack of respect by yelling at and criticizing him/her. Although teachers can make mistakes or lose their temper, other teachers purposely critique or pick on certain students. Teachers should fix this problem by treating all students equally and by making amends through raising a student's mark. People should learn from their mistakes and try their best to avoid repeating them. This will help individuals to become better people. Teachers should place their faith in God, but many teachers lack knowledge or belief in God. While teachers won't lose their jobs for failing to believe in God, they will lose their jobs if they have performed poorly or committed a sin. Teachers need to stop focusing on the laws and government, because their job of teaching students shouldn't rely on these factors. Many students are failing and receiving poor marks, which indicates that some teachers are failing to properly perform their job. Teachers will pressure and rush students with strict deadlines and many assignments, such as homework, assignments, tests, and finals, all of which students must pass in order to reach the next level of achievement. Students cheat because they feel the pressure to succeed but believe that they lack the ability to do so without an additional advantage. In this case, the teachers are at fault because they make learning extremely difficult. Students should have the right to ask the teacher any questions, especially if students have difficulty with the material. Students can obtain help from a wide variety of sources, including teachers, tutors, friends, and classmates. Rather than simply providing the student with the final answer, these individuals should help students to learn the process of properly solving the problem in order to teach them the material. When teaching or helping, people should guide the student nicely and with respect so that they avoid abuse, thus enhancing the learning process. For people that help other individuals, such as classmates, friends, and tutors, they shouldn't just complete another person's work; they should actually help the person to understand the material. Contrary to the opinion of some teachers and tutors, most students actually want to learn the material; the students aren't lazy or looking for someone to do their work. Rather than continuing to give a student poor grades, teachers should try to obtain help for the students. Teachers shouldn't give a student poor marks because they don't like the student or because of other factors such as race, religion or culture. This behavior is illegal and the teacher will lose their job for doing that. Students need good marks and have to work hard, so teachers should show biases or discriminate against the students unless their performances are actually very poor. Parents that have concerns about their children's academic performance or the teacher's behavior should write a letter to the teacher or speak to the teacher personally in order to discover the problem with the student. However, parents should exercise caution from sounding threatening or accusing towards the teacher, since the teacher may interpret the parents' or students' letter as a threat to their safety, which will cause trouble for both the parents and the student. Parents and students want to solve problems and improve the students' academic performance rather than harm the teacher. If parents have innocent intentions, they shouldn't be accused of trying to harm the teacher or get in trouble when they speak to the teacher's superior, such as a principal or dean. On the other hand, teachers and other students should refrain from threatening or upsetting another student, especially since a few students actually are criminals and may hurt or kill someone who threatens them. Some teachers make students' lives difficult by labelling them, criticizing them, or giving them low marks; however, teachers should exercise caution because they may offend or upset the wrong student. Similarly, other students should avoid snitching or ratting on other students because these students may want revenge and try to attack them.

When teachers perform poorly or exhibit discrimination against students, students have the right to complain about bad teachers. Most schools provide students with warnings, temporary suspensions, or light penalties before they kick students out for cheating. Students that have been caught cheating should learn from their mistake and avoid repeating it, especially since the future consequences will be worse, such as expulsion from school. When students continue cheating, it could ruin their lives, because they will lose the opportunity to obtain the academic achievement that they otherwise would have acquired if they hadn't been caught cheating. In post-secondary institutions such as university and college, students that cheat usually don't receive warnings or second chances. They will get expelled from that particular institution and will likely lose the opportunity to attend another school because they will receive a bad reputation from their offense. In addition, the student could also jeopardize their relationship with other individuals in their lives, especially family members or spouses that paid for their education. Since the university or college won't refund cheaters with their money, the person who funded the student's education won't get their money returned and will feel as if the student wasted their money. This could ruin relationships in the student's life.

Courses have varying levels of difficulty, and students have different ability levels, which mean that some courses are easy while others are difficult. Regardless of a student's ability level or age, all students should receive equal treatment. Teachers and other school officials should treat all students the same, regardless of their gender, age, skin color, religion, orientation, or nationality. Specifically, all students should have equal opportunity to succeed in school; teachers shouldn't interfere with a student's opportunity because of their previous skills, programs, experiences, or abilities. Students should have the chance to learn new material or programs at any stage in their lives, and proper training will help them to achieve this goal. Teachers can't stop students from attending certain programs or fostering certain career goals. Students shouldn't let bad teachers discourage them from learning certain materials or taking certain courses and programs. While most teachers are good, some teachers are bad because they aren't honest with students and they show discrimination against students.

Behavior Control

There are several actions that people can take to ensure that they stay out of trouble. For example, if someone stops a person to talk to them, they should reply, but they shouldn't talk too much or give too much information. If people don't want a problem, the best strategy involves remaining quiet. People that keep quiet are not necessarily a hypocrite, snob, antisocial, shy, or scary. Most people don't judge others that keep quiet; however, people that talk a lot will experience more problems than people that stay quiet. For instance, people shouldn't become offended or overreact to minor incidents; they should only react to major offenses. However, in all cases, people should make their best efforts to stay out of trouble.

Regardless of whether or not a person's first language is English, they should respect other people. Conversely, people should respect other individuals despite any language barriers. Nobody should disrespect or insult another person because of his/her language, nationality, culture, skin color, or religion. People can speak any language in any country. Nobody should tell a person to speak only the native language or official languages of the country. In Canada, people should be able to speak any language that they want, even though the official national languages are English and French. People can also learn other languages from their friends and family members and speak those languages in Canada or any other country that they choose. Just because a person knows a certain language doesn't necessarily mean that they're from a country that speaks that language. People have different levels of respect for different languages; for example, languages that are considered international have more regard than those that are not international. Some people disrespect others that speak non-official languages or languages that do not have international status.

Some people may have difficulty with important paperwork, such as government documents, schoolwork, and applications. People that speak the native languages should help these individuals without giving them disrespect or insulting them because they lack comprehension of the national or official language. Rather, individuals that understand important documents should help other people complete those documents by explaining the paperwork to them, translating the language, or helping them with the answers. People can help others without necessarily doing their work for them. People should use common sense and think about their actions.

Some parents don't like to help their children and attempt to abuse them, which is wrong and illegal. People can talk to their family and close friends about religion and politics, but they have to exercise caution, because some friends take offense to certain viewpoints or conversations. In fact, individuals shouldn't discuss religion and politics with people that they don't know very well, especially since those individuals may become upset and even become aggressive or try to attack someone.

The following list provides some rules about behavior:

- Don't insult or disrespect people if you don't want people to disrespect you

- Don't' judge people unless you want to be judged
- Don't take people's lives if you don't want other people to murder you
- Don't be aggressive, insulting, abusive, or violent with other people unless you want them to retaliate in this manner
- Don't lie or steal unless you want people to lie or steal from you
- Don't say negative things about other people unless you want people to act in the same manner towards you
- Don't treat people badly unless you want people to treat you badly
- Treat others in the way that you want to be treated by treating people with respect, equality, and rights
- People can choose who they want to select as their friends; however, regardless of who people select as friends, they should respect everybody. Despite the fact that everyone is different, individuals still need to respect one another and treat each other with courtesy. This attitude would bring peace to earth and avoid issues such as war, violence, and fighting.

Although everyone has free will, people should still make intelligent choices and avoid making poor decisions and mistakes. The following list discusses the elements and characteristics that individuals need in order to make intelligent choices:

- love
- perseverance
- honesty

- trust
- accepting others' differences
- goodwill
- courage
- valuable culture and traditions
- overcoming challenges
- believing in oneself
- friendship and family
- making good choices
- teamwork
- self-confidence
- happiness

In some other countries, especially the United States and Latin America, individuals can't make conversation with strangers like they can in Canada and Europe. In these former nations, people take offense when other individuals speak to them. For instance, people can't talk to business-men or police; in the case of the police, officers may take offense and put people in jail for speaking to them. Also, men aren't allowed to speak to women in the United States, Latin America, and some parts of Canada, like Toronto.

The Bible states that if God and the people forgive the mistakes of others and apologize, they will also receive for-giveness. However, once people are forgiven for their behav-ior, they should stop their mistakes and avoid repeating them again. If people that have done wrong apologize and discon-tinue their behavior, individuals should grant them forgive-ness. By providing one another with forgiveness, people can bring peace into the world and eradicate war.

People shouldn't allow others to become their enemies over small matters or little mistakes. Individuals shouldn't want to take revenge on another person because of a small error; however, if someone commits a major offense against another individual, then the offended person can make the offender their enemy. The best strategy involves stopping an enemy from his/her behavior and showing them humanity. People should show others that they are human and don't deserve disrespect.

Some civilians and police commit crimes or refuse to stop criminal behavior. If someone commits continual crimes against an individual, the individual shouldn't forgive them because they have enacted major offenses against that person, such as killing a person's innocent family members. Criminal people and corrupt police officers don't deserve forgiveness; rather, they deserve to die by another person or by the government or to receive life imprisonment.

Some of the behaviors that will guarantee a person's safety involve the following precautions:

- Avoiding crime
- Avoiding suspicious behavior
- Avoiding terrorist activity, including discussing terrorism or being associated with terrorists
- Avoiding discussion about politics or religion
- Avoiding discussion about politicians, government members, or police officers

Some people possess knowledge about politics but avoid discussing these issues because they want to avoid trouble. Smart people also avoid breaking the laws and rules of their country and other countries. People should respect the laws and demonstrate honesty with the police and government. No individual is perfect and all people make mistakes.

However, people should apologize for their mistakes and receive forgiveness for these errors. People should always tell the truth; otherwise, individuals will fail to trust them and believe that they are liars or hypocrites, which will get them into trouble. God wants people to tell the truth and perform moral actions. Some individuals that have embraced the truth include Martin Luther King, Malcolm X, Nelson Mandela, Rosa Park, Tom Douglas, Mfumu Kibangu, Assange, and Edwin Snowden.

People shouldn't fear death because the truth is the most important thing in the world. Individuals need to tell the truth without worrying about how corrupt police or government will deal with them. People that don't expose the truth will spend the rest of their lives in shame. God is right and almighty; he wants people to tell the truth and so people should follow God's word.

Furthermore, people should avoid discrimination against others and treat each other with the same amount of respect regardless of skin color, religion, race, or nationality. All people, including whites, blacks, Hispanics, Arabs, Asians, Natives, and Mulattos, deserve fair and equal treatment. Similarly, all religions, including Muslims, Christians, and Buddhists, all deserve equal respect. All individuals, regardless of race or religion, are human beings, and everyone should realize this fact.

In addition, people worry too much about what others think of their physical appearance or tend to judge others by their looks. People can go to the gym to burn fat or build muscle and nobody should judge them or tell them what to do. When people exercise, they should start slowly and take their time in order to avoid hurting themselves. People shouldn't listen to what others say; they should have patience and not force themselves to do more exercise than they can handle. If people take their time, positive changes will eventually come. The body is important and people should concentrate on their health. Specifically, muscles are important because people can defend themselves from attacks. When people have strong muscles, they can deal with an attacker more easily. Muscles also protect a person from permanent harm, and they will heal more easily. In addition, people should take training or self-defense courses in order to learn how to protect themselves. At first, these courses may be difficult, but after practicing for a long time, the courses will become easier. People should know how to defend themselves in case they experience an attack from another individual. However, people need to realize that they shouldn't build their muscles or learn fighting techniques in order to attack another individual, because assault represents a criminal action. People should only fight if another individual attacks them; however, the best strategy involves avoiding a fight if possible. People will feel more reluctant to start a fight with a strong, muscular person because they will be more difficult to harm or kill. In this way, building muscles and taking defense courses allows a person to avoid harm rather than to start fights. People shouldn't assume that muscular people are bad; some police may see a muscular person and automatically think that they want to start trouble. However, the police shouldn't make this assumption and should treat everyone equally. Police should only start fights with bad people rather than with good people; also, police should never start fights with women. In particular, police and civilians should never touch, hit, or beat a woman. Police who assault women should lose their jobs. When people are young children and teenagers, they may fight with their sisters and female friends, but adults shouldn't behave in this way. Men should defend their mothers and sisters from assault or murder. People that defend their female family members are not breaking the law. If a person attacks an individual's mother, grandmother, wife, girlfriend, or sister, a male family member can defend them without being charged. However, men are prohibited from the following actions:

- to fight with a woman
- to touch a woman
- to beat a woman
- to yell at a woman
- to abuse or mistreat women

In particular, husbands and boyfriends should never perform these actions on their partners because these actions are illegal and will result in jail time. Women bring babies into the world, so they are particularly vulnerable while men are not as fragile as women. As a result, men can't beat or kill women. While women can legally fight with one another, they shouldn't fight because fighting represents an immoral action. Like men, women should exercise and take self-defense classes in order to defend themselves from attacks. Men shouldn't assume that women work out in order to attack other people. Women can only fight when other people want to attack them or rape them. They should also protect their own children from an attack, especially those from their husbands or boyfriends. As in the case of skin color and religion, people should treat men and women equally. Some countries don't provide women with the same equal rights that they receive in Canada. In these countries, the governments abuse women and allow their husbands or boyfriends to beat and kill them. In North America and Europe, democratic countries provide women with the same rights as men and prohibit men from abusing women. However, some of the police in these nations are still abusive and sexist towards women. Other officers provide women with more lenient punishments and sentences. Both attitudes are wrong; women that commit crimes should have the same punishments as men who commit the same offenses. On the other hand, innocent men and women should not have to go to jail if they didn't commit any crimes. Police, government, and civilians should treat men and women with the same respect and should avoid discriminating against one sex or another. People that elevate one sex above the other are committing sexism, which is wrong. Also, men and women should respect one another equally, and spouses should treat one another with respect.

People need to think about their behaviors more thoroughly. People cannot insult or disrespect other people because of their gender, skin color, nationality, or religion. If a person's spouse respects them, that person should also treat their spouse with respect. Partners should give each other equal treatment and courtesy. Women can only hit men if the man does something wrong; however, men are never allowed to hit a woman because it is against the law. Even if the woman does something wrong to the man, men can never hit a woman.

People need to respect each other and the law in order to stay out of trouble. If people can control their own behavior, they will be fine.

Transportation

There are several modes of transportation in major cities. Some of these public transit options include the tram, light rail transit, metro, trolleybus, railway, sightseeing bus, and trackless train. Small towns and villages don't require these transit options because they don't have a large area or a big population. Small cities only require regular city buses. Buses are divided into city buses and regional or intercity buses. While intercity buses travel from city to city, intracity buses only travel within a particular city or town. Both types of buses must follow designated routes and stop at particular places. Intercity buses go through a wide variety of different municipalities, including large cities, small cities, towns, and villages. In some cases, these buses can travel from one province or state to another. Some intercity buses can also cross the border between Canada and the United States. There are laws governing the routes of intercity buses. When buses cross the border, they must follow certain rules, especially the rules of each country. One example of an intercity bus is the Greyhound bus, which travels throughout different states, provinces, and countries, following predetermined routes that take passengers to particular stops.

Other modes of transportation include sightseeing vehicles, which can include buses or trackless trains. These vehicles are designed to show tourists around a particular city, pointing out certain attractions or historical sites. Railways and cable cars take tourists through the mountains and other scenic routes between large cities. Trolleybuses take tourists or locals from one stop to another within major cities. These buses use environmentally friendly means of energy and minimize pollution as well as environmental damage. Trolleybuses, in addition to metros or underground subways, protect the residents of a major city from pollution-related diseases and save the government money to spend on important issues. These forms of transportation are used in cities that tend to have extremely large populations and/or pollution problems. Cities with smaller populations or that lack pollution issues generally don't need trolleybuses. While trolleybuses are slightly faster than regular buses, they protect against pollution and help to keep the city clean.

The tram, LRT, and underground railway are faster than both regular buses and trolleybuses. Large cities require these modes of transportation in order to ensure that local residents transit to and from work and school. Many people don't have time to sit in traffic, so they tend to avoid cars or buses during rush hours. Trams and metros help people to avoid rush hour traffic. However, smaller cities and towns generally don't have metros because they are not sufficiently populated or busy. Medium-sized cities usually have trams and LRTs because these modes of transportation are cheaper. For example, Calgary, which is larger than Edmonton, has more light rail transit than Edmonton. The Calgary LRT extends across the entire city, while Edmonton's LRT only has one main line. However, as Edmonton is expanding, its LRT routes are increasing to accommodate the growing population. In the future, Edmonton plans to expand its LRT into neighboring communities such as St. Albert and Sherwood Park. Edmonton is growing into one of Canada's largest cities, which also includes Calgary, Vancouver, Toronto, and Montreal. Another large Canadian city, Ottawa, which is Canada's capital city, should have trams, LRT, or metro because it has a busy population.

Poor countries don't have transportation modes such as buses, trolleys, railways, trams, and metros, because the governments of these countries can't afford such infrastructure and because their populations are not sufficiently large to justify the expenditure. Only developing countries such as Canada, United States, Greenland, Australia, New Zealand, European Nations, Asian countries, and South America can afford these transportation modes. The Internet distinguishes among three main modes of transportation in each developed city, including:

- Tram World Cities
- Metro World Cities
- Trolleybus World Cities

The countries in North and South America generally don't have high-speed trains because they currently lack the need for this method of transportation. However, in the future, perhaps in 10 or 15 years, these nations might need high-speed trains due to the expanding population. Countries that require high-speed transit, such as European and Asian nations, have extremely high populations with busy lifestyles, including school, work, and extracurricular activities. These trains allow travelers to commute quickly from one town or city to another without wasting significant amounts of time among traffic or slower transportation. In addition, high-speed trains keep the environment cleaner and represent a fiscally responsible decision because they save money on parking and fuel. Gas not only costs commuters significant amounts of money but also harms the environment and the population. The high-speed train is faster than cars, buses, trolleys, metros and LRTs. In the future, the human population will continue to grow at exponential rates, so high-speed trains will become increasingly important to serve large populations and enhance the efficiency of commuting. These trains will cover all residential areas, including towns, cities, villages, and large metropolises. Wealthy countries, such as Canada and the United States, are sufficiently affluent to build high-speed trains; however, underdeveloped or developing countries may not be able to afford this means of transportation. The government can use taxpayer money to build high-speed trains. Taxpayers won't necessarily have to pay more taxes, and the government can continue to tax people in the same way, so that wealthy people pay more taxes than poorer people. Tax is important because it allows the government to afford important necessities, such as healthcare, education, and transportation. However, people should still keep a substantial amount of their earnings so that they can afford their basic necessities and enjoy their lives. In the future, people can still use oil and gas, but they should reduce their use of these fossil fuels because they harm people's health and the environment. The government should spend most of its money on building safe roads, schools, companies, and health facilities. In addition, it should pay government workers, such as military, police, construction workers, teachers, and healthcare professionals. Finally, the government should provide money to healthcare and to individuals with disabilities. Once this money has been used, the government should use the remaining money to build high-speed trains that have reinforced safety and security. Specifically, the government can hire additional security personnel and high gates to protect against injury and death. The land currently has enough empty space to build high-speed trains without jeopardizing housing, businesses, farmland, and parkland. Once the train is built, it will travel all across Canada and the United States as well as through other countries. The train will travel from city to city and through different states and provinces.

Due to their lower population, smaller towns and villages won't need high-speed trains; however, they can use buses or taxis to commute into the city or another town. The government can't make the excuse that high-speed trains are expensive because many modes of transportation are expensive and cost money. The government needs to create an efficient plan for high-speed train travel. Unfortunately, there are many corrupt governments and bad politicians so the future is always uncertain to some extent regardless of the political system: dictatorship or democracy. Politicians can lie and say that they will build a high-speed train just to win the election, and, once they have won the election, they may never build a high-speed train. Politicians need to use common sense and to perform actions that benefit the population rather than themselves. Some politicians want to stop the development of high-speed trains because they fear that these trains will harm the economy by eliminating other transportation businesses, including cars, planes, and buses as well as crucial industries such as oil and gas. However, trains will not hurt the economy because people will continue to use conventional modes of transportation. Governments should look to European countries as a model of intelligent planning with high-speed trains. North America needs all modes of transportation, including high-speed trains, cars, planes, trucks, railways, and buses. In addition, countries need tourist transportation, including trolleys, buses, Greyhounds, and metros. High-speed trains will not affect other modes of transportation, and, since North American governments have sufficient money to spend, they should develop high-speed trains.

In a democratic country, citizens can vote for any politician or political party that they believe will make a good leader. Nobody can stop a person from voting for any leader that they choose. In fact, people can even choose to refrain from voting at all. Many people complain about the government or the current political situation, but people shouldn't complain about minor issues, especially if they voted for the party in power. In Canada, only people with citizenship can vote; however, citizens can also choose not to vote. People must respect the political choices of all Canadian citizens, even if they disagree with their choice of candidate or their decision to refrain from voting. Many politicians are bad leaders that only want people to vote for them, and, once elected, they don't make any good changes to the country. If people don't like the party that they voted for or the leader in power, they can vote for a different person next time. Many people complain about the political situation and yet they continue to vote for the same leader, which makes no sense.

In many countries, including Canada, United States, Australia, New Zealand, and South American nations, most people prefer driving to other modes of transportation. However, not all individuals own cars, because they usually have family members or friends to drive them to places. Even when people ask others for a ride, their friends or family members can't always accommodate their wishes, especially because everybody has busy lives and many commitments. Since people don't always have access to a vehicle, the government should build high-speed trains that will enable individuals to reach their destination quickly and efficiently. In the future, populations will continue to increase and people will need to reach their destinations more quickly, making high-speed trains a necessity. People will want to commute to work or travel across the country without using cars, planes, or other conventional modes of transit. Some politicians, such as Republicans, want to stop the plans to build high-speed trains because they want to keep the money and the power to themselves while denying civilians rights, freedoms, and happiness. Public transport such as high-speed trains will enhance the ease of travel for everyone while also saving money and helping the environment. While most people will use high-speed trains, Republicans and other wealthy individuals can continue to use their own vehicles or planes for transport. This way, everybody will be happy. A few years ago, there was discussion about building a high-speed train between Edmonton and Calgary; however, this plan never happened. North American governments are selfish and prefer to spend money on oil and gas, which not only harms the environment but also brings sickness and disease to people. These governments need to spend their money on smart choices such as high-speed trains.

The Canadian Prime Minister wants to build an oil pipe underground from Canada to the United States. This plan doesn't make any sense because it will harm the environment, ecosystems, water, farmland, and people. In addition, oil pipes can cause diseases and kill people so the leaders need to find a better solution. President Barack Obama was correct in refusing to allow this oil pipe to be built. Although people may disagree with the Canadian Prime Minister, it doesn't mean that people are against him or don't respect him.

Not only do Europe, Japan, and China use high-speed trains between cities, but they also use public transportation, such as buses, within cities. Even villages have buses because many people don't own their own vehicles and everyone needs to go to the city or another town for work, school, or business. Public transit provides people with options, especially in the case that people don't own their own car. Cities have much more extensive public transit systems than towns and villages, although smaller municipalities still have a few buses and taxis. North Americans should be able to use their bikes for transportation in the summer time. Governments should build safe bike paths in more cities so that people can ride their bikes safely beside the roads.

In many countries, including Canada, United States, Alaska, Greenland, Mexico, Australia, New Zealand, South American nations and South Africa most people prefer driving to other modes of transportation. However, not all individuals own cars, because they usually have family members or friends to drive them places. Even when people ask others for a ride, their friends or family members can't always accommodate their wishes, especially because everybody has busy lives and many commitments. Since people don't always have access to a vehicle, the government should build high-speed trains that will enable individuals to reach their destination quickly and efficiently. In the future, populations will continue to increase and people will need to reach their destinations more quickly, making high-speed trains a necessity. People will want to commute to work or travel across the country without using cars, planes, or other conventional modes of transit. Some politicians, such as Republicans, want to stop the plans to build high-speed trains because they want to keep the money and the power to themselves while denying civilians rights, freedoms, and happiness. Public transport such as high-speed trains will enhance the ease of travel for everyone while also saving money and helping the environment. While most people will use high-speed trains, Republicans and other wealthy individuals can continue to use their own vehicles or planes for transport. This way, everybody will be happy. A few years ago, there was discussion about building a high-speed train between Edmonton and Calgary: however, this plan never happened. North American governments are selfish and prefer to spend money on oil and gas, which not only harms the environment but also brings sickness and disease to people. These governments need to spend their money on smart choices such as high-speed trains.

The Canadian Prime Minister wants to build an oil pipeline underground from Canada to the United States. This plan doesn't make any sense because it will harm the environment, ecosystems, water, farmland, and people. In addition, oil pipes can cause diseases and kill people so the leaders need to find a better solution. President Barack Obama was correct in refusing to allow this oil pipe to be built. Although many people may disagree with the Canadian Prime Minister, it doesn't mean that people are against him or don't respect him.

Not only do Europe, Japan, South Korea and China use high-speed trains between cities, but they also use public transportation, such as buses, within cities. Even villages have buses because many people don't own their own vehicles and everyone needs to go to the city or another town for work, school or business. Public transit provides people with options, especially in the case that people don't own their own car. Cities have much more extensive public transit systems that towns and villages, although smaller municipalities still have a few buses and taxis. North Americans should be able to use their bikes for transportation in the summer time. Governments should build safe bike paths so that people can ride their bikes safely beside the roads.

Interracial Relationships

Any person should be able to date or marry someone of any race. For example, a black man can have a relationship with a woman of his own race or of another race, including white, Aboriginal, Middle Eastern, East Indian, Latino, or Asian. No person or social institution, including friends, family, police, or government, should be able to force or influence a person to date only within their own race or within another race. Everybody is different and has their own values and beliefs, but people have the right to do what they choose, especially in a democratic country. Nobody can stop people from having the right to form their own values and make their own choices. People need to respect everyone's values and choices even if they don't personally agree with those decisions. Thus, the race of one's partner shouldn't matter, as long as they are a good person. If a person's girlfriend, boyfriend, husband, or wife treats them well and his/her family respects the other person's family, then the skin color of each person shouldn't matter. Each person needs to treat their significant other and each other's families with respect.

People should consider interracial relationships normal because there is nothing wrong with dating or marrying someone of another race. People meet many attractive individuals from around the world regardless of where the person comes from or where they travel. For example, as a black man, I find that the most beautiful women are Latinos, Filipinos, and Hispanics. However, everybody has their own opinion about which people they find the most attractive. All people want to date and marry someone that they consider attractive. For example, men want to have relationships with beautiful women and women want to date or marry handsome men. People are less likely to cheat on their partner if they find their partner attractive. Although it's important for people to have relationships with someone they consider attractive, their partner should also have good characteristics as well. The superficial characteristics such as age, religion, and race shouldn't matter in a partner, as long as the partner treats them well.

The act of cheating on a boyfriend, girlfriend, husband or wife is always wrong, and a person's partner should also refrain from cheating on them, especially if they have not cheated on their partner. Two partners should stay together with each other and stay out of trouble. Many people cheat on their partners if they find that their partners are not very attractive, so they decide to sleep with someone more attractive. The following questions can be asked about why people cheat on their partners:

- Why do people cheat on white women or men?
- Why do people cheat on black women or men?
- Why do people cheat on Native or Metis women or men?
- Why do people cheat on Asian or Filipino women or men?
- Why don't people want to cheat on Filipino women or men if they are attractive? Some people prefer Filipinos, approximately half of the people in the world, but other people prefer Latina or Hispanic women or men, especially Brazilian women, since they are very beautiful

- Why do people cheat on brown or Arab women or men?
- Why do people not cheat on Latin Europeans or Hispanics?

If a person is very attractive and has a nice body, as in the case of Latino women, then men will want to keep them and spend their whole life with these women. People in relationships with Latino women generally don't cheat because they will want to pay all of their attention to these women. In addition to their beauty, Latino women possess desirable characteristics, including the ability to cook, take care of a house, and raise children while a man goes to work and makes money. If a man cheats on a Hispanic or Latino woman, then he makes a very stupid mistake by destroying his chances to have a permanent relationship with a beautiful woman. Once men have been in a relationship with a Hispanic woman, they know her characteristics and desires, so they shouldn't make the foolish decision to cheat on them. If the Latino woman discovers that her partner has been cheating on her and breaks up with him, then it will be his fault and not hers.

Most people's families and friends tell them about their experiences in relationships and inform them of the desirable qualities and characteristics in a romantic partner. Although both sexes are picky, women tend to demonstrate more scrutiny than men. Women look for the following characteristics in their partners:

- Women don't like unattractive or overweight men
- Women don't want men with a lot of hair on their faces and bodies, especially moustaches, beards, chest hair, and underarm hair

-   Women don't like men who dress sloppily or fail to groom themselves

If men meet these physical requirements, then women will like them and wish to date or marry them. Otherwise, women don't desire men who don't take care of their appearance. If men want a chance to improve themselves, they should listen to friends and family members to receive advice about dressing and grooming. Men that want women to find them attractive should do the following things:

-   Behave well and treat women properly
-   Lose weight and gain muscle
-   Shave the face and groom the underarms
-   Shave the chest and other body parts at least every two weeks
-   Dress properly and nicely. The choice of clothing shouldn't matter as long as you are clean and presentable in all public places, including schools, communities, parties, and clubs. In particular, your clothing shouldn't be shabby or dirty
-   Make sure not to have a bad odor. Men shouldn't have any smell except for a sweet or attractive smell; otherwise, women will reject them or walk away from the. Women think more independently than men, so women will reject or dump men that don't meet their expectations.

If men follow the proper instructions on their appearance and behavior, they will attract many beautiful women rather than ugly women. By attracting beautiful women, men have the best chances for having a wife and children in the future.

For example, if a man is from Haiti and speaks French, he can have a wife from Mexico or El Salvador who speaks Spanish. This couple and their two children can live in Canada and the United States. However, they need to learn to speak English properly and to teach their children how to speak English so that they can attend school. People shouldn't have a problem with interracial marriages, especially if they have a wife from another country that has a different culture or speaks a different language. Although several challenges exist in interracial relationships, people can work hard in order to enjoy their relationships. When people have children, they should teach their children about their languages and cultures before the children get too old to learn. In addition, interracial couples should teach each other their own cultures and languages.

In the past, people divorced from one another; however, divorce is much more common today than it was in the past. Since divorce is very common, the government should make the process easier and less expensive for people. Regardless of whether people believe that divorce is moral or immoral, the laws should be fair and just for everyone. In the past, people didn't have the opportunity to divorce from their spouse because divorce was very expensive, especially in the 1950s and 1960s.

People have the right to divorce their partner when they have legitimate reasons for wanting to break up their marriage. The following situations represent good reasons to want a divorce:

-   abuse
-   yelling
-   assault

- cheating
- financial problems
- if someone's partner has committed a crime
- if someone's partner has threatened to kill them or their life is in danger
- if someone's partner uses violence against them
- if someone's partner refuses to take responsibility for their family or children
- if someone's partner treats them unfairly

While the list above provides legitimate reasons for divorce, people shouldn't divorce their spouse if there is no real problem in the relationship. Since divorce isn't ideal, couples should try to work their relationship out so that they avoid divorcing from one another. Even if people are divorced, they can still remarry and divorce again; although people should try to avoid repetitive divorces, the government shouldn't tell them what to do. Ideally, husbands and wives as well as boyfriends and girlfriends should respect one another. People should only end their relationships if the other person doesn't treat them very well. If both people treat each other well, then there is no reason to end the relationship. People can only find new partners after they have broken up with their previous partner. Conversely, people shouldn't see other people while in a relationship, because this constitutes cheating.

Before someone decides to date or marry someone else, they should become acquainted with that individual as a person. If a person has a bad personality or character, then they don't make a suitable partner. On the other hand, people with good characters make appropriate partners, which helps them to succeed in life. Thus, people should get to know their partners before committing to them in a relationship.

Marriage preparation and courtship represent important processes in early adulthood. Although laws don't necessarily exist for these processes, people should get to know their partners in order to ensure that they are protected later in the relationship. During courtship, people should get to know their significant others in several ways:

- Become acquainted with the person and their characteristics
- Find out how many times a person has dated and broken up with their partner
- Find out how many times the person has married and divorced
- Find out how many times the person has had sex
- Schedule a blood test for you and your partner in order to determine if your partner has any sexually transmitted diseases, such as HIV/AIDS
- If your partner doesn't have HIV/AIDS or other diseases, you can use condoms so that you are safe and don't contract any other diseases
- If your partner has HIV/AIDS, you should break up with that person and get a new partner.
- Partners should trust one another and ask each other honest questions while providing honest responses to their partner. People shouldn't become offended when their partners ask them honest questions.
- People should talk with their partner on a daily basis and try to visit the person as much as possible. If it's not possible to see your partner every day, you should keep in touch with them via technology, such as email, cellphones, Facebook, and texting.

When people have sex with their partners for the first time, they should use a condom. People should exercise caution when using condoms, especially since condoms can be used, expired, or damaged. Thus, people should only use condoms that are brand new and have been tested for defects. If people fail to use a condom or use a damaged condom, they may become sick or contract a sexually transmitted disease. Some people have diseases such as AIDS and may not be honest with their partner, leading to the spread of disease. In order to guarantee safe sex, it's best to use two or three condoms in case one is ripped or broken. People should pay attention to make sure that the condom hasn't been damaged in any way. Not only do condoms help to protect from sexually transmitted diseases, but they also assist in preventing pregnancy. Although a couple may want children in the future, if they don't want children at the present time, they should use condoms to prevent unplanned pregnancies. Many religions and individuals believe that abortion is immoral, so if a woman becomes pregnant, she feels obliged have the child. Men can't force women to have an abortion; if a man encourages a woman to terminate the pregnancy and she experiences complications that lead to illness or death, the man can be charged with a crime.

Some religions and governments prohibit or highly discourage sexual activity before marriage. In these countries, people that engage in premarital sex may be arrested, imprisoned or even killed. Other countries prohibit relationships between same-sex couples, such as gays and lesbians. In fact, the Bible and other religious scriptures even condemn premarital sex as well as gay and lesbian relationships. However, it's wrong for people to kill each other or for the government to put people in jail because they have sex before marriage or engage in same-sex relationships. The Bible states that people should only have one wife. In some countries, people have more than one wife or husband, but Canada prohibited people from having more than one marriage partner. Regardless of whether someone follows the law or whether they treat their spouses well, Canada, some other countries and some places of the United States disallows people from having many wives.

The apparent relationship between former American President Bill Clinton and Monica Lewinsky was immoral because he was married. Also, Monica Lewinsky lied to the police and media, claiming that Bill Clinton raped her; however, Clinton didn't actually rape her. Lewinsky just wanted to receive his money from a lawsuit against Clinton. Clinton's wife defended him and protected him against Lewinsky's allegations, which ultimately lacked proof.

Some men assault girls and young women by fooling them into thinking that they like them. These men will take their victims to secret or hidden places so that nobody can know about the assault. Sometimes, assailants will give their victims alcohol or drugs to put them to sleep so that the women are weak or unconscious, making them easy victims. Also, if women are drugged, they won't remember the attack, and the men can get away with assaulting them. In some cases, men will even kill their victims so that they can't tell the police about the incident.

Although most people want to date or marry someone, not everybody chooses this path in life. People shouldn't be forced to have a relationship with someone; however, even if someone doesn't want to date or marry a certain person, they shouldn't be rude to that person. For example, people can reject someone nicely without disrespecting them or insulting them. People should respect other people's feelings, especially if they want to also receive respect from others.

People shouldn't let others judge their clothing styles. It's not important whether or not someone is wearing the latest trends in clothing, although older styles, such as baggy clothing, don't exist anymore. The way in which people choose their fashion shouldn't matter, as long as their clothes are presentable, clean, and appropriate. People should choose clothing that would be appropriate in public places, such as clubs, parties, churches, schools, and communities. This way, people will receive respect from everyone in the community and in society, and attractive members of the opposite sex will find them appealing. Furthermore, individuals shouldn't judge the clothing styles of other people, because everyone has different fashion ideas. Everyone has unique styles based on how they feel comfortable and different tastes in clothing. People should respect others' unique styles and refrain from judging others; otherwise, those other individuals may also exercise judgment.

Some people came to North America or Europe from other countries when they were young children or teenagers; other individuals were born in North America but their parents emigrated from another country. It's understandable that these individuals would follow North American culture because they were raised in a white person's country. People shouldn't judge others because of their cultural upbringing, regardless of where they live or have lived. Some people still remember their previous country or their parents' country while others have forgotten their birthplace or lack knowledge of their parents' original nation. It's also good when people remember their parents' former country and can speak the mother tongue language from that country as well as North American language and culture.

Interracial dating occurs when someone dates or marries a person outside his/her race and/or culture. People should be able to date anyone that they choose, regardless of that person's race, culture, religion, or skin color. Others should respect interracial couples and refrain from judging them. While some people believe that those who date someone of another race are against their own race, religion, nationality, or family, this belief lacks credibility. In particular, people's families shouldn't judge their choice of romantic partner, because a person's individual choice should be respected. As long as people respect their own culture and family, they should be able to date whoever they want.

Caucasian Divorce

In the countries dominated by Caucasian individuals, immigrants and people of other races need to follow the rules of those countries. One set of rules involves those governing divorce. In some countries, if a man divorces his wife, he must pay his ex-wife money for the rest of his life or split his assets with her. However, in other countries, a man only needs to send money to his children and to care for these children for the rest of his life. Another law concerns remarriage; for example, a man that divorces his wives can remarry to another woman and have children with his new wife. Also, the ex-wife can marry another husband and have new children with this man. Normally, if the wife divorces the husband, the children can still keep the father's last name; however, the wife is not required to keep her ex-husband's last name, so she can change her married name back to her maiden name. When a woman remarries to a new husband, she can change her name to his last name. In most countries, the husband never takes his wife's last name. The wife has to take her husband's name because God created men before women. The Bible states that God created Adam and then made Eve so that Adam could have a wife. Therefore, the custom of a woman taking her husband's last name results from the Bible rather than from a sexist policy designed to elevate men over women. Most Caucasian societies respect both men and women in an equal manner.

However, Caucasian societies contain some questionable rules about divorce. These rules and laws lack logic and fairness. For instance:

-   Why does a husband have to pay his ex-wife alimony for the rest of his life, even when the children become adults?
-   Why, even when the ex-wife marries another husband and has children with that husband, does a man have to continue paying alimony?
-   Why does a woman always have to take her ex-husband to court so that he can be charged and threatened by the police?
-   Why do white women teach immigrant women ways to mistreat their husband and brainwash immigrant women into believing that their husband mistreats them even when he is a good husband?
-   Why do white women and Hispanic women continue ruining their ex-husband's life even after they have been divorced? Do these women only want their ex-husband's money?

These rules don't make any sense and need to be changed.

Health Food

Food represents an important aspect of human life, as people need to eat in order to survive. As a result, people should know how to cook food properly by adding only a small amount of salt and pepper to enhance the taste. People can drink juices or pop with a small amount of sugar. If people only ate enough to become full, then everyone would have access to food. Many people lead very busy lives, so they want to eat quickly so that they can focus on their work. Individuals acquire their energy from food in order to perform daily activities, so that they are not hungry. Everyone prefers food that has a good taste; however, people need to learn how to eat healthy foods. Many businesses, like supermarkets and restaurants, sell food and beverages in order to make money. The sale of food helps the economy and allows the government to tax foods. However, companies that sell food and drinks should ensure that the food doesn't contain chemicals and fat. The unnatural ingredients in food can make people obese and create diseases such as diabetes, heart disease, and cancer. Many people have become sick and even died from eating unhealthy foods, which is also known as fast food or junk food. Some of this food includes sugar, candies, and pop. These foods are very bad for the human body in a similar way to drugs. Like drugs, fast food contains harmful or poisonous substances that gradually kill the human body.

Many companies advertise the sale of junk food in order to make it appealing to the public. These businesses only care about making money rather than the health of the population, and they will not stop selling unhealthy food. The government also allows these businesses to grow because of the tax money. This attitude is wrong because unhealthy food poses a serious risk to the population. While some people care about their bodies and their health, other people aren't concerned with the type of food that they eat. People should not only care about their own health but also about the health of the entire human race. In Europe, companies used to sell unhealthy foods, but now businesses have found other ways of making money because the governments have realized that junk food harms people. Restaurants like McDonalds, KFC, A&W, and Wendy's sell fast food that causes damage to the human body and can even kill people over time. The perpetuation of these businesses ultimately causes significant healthcare expenditures for issues such as obesity and diabetes. European governments have realized that fast food restaurants cause more harm to society than the money they provide the economy, so they have restricted unhealthy foods. People should exercise responsibility for the foods that they consume and learn to control their own eating habits. The European governments want to ensure the health of their citizens, and North American governments should follow their example and ban fast foods. If North American governments try to restrict junk foods, the elite will oppose the government because the fast food industry represents a significant source of income for the economy. However, North America should ban chemicals, fats, and sugars from foods and drinks in order to increase the health of the population and eliminate obesity. The mentality of

North American governments, especially the Republicans, completely lacks sense. They make life difficult for their citizens not only through the perpetuation of unhealthy eating but also through threats and violence.

Although people can eat the occasional amount of junk food or fast food, they should mostly consume natural fresh food, such as fruits and vegetables. These foods are very good for people because they don't have chemicals and provide important nutrients. Unlike junk food, healthy food doesn't cause diseases such as obesity, cancer, or diabetes. Natural food, fresh food, and spicy food are better than foods with preservatives and other chemicals. Also, people should drink more water and avoid juice and pop. People can drink pop or juice once in a while but not every day. People that live in rural areas and work on farms generally tend to eat natural, fresh foods and drink water every day. Since these people grow food for a living, they know more about healthy eating than people that live and work in the city. Individuals that eat healthily from the time that they are young will stay healthy even when they are older. Many people don't realize that slimmer people are healthier and receive more respect than heavier people. In addition, slimmer people won't die as early as heavier people, and they can grow old without encountering any health problems. When people eat healthy foods, they get stronger and avoid diseases. Although older people lack the energy and health of younger individuals, people that have eaten healthy foods for their whole lives will avoid problems like deafness and blindness as well as medical conditions. Some people live into their late nineties and they should thank God for their good health and long life. In comparison to overweight individuals, slimmer people have longer lives. Fat people will have a heart attack or other medical issues that will shorten their lives. In addition to food, the environmental health also determines people's lifespan and health. Some people come from places other than North America, where there are fewer vehicles, less pollution, and fewer diseases. These environments enable people to live longer lives due to the decreased amount of chemicals and pollution.

Some mothers lack knowledge of proper nutrition during pregnancy. Specifically, they eat unhealthy foods, which results in a less healthy baby. In addition, some mothers feed their babies or young children chemically enhanced or fatty foods. These foods cause children to gain excess weight or acquire medical conditions such as diabetes. Mothers should always prepare healthy food and snacks for their children as well as teach their children how to eat properly so that they can make their own healthy meals. In some cases, children don't listen to their mothers' advice and eat unhealthy foods despite receiving proper teaching and adequate nutrition from their mother. Many mothers in North America have caused their children to acquire an addiction to chemically-altered or fatty foods by feeding children these foods when they were young. In some cases, the mothers didn't realize that the food was unhealthy; however, the children developed a taste for these foods and continued consuming them as adults.

Individuals that are overweight try to lose weight through pills, surgery, or exercise. While some people can lose weight, others experience difficulty in shedding excess pounds. The majority of overweight people tend to struggle to lose their weight. Some of them try to stop their poor eating habits; however, in many cases, people revert to their old habits and continue eating badly. Although some people blame their parents for their weight problems, they should forgive their parents because in many cases, people are responsible for their own habits. In some situations, parents told their children how to eat properly but the children ignored their parents, so, in these cases, these individuals are responsible for their own problem.

The popularity of junk food in North America represents a pattern that also includes the selling of drugs and weapons. While many people don't consider obesity as big a problem as drugs and crime, all of these phenomena contribute to the deterioration of North American society. In order to improve their health, people should implement the following suggestions:

- People should engage in regular daily physical activity to burn their fat and build muscle
- When exercising, people should start slowly and take their time in order to achieve a certain level of fitness; they should avoid overdoing exercise so that they don't get hurt
- Some people can lose their weight quickly in a short time period, such as two months, but for other people, it takes much longer
- People should still consume an adequate amount of food, but they should avoid overeating and stop eating unhealthy foods
- Individuals should understand that weight loss is not easy, but they should continue working hard and not give up. They should keep working hard until the weight starts to disappear. They should put their faith that God can help them to heal.

- Although people will become hungry, they should avoid the temptation to overeat
- People should only eat healthy foods and beverages
- Individuals should avoid junk food, especially from restaurants such as McDonalds, KFC, A&W, and Wendy's. These places, as well as other fast food joints, contain chemically-processed and fatty foods that lead to weight gain. People need to take responsibility and control their eating habits.
- People that want to attract a nice-looking partner in order to marry and have children should eat properly and stay slim. In particular, women are pickier than men, and they prefer men that are slim and have muscle. Most women don't want to date or marry an overweight man; in fact, some rude women will even tell them to find a fat woman to date.

People that want to lose their weight quicker should avoid using pills or medicine, because most of these products are scams and don't actually help people to lose weight. However, prune juice helps people to lose weight, especially if people have two glasses per day, three or four times a week. Although it takes time, people need to be patient and continue taking prune juice. This juice eliminates all dirt and bacteria from the intestines and cleans the stomach. In addition, people can also eat spicy peppers or natural sambal; while this remedy is very hot and causes pain, it also helps to eliminate bacteria quickly. Even when consuming these weight loss foods, people still have to go to the gym and exercise every day without quitting or giving up.

Most places in the world have natural foods without chemicals, including Caribbean Islands, Middle East countries, Africa, Asia, and Latin America. People in these countries eat fresh and natural foods, which are much better than processed junk food. Although Europe restricted fast food, North America still contains a significant amount of unhealthy foods. The American and Canadian governments will continue to encourage the existence of fast food restaurants and the consumption of processed foods. This is unfortunate because these foods will continue to make people sick and unhealthy.

Life and Death

God gave people free breath to live in this earth. As a result, we should be thankful to God and respect him for giving us life. People that believe in Jesus Christ and have received his body and blood will have eternal life after they die. Although the body of Christians will eventually perish, their spirit will live forever and they will live with God in heaven, especially if they have lived a good life on earth. People that have followed all of God's laws and have not sinned will gain eternal life. Since God and Christ gave us breath and life, we should remember them and respect God by performing good actions and avoiding sin.

While some individuals believe in God and Jesus, other individuals don't follow the Christian religion. However, present and past evidence show that God and Jesus exist. Like Jesus, some people have come back to earth in their spiritual form. Jesus raised Lazarus and other people from the dead; in fact, Jesus himself came back to earth after his death. Jesus' body went to heaven, but his soul remained on earth similar to the way in which Prophet Ella's body went to heaven and he never actually died. After Jesus was resurrected, he showed his body to his disciples. In addition, some women realized that Jesus' tomb was empty, and they met an angel of God, who was Jesus. Although some people believe that the disciples and women imagined Jesus' spirit, the Bible speaks the truth about his resurrection. While some history and other major texts lie, the Bible always tells the truth.

Today, people are less likely to return from death than they were in the past. Although individuals committed some sins in the past, people today commit many more sins. As a result, when most people of the current era die, their spirits die with their body and their souls don't go to heaven. The Bible states that heaven is only for the good people and hell is for the sinners. People that commit sins on earth go to hell, where they burn for all of eternity. While individuals that lived a good life go to heaven, people that committed evil on earth will stay in hell. Although God tells us to refrain from judging people, God is the ultimate judge, as He decides which individuals go to heaven or hell upon their death. Furthermore, when the world ends and Jesus Christ returns to the earth, God will judge all of the wrong that people have committed. As a result, we have to be prepared for God's final judgment and change our behavior to ensure that we are performing only good actions. We should avoiding insulting other people unless they have done wrong to us. Nobody in this world is perfect; only God, the Creator, is a perfect being. Some people oppose God or don't believe in His existence. People shouldn't insult or lie to God or believe that we are better than Him. Nobody on this earth is more perfect or better than God because He created everything on this earth, including human beings. God has the power to decide someone's fate, so people should exercise caution in how we perceive and act towards God as well as refraining from sin. Although everyone commits some sins and should be forgiven by others as well as by God, we need to control ourselves and avoid repeating our sins. If God forgives us for our sin, we should never repeat this mistake again. Individuals that sin repeatedly will die early and they won't have a long life. Individuals that want to live a long and healthy life need to avoid sin and commit moral actions by respecting the rules and God's laws.

Some people live a very long life, living well into the 90s and even over 100. When people become very old, they start to experience health issues, such as weakness, fatigue, illness, and blindness. However, some seniors are still fairly strong and healthy despite their old age; these individuals can still speak, walk, hear and see. People can minimize the effect of aging by consuming healthy foods for their entire lives. In addition, God gives people long and healthy lives because they don't commit sin or eat unhealthy foods. Only a small percentage of people have long lives, so they should thank God and be happy without complaining. However, all of us eventually die because God designed us as mortal beings. The only being that can live forever is God. God's original plan was for human beings to live forever; however, when the first humans, Adam and Eve, disobeyed God, he punished all humans for their sin by introducing death into the world. If it weren't for Adam and Eve's mistake, there would be no death or evil on earth.

The Bible states that humans came from dust and return to dust upon their deaths. When people die, individuals should bury them. Although some people choose to cremate their loved ones, this method of dealing with the dead represents a sin. In some cases, individuals lack sufficient funds to bury their loved ones, so they choose the cheaper method of cremation because burial at a cemetery is expensive. If people have a good job or own their own business, they should save money to bury their family members in the future because when they get old, they want to be buried by their own children. People can renew their parents' burial plot so that their parents' bodies can stay underground and they won't need to have their parents cremated.

Music and Sport

Most people in the black culture like hip-hop and rap music, as these individuals grew up listening to this type of music. However, people in the current generation can choose from many different types of music, including techno, house, reggae, rhythm and blues, rock, pop, and heavy metal. Everyone has different musical preferences and listens to different types of music. People shouldn't judge others because of their musical tastes.

Individuals of African heritage prefer hip-hop, rap, rhythm and blues, and reggae. Among these styles, hip hop represents the most popular type of music for blacks of the current generation. Although individuals may believe that rap and hip-hop are different types of music, they are actually very similar.

Within any musical genre, older musical styles are referred to as old school, while newer subgenres are called new school. Most young people prefer new school music because they generally don't listen to their parents' or grandparents' music. However, old school music is preferable to newer types of music. Newer musical styles, especially those in the rap and hip-hop genres, contain inappropriate content:

- sex and women
- gays and lesbians
- money and power

- crime and drugs
- violence
- insults, harassment, and racial slurs
- videos that show naked women

This content contains negative educational value for children, as it teaches members of the current generation about detrimental ways of living. This music instills the following messages into children:

- People will spend the rest of their lives in ways that bring them closer to death, including the use of crime, drugs, and violence
- People will always get into trouble with other individuals and will spend time with people that represent a bad influence on them
- People will always have problems with major institutions, such as schools, workplaces, the government, and the police
- People will experience difficulty with immigration and embassies
- People will experience harassment, violence, and death from the police

Before this style of music started in the 1990s and 2000s, rappers and hip hop artists had respect; however, the current music has changed significantly, illustrating major differences from old school and new school rap. Previous music contained strong educational values, while current music has little value, encouraging people to live immoral lives filled with sex, crime, drugs, and violence.

Some of the old school rappers include 2Pac, Notorious BIG, Snoop Dogg, Dr. Dre, Ice Cube, Eminem, 50 Cent, G-Unit, D12, Run DMC, Vanilla Ice, Jay-Z, Foxy Brown, and Nas. Although these musicians use course language and curse words in their music, they came from a difficult background of gangs, drugs, crime and violence. Their families were in poverty and they didn't experience the opportunity to attend postsecondary school and obtain a good job. This situation provides an example of discrimination, as most rappers, who are black, were denied the opportunities provided to whites, Asians, and Hispanics. In their lives, these musicians experienced racism and adversity from society, including schools, workplaces, citizens, military, and police officers. As a result of the struggles that they experienced, rappers sing about violence and use foul language. However, due to their circumstances, they shouldn't be faulted for their music, as it provides a way to express their feelings, such as anger and frustration.

Unlike new school rappers, old school rappers don't sing about murder and revenge or insult other people, such as rival gangs and police officers. However, both old school and new school rappers will insult someone if they feel as if they have been wronged. They may also sing about taking revenge on individuals or groups that have offended them; while old school rappers only take offense to major issues such as the murder of a friend or family member, newer rappers propose killing someone even for a minor insult, which is not right. People need to respect rappers and avoid causing trouble with them because they may take revenge.

Although some individuals believe that rap and hip-hop music focuses mainly on issues such as drugs, violence, and gangs, this type of music recounts the life experiences of the rappers. As previously mentioned, old school rappers don't swear to impress people; their course language reflects their frustration with their personal circumstances. They don't swear intentionally outside of their music or purposely expose children to their bad language because they don't want young children to learn about cursing or other negative aspects. Children that become exposed to bad language or detrimental issues such as drugs, crime, and violence will act badly by disrespecting their parents and other authority figures. When they become adults, they will commit crimes, use drugs, and act violently towards others. Since children don't understand the difference between right and wrong, young children shouldn't listen to rap music because it will have a negative influence on them. On the other hand, adults can listen to rap music because their values are already established.

The government and other public authorities complain about old school rap music that contains swear words; however, they should focus on the content on music rather than superficial elements such as the language. Instead, people should protest against the violence and sexual situations portrayed in new school rap music, because this content teaches children about inappropriate aspects of life. Rappers only use course language when they become upset about an unjust situation in their lives. However, not all rappers use curse words because some rappers have never experienced the difficult lives that blacks face. High-quality rap music provides inspiration for learning many positive aspects of life rather than focusing solely on the negative aspects. Old school rap featured many quality artists, such as 2Pac and Notorious BIG; while Notorious BIG played freestyle rap, 2Pac conveyed the reality of life in a way that no other rapped succeeded in doing. As a result, 2Pac was the best and most genuine rapper. In the same way that Michael Jackson was the king of pop music and Aaliyah was the queen of rhythm and blues, 2Pac was the king of rap music.

Some rappers make fun of other people based on their demographic characteristics, such as age, race, skin color, religion, or sex. In most of these cases, rap songs ridicule women, especially young and beautiful women. Some rappers don't mean any harm and intend only to make a joke; however, people shouldn't make jokes about people they don't know, as the object of the joke may take offense to the joke. Rather, people should only tease or joke with acquaintances, friends, and family members. Furthermore, people shouldn't use negative or inappropriate language to refer to women. In some cases, individuals should only tease their wives or girlfriends; however, even these intimate acquaintances may take offense to such remarks. Some of inappropriate terms used to refer to women include pussy, chick, chicky, whore, and bitch. Rappers, along with other men, can use this language in reference to women. In some cases, these terms indicate that a man finds a woman very attractive; while a few women won't take offense to these terms, other women find them very offensive. Despite this disparity in opinion, these words show a lack of respect towards women, and, in order to respect women, men should avoid using this language.

In the 1990s, there was a rivalry between East Coast and West Coast rappers. These two groups of musicians used to hate each other and threaten to wage war with or kill one another. For example, 2Pac and Notorious BIG couldn't hang out together because their association would increase the animosity between the two gangs. However, this rivalry has dissipated, and all rappers now associate positively with one another. Hip-hop and rap music should emphasize peace rather than violence, hatred, or killing. According to God and Jesus, all of us are brothers and sisters, and, we should treat each other accordingly.

Another set of problematic terms in rap music revolves around the use of the word "nigger" or "nigga." In black culture, it is offensive for a non-black person to call someone of African heritage a "nigger." For example, Caucasians, Arabs, Hispanics, Latinos, Mulattos, Indians, and Aboriginal people should not refer to a black person as a nigger; this term contains disrespect when used by a person of a non-black race and demonstrates racial prejudice. Since black people don't use racially inappropriate terms towards members of other races, non-black races shouldn't use derogatory terms towards blacks. Similarly, rappers and other citizens should respect women by refraining from inappropriate words such as "bitch" and other negative terms. Sometimes, women that dislike each other even use this term as an insult; however, women shouldn't use these derogatory terms towards each other because they not only insult a particular woman but they also insult all women.

Another issue in music involves cheating, especially in terms of one musician copying or imitating another. In school, teachers and principals have strict laws against cheating and punish students that they catch cheating. However, musicians that copy other artists don't incur penalties. Since cheating in school resembles cheating in music, then both students and recording artists that cheat should receive a punishment or penalty. Artists that copy the melody of other artists are not cheating; however, they should ask the other musician for permission to use his/her music. If the original artist fails to provide the other musician with permission, then the second musician shouldn't copy the first one; otherwise, he/she may get caught and have to go to court. Before he became famous, Michael Jackson copied the music of other artists. However, once Jackson achieved fame, he made his own music, and, as a result, people liked his music and he became rich. People that copy the music of other artists lack knowledge of music and will never learn about music or become famous by copying others.

People that want to enter the music industry need to gain a significant amount of practice and experience. The process of breaking into the business and becoming famous contains many challenges and only a select few individuals successfully accomplish this feat. Individuals that want to become a musician shouldn't copy other artists in order to make money for themselves. Although some rappers copy aspects of other rappers' melodies, they generally ask for permission and use their own lyrics. Singers should accord other musicians this type of respect rather than simply copying their music without asking. Musicians that create their own songs contribute genuine music to the industry, while singers that copy other artists don't make real music. In order to succeed in the music industry, musicians should make their own music. True music is a blessing of God, and successful singers should thank Him for their gift.

With regards to music and sports, some people have stereotypical perceptions of individuals' tastes and preferences. Some of these stereotypes are illustrated below:

- People that like boy bands, such as Backstreet Boys, N-Sync, and O-Town are people that are considered "for the guys"
- People that like girl bands, such as Spice Girls, Girl Thing, and Girls Aloud are either women or homosexuals

- People that like country music are older white people
- People that like rock, pop, and heavy metal are generally whites
- People that like techno or European music are white teenagers or young adults
- People that like Salsa, Rumba and Tango are Spanish people
- People that like Jazz and classical music are senior citizens
- People that like hip-hop, rap, and rhythm and blues are black people
- People that like soccer are Latin Americans and Europeans
- People that like basketball are black
- People that like winter sports, such as hockey and curling, are white people
- People that like karate, judo and kung-fu are Asian people

However, these musical and sports stereotypes are false, because factors like skin color and nationality don't dictate people's preferences or interests. For example, hip-hop and rap music contains some artists of Spanish origin, such as Pit Bull and Fat Joe, as well as white artists, such as Eminem, Beastie Boys, and Vanilla Ice. Although hip-hop and rap mostly contain black artists that perform for black audiences, people shouldn't judge others' preferences on this basis or make assumptions about the relationship between color and musical preference. People shouldn't call rap "black music" because this type of terminology insults and offends people. Another case that challenges musical stereotypes involves

Charlie Pride, who was one example of an African American country music musician. In sports, many people assume that only black people play basketball; however, many white and Asian individuals also participate in this sport. Many black people and African countries play soccer, which most people assume is dominated by whites and Hispanics. Soccer represents a multicultural sport that many people from all over the world play and watch. In Canadian society, a larger number of women than men play soccer, which contrasts with the situation in the rest of the world, where larger numbers of men play soccer. In addition, soccer is a fairly rough sport, which makes it more suitable to men than women. Gentler sports, such as tennis, are more ideal for women. However, I respect both men and women, and I strongly believe that both sexes can play any sport that they wish. Women can play rougher sports such as football, soccer, or fighting sports, while men can play lighter sports such as tennis. People shouldn't make assumptions about suitability to a sport based on factors such as sex and race, and individuals shouldn't judge others regardless of which sports they play. People should play sports in which they take an interest as well as for which they have skills and God-given abilities. Individuals shouldn't exercise judgment against one another, especially when others don't judge them. The only being that can judge other people is God.

When I was a young boy, I thought that the sport of bobsledding was only for white people that lived in winter countries with snow. I didn't know how individuals could practice bobsledding if they lived in tropical countries without snow and ice. Later, when I grew up, I realized that nationality, geographic location, and skin color doesn't determine an individual's participation, interest, or expertise in a particular sport. Athletes can excel in any sport as long as they train and practice that sport. For example, the film "Cool Runnings" conveys the true story of Jamaican bobsledders who were the first black people to win a bobsled championship in Calgary, AB, Canada in 1988. As a result of their fame, other black people from Jamaica compete and even excel in bobsledding. In addition to bobsledding, Jamaicans also excel in other sports, including running, in which they qualified for the Olympics as well as winning championships and medals. Athletes that represent their country successfully help to create a positive image for that country.

Discrimination and Racism

Discrimination and racism occur everywhere in the world. Caucasian people are the first group of individuals who created problems such as colonial struggles, suffering, supremacy, segregation, pain, discrimination, and racism. White people provide a poor example to other nations, teaching all cultures about aspects such as discrimination and racism. Caucasians have always believed that they are superior to people of other races; however, this belief is misguided.

To this day, discrimination and racism occur in many European countries, including

- Netherlands   - Belgium   - Luxemburg
- Germany   - Switzerland   - Austria
- UK   - France   - Spain
- Greece   - Russia   - Scandinavia
- Portugal   - Italy   - Ireland

In addition, several non-European countries also feature racism and discrimination, including

- Canada   - Australia
- United States - New Zealand
- South Africa   - China
- Japan   - South Korea
- some countries in South and Central America

Immigrants of other nations are also victims of racism and discrimination by the citizens, police, and government of these countries. In particular, black people experience the worst discrimination, especially in terms of police brutality. Although racism was worse in the past, especially in the United States and South Africa, discrimination still represents a major problem because white people, and, to a lesser extent, other races, such as Arabs, Hispanics, Asians, and Mulattos, receive greater opportunities in life than black people. The diminished opportunities that blacks receive occur in all countries, especially in European nations, Australia, New Zealand, South Africa, South Korea, China, and Japan. Regardless of a person's skill or behavior, most countries care more strongly about skin color than they do about personality and attributes, which represents a racist attitude. The following examples detail the ways in which black people experience racism and discrimination:

- Black people are restricted in their opportunities for higher education
- Blacks are limited in their career opportunities, with their chances limited to minimum-wage jobs such as custodians or laborers
- Some companies won't hire people because they are black
- Black people that experience difficulties with the government, police, schooling or education won't receive help from the government, lawyers, or police officers, even when they are victimized by theft or another crime
- If a problem arises or people suspect that an offense has been committed, black people are automatically

blamed, even if they are innocent. Some citizens or police even bother black people to provoke them into a fight. If blacks fight back for self-defense, then they often get in trouble with the police

- If the police suspect trouble, they automatically assume that a black person has committed the crime even if they are innocent. Although the police don't have proof and may need more information, they will still assume that a black person is guilty
- Police are unnecessarily brutal and aggressive with black citizens. Rather than asking a black person about a particular situation, they will become aggressive or arrest the black person. If a black person resists arrest, they will go to jail or get killed.
- In prison, many black people were poisoned or killed by brutal police and security guards. Police and guards beat up black people freely, especially when black people experienced issues with other citizens. In fact, there have been situations where police have seen black people on the street and shot or killed those people.
- Police constantly harass black people and ask for their ID or government documents to prove their citizenship status. If black people don't have their citizenship status, lost their documentation, or failed to renew their passports, the government will arrest them and potentially deport them back to their country.
- The police, government, and citizens of the country treat blacks poorly, limiting their rights and freedoms, especially in comparison with the rest of

the citizens. They segregate blacks from other races and provide blacks with inferior treatment.

- If blacks try to protest and fight for their rights, the police will stop them or even shoot them for protesting. Similarly, some racist citizens that see blacks on the street will beat them up, stab them, or even shoot them for no reason. The police won't stop this behavior because they also discriminate against black people as well as other immigrants.

The government and police try to brainwash their citizens against blacks and immigrants of other races by establishing an "us" vs. "them" mentality as well as by using propaganda that states that they are "protecting our country" when harming blacks. This propaganda influences the citizens to believe that black people are dangerous enemies rather than citizens of the country; such behavior represents racism and discrimination by the police, government, and citizens. These actions occur in many countries, including the following:

- European nations   - Brazil
- United States   - Chile
- Australia   - Argentina
- China   - Paraguay
- Japan   - Uruguay
- South Africa   - Belize
- New Zealand   - Mexico
- South Korea   - El Salvador
- Columbia   - Venezuela

In these nations, the police use violence and threaten immigrants, especially black people. Citizens also exhibit discrimination and racism against black people. Many immigrants and blacks feel afraid to go outside of their homes because they believe that their lives are in danger. Black people lack the rights and freedoms granted to other citizens. For example, black people are denied the right to borrow money or to save money for purchasing a house or opening their own business. Several other instances of discrimination against blacks involve the following:

- Black students have always been labeled with learning disabilities or psychological problems even though they lack these issues
- Schoolteachers and principals exhibit racism against black students. In the past, the government established separate schools for blacks and whites. Even today, black students still experience abuse from teachers, principals and police.
- Many black people have only been afforded a minimal education, which results in their unemployment, low-income status, and homelessness. Governments won't allow black people to obtain higher educations; even if they finish high school, they won't have access to better jobs.
- Caucasians discriminate against blacks and other immigrants that have accents and language barriers. Even in the case that blacks possess strong language skills, they are still denied access to good jobs because of their skin color

European countries have historically exhibited strong racism against blacks. In the past, Germany and Russia burned down refugee villages to kill immigrants and refugees, especially black immigrants, during the 1980s and 1990s. Among all European nations, Germany has exhibited the strongest degree of racism, especially under the reign of Adolf Hitler.

The following scenario involves a man named Zeca Schall, who is a black politician in Germany. He was the victim of abuse from the far right wing government because of his left-wing stance and his skin color. When he had a political campaign approaching, he felt threatened by the opposition and had to enlist police protection around the clock.

Schall originally came to Germany from Angola more than twenty years ago and obtained German citizenship by marrying a German woman. After his arrival in Germany, he became a member of the Centre for Christian Democrats in the CDU party. Not only was Schall a member of the CDU, but he was also a volunteer firefighter at a local fire department in Germany. Because of his political affiliation, the National Democratic Party has wanted him out of Germany; however, the German government lacks the ability to kick him out of the country. The government and his political opponents refer to him as "Cota Nigro," showing racism and discrimination. Although Schall possesses a higher education and German citizenship, people still exercise prejudice against him because of his skin color. The NDP denied accusations of this racist behavior and tried to play down their actions as part of a political campaign. The CDU claims to fully support Schall against the hate campaign in North Germany. Schall's house was broken into and shootings occurred in his hometown. This was a disaster, especially since Schall was a good person and had lived for many years as a German citizen. Schall was totally shocked and couldn't believe that people would treat him in this manner, especially since he had a high post as the CDU Export Integration of Minorities. Schall experienced several death threats against him mainly because of his skin color. Overall, this example demonstrates the severe extent of racism that still occurs in countries such as Germany.

In addition to Germany, Spain and Russia also exhibit discrimination and racism against blacks, especially in their refusal to give proper medical treatment to these individuals. When black people are very sick, medical professionals will give them a bad nail to put into their bodies in order to cause death.

Slave Routes

The Europeans enslaved the black people from Africa, taking them from their native country to many other places in the world, including North America, South America, Caribbean Islands, and Central America. In addition, Europeans took Indians, people with dark brown skin, from India, Sri Lanka, and Bangladesh to places such as South America, Caribbean Islands, and Central America. In contrast, the brown people with light skin were never slaves; rather, they came to North America and other locations as immigrants and performed cheap labor. Although the dark brown people were enslaved for a short period of time, Africans were treated more harshly and enslaved for longer periods of time. The brown people gained their freedom earlier than the blacks did, and the Africans travelled farther distances than the browns; thus, the Africans experienced much harsher conditions in their slavery.

Many individuals believe that the United States was the only country to use slaves directly from Africa; however, other countries, such as Canada, also engaged slaves from Africa. In fact, Canada has an increasing number of African-Canadians today. Nevertheless, Canada didn't use slavery to the same extent as the United States. Rather, the United States used more slaves from Africa and for a longer period of time. In fact, black slaves from the United States escaped to Canada in order to regain their freedom. As a result of this escape, the slaves and their descendants became African Canadians.

Although the Dutch people from the Netherlands were the first nation to employ slaves, the British made much more extensive use of slaves. The following European countries participated in the slave trade:

- Netherlands	- Germany
- Belgium	- Switzerland
- Luxemburg	- Austria
- England	- Wales
- Scotland	- Ireland
- Scandinavia	- Russia
- Poland	- Romania
- Spain	- Portugal
- Italy	- Greece
- France	

Europeans used slaves for planting items such as cotton, sugar, and coffee as well as for farm labor. During slavery, black people worked for free and didn't receive payment by their American and European masters. In addition, the slaves received poor treatment by their masters; they were treated like animals and subject to harsh working conditions. For example, they didn't receive breaks, they weren't allowed much sleep, they weren't permitted to obtain education, and they didn't have any freedom. Blacks suffered and struggled for their entire lives at the hands of white people. If slaves made a mistake in their work or they tried to run away, they would receive cruel treatment, which may involve beatings, rape, torture, or death by their white masters. Slaves were only given minimal amounts of cheap food or clothing, and they had to eat on the floor like animals. As a result of their malnutrition, many slaves became sick or died. White people also abused slaves frequently, with hanging, starvation, and cutting of the limbs. Slavery represented a low point in history, as slaves experienced terrible treatment by their white masters. Fortunately, slavery no longer exists in most countries, including USA, Canada, Caribbean Islands, Central America, and South America.

Although slavery occurred in the past, many people become upset when learning about slavery through their ancestors or from history books. Many sources, including books, documentaries, films, and TV, discuss slavery and the slave route. During the time of slavery, black men couldn't date or marry white women, because they would go to jail or die at the hands of white men. However, white men could date, marry or sleep with black women without suffering punishment or death. Similarly, while white men could impregnate black women, black men couldn't impregnate a white woman without suffering disastrous consequences, such as death, and they would certainly never be allowed to see their child.

While Aboriginal people were never slaves in the same way that Africans were, the Europeans, Americans, and Canadians still mistreated Native people. Aboriginals were killed by the British, French, and Spanish people who invaded North, Central, and South America, taking away the Aboriginals' land. In addition, the Europeans forced Aboriginals to lose their culture, language, and religion. Natives weren't allowed to speak their own language or teach their culture to their children. Rather, the Europeans forced the Aboriginals to speak the European languages, including English, French, and Spanish. The Native children were taken away from their parents and sent to another province or state. The parents didn't know where their children were and were not permitted to visit their children. Similarly, children weren't allowed to come back and visit their parents. The Europeans brought corruption and segregation to the Americas; the white man dominated the rest of the world because whites believed that they were superior to every other race. The whites prohibited Natives from having basic human rights; Europeans killed and raped Aboriginals, often resulting in pregnancies.

Today, some countries still employ slavery, such as Latin America and Arab countries, including Northern Africa and the Middle East. Arabs, as well as some places in India, still use black people as slaves. In the past, India designated small children and teenagers and slaves to adults.

Civil War

In the 1950s, a moderate amount of racism and discrimination existed in the United States. However, in the 1960s, these issues escalated. The climate of America involved intense hatred and racism between blacks and whites. In addition, a series of laws segregated blacks and whites in the United States, giving whites preferential treatment. These laws included the following:

- Black people and white people couldn't associate with one another or speak to one another. Blacks and whites had separate neighborhoods and couldn't visit one another's neighborhoods. If black people were in a white neighborhood, they would be arrested or shot by the police
- Black people couldn't obtain sufficient education to receive high school diplomas or to go on to post-secondary education. These educational restrictions prevented black people from obtaining a better job and a better life
- Black people were prohibited from certain professions, such as police officers, doctors, military personnel, technicians, mechanics, and lawyers. Additionally, blacks were not allowed to own or operate their own business

- Black people didn't have equal rights and weren't treated with respect. Black people couldn't even enjoy their own lives or experience a true sense of freedom. In fact, blacks were not allowed to vote
- Blacks and whites had to use separate facilities from one another. For example, blacks and whites couldn't sit beside one another on the bus or they couldn't eat and drink with each other. In fact, black people and white people had to use separate water fountains. In addition, they had to play sports on separate teams and use different modes of transportation
- Black people were prohibited from certain buildings and public places, including restaurants, movie theatres, beaches, and swimming pools

These examples of discrimination show that blacks have always endured racism from white people. In addition to these aforementioned restrictions, blacks also suffered verbal insults, such as "Nigger" and "Negro," from white people. If whites, policemen, or members of racist organizations, such as the KKK, saw black people in the street, they would harass, threaten, or attack blacks. Whites also burned down the houses of black individuals or families. Both police officers and members of the KKK killed blacks with various weapons. The laws also favored Caucasian individuals; for example, if a white person assaulted or killed a black person, the white person wouldn't get arrested, but if a black person assaulted or killed a white person, they would get arrested. Additionally, police disrespected, insulted, threatened, arrested, or killed black people for no apparent reason, even assaulting black individuals in public places. Some examples of police brutality against black people include the following:

- Police officers assaulted and arrested innocent black people for no reason
- Police officers murdered black people because of their skin color
- Firefighters embarrassed and harassed black people by spraying water on them
- The police and military used their dogs to attack and murder black citizens in countries such as the United States and South Africa

Rosa Parks was a black woman that was arrested for refusing to give up her bus seat to a white person. At that time, black people had a designated seating area near the back of the bus, while white people could sit anywhere that they wanted. When the bus driver asked her to move and give up her seat in the colored section to a white person, she refused. Although she didn't break any law, the bus driver called the police, and the police arrested her for her actions. Rosa Parks became an activist for black people's rights; however, she faced significant racism, including arrest, prison time, and death threats.

In addition, Presidents Abraham Lincoln and John F. Kennedy were assassinated because they wanted to treat black and white people equal and with respect; they strongly opposed racism and discrimination against blacks. While some people agreed with the aspirations of these presidents, many other individuals disagreed with the idea of giving blacks and whites equal rights and freedoms. Similarly, Martin Luther King and Malcolm X were killed because they fought for the rights of black people, trying to ensure that blacks were treated equally to white people. In South Africa, Nelson Mandela also attempted to change the laws restricting the rights and freedoms of black individuals; however, he went to jail for 30 years as a result of his efforts.

Today, black men can date, marry, and have children with white women and women of other races; however, black men could only date or marry black women in the 1960s. If black men tried to have a relationship with women of other races, they would endure arrest, imprisonment, or even death. On the other hand, white men have always been allowed to date, marry, or have children with black women as well as with women of other races.

Although discrimination and racism still exist in places like the United States and South Africa, these issues are not nearly as bad as they were in the past. Nevertheless, certain racial groups, such as Caucasians, Hispanics, and Blacks, still dislike each other, especially in Latin America, the United States, and even Canadian cities such as Toronto, which lies near the border of the USA. In some cases, people of one race can't have a conversation with a bus driver, police officer, or other individual because they may insult that individual or even act aggressively towards them. However, in most of Canada and Europe, with the exception of Germany and Spain, people of all races can talk with police officers or bus drivers.

While some black people exhibit racism, most black individuals treat each other as well as people of other races with equal rights and respect. The majority of black people don't threaten people that don't bother them and they don't attack people who don't start a fight with them. Blacks generally don't kill people who haven't attacked their own people and they don't hate people that don't hate them. Black people will only become aggressive in the following situations:

- Black people will only kill other people if those individuals kill their family or friends
- Black people only hate people that hate them
- Black people will only threaten or use violence against people that threaten or use violence against them

Most black people don't oppose anyone or discriminate against members of other races. In fact, people shouldn't take revenge unless another person has committed a major offense against them. The police don't have any right to arrest, threaten or kill people if a person tries to defend themselves or their people. Individuals should learn self-defense so that they can protect themselves as well as their family and friends from unsolicited attacks. Some people would prefer to die defending their rights rather than to live in fear of the police and government. Individuals can use their own weapons against the police and military in order to defend themselves or to revenge officers or armies that failed to respect them and took away their rights. Police should only defend themselves if their lives or the lives of innocent people are in danger; they shouldn't attack innocent people on the grounds of racism. White police are the biggest culprits in attacking individuals of other races; although one can claim that this statement represents a stereotype or racism, statistics prove that white police discriminate more than officers of other races.

Black people have declared their rights on this Earth to be treated as a human being. They should receive the respect and equality afforded to all other humans in the world. Blacks are not animals or an inferior species; blacks are human beings and deserve the same rights, respect, and freedom granted to other races.

Black Community

Unfortunately, many black people foster hatred for one another and kill each other. Most races don't exhibit as much internal animosity as blacks do for one another. Other nations solve problems and make solutions rather than showing hatred and jealousy for one another. Black people should use similar ideologies to improve their communication and relationships with each other. For example, white people or Caucasians perceive one another as brothers and sisters, treating each other with respect for the most part. Although whites and other races make mistakes and can treat one another poorly at times, they don't allow other races to deceive them about money and politics in the way that blacks are manipulated. Blacks should act intelligently and defend members of their own race and community rather than hating and trying to hurt one another. Blacks shouldn't allow other people to manipulate them into hurting one another. For example, some Caribbean people and Afro-Americans are against Africans although their own relatives came from those countries when they were slaves. Blacks allow white people to manipulate them into hating other black races. Specifically, whites claim that the managers of African villages sold their own people into slavery; however, white people are lying about this fact because whites forced blacks into slavery. When the slaves were sold from Africa, they were supposed to return to Africa; however, the slaves never returned to their native country. Slaves were permanently taken from their family and never got to see their parents or family members again. Caribbean people and African Americans can't deny their history despite the fact that white people try to persuade them to do so. Most black people originally came from Africa; thus, all blacks are related to one another through their common ancestry.

In the United States, many black people dislike one another. They complain about each other, hate their own race, and try to harm one another. In fact, even some black people try to bleach themselves in order to change their skin color to white. Blacks shouldn't try to change their skin color; they should show pride in their race and identity. White people have turned blacks against one another by enslaving them, which has represented a humiliating experience and caused blacks to feel ashamed of their own identity. People that try to change their skin color only end up harming themselves by causing health problems and incurring severe financial expenses. For example, Michael Jackson, who was trying to bleach his skin to make himself white, ultimately died in 2009 partly due to this issue.

Many black people don't realize that if they don't respect themselves and their people, that no one else will have respect for them. Blacks who despise themselves and their skin color set a bad example for Caucasians and other races to further discriminate and oppress blacks. Even if other races don't like blacks, they will respect black people if blacks show self-respect and pride in their own color and race. Blacks that hate themselves and other people of their race can't blame other races that show prejudice and racism against them. However, in the case that blacks respect themselves and other races still disrespect them, they have a legitimate complaint. In the past, when Jewish people were slaves of Caucasians, Jewish people declared their rights and white people paid them back. Blacks should follow the example of the Jewish people and show greater respect for themselves in order to earn more respect from other races, especially Caucasians. Whites should pay blacks back for their history of enslavement rather than continuing to oppress and threaten blacks.

Ruling the World

Caucasians have travelled around the entire world and explored everywhere, including the Americas, Asia, Australia, New Zealand, and Africa. Caucasians originally came from Europe and brought many negative aspects to the world, including colonization, suffering, depression, and segregation. In fact, they even oppressed people in their own land through racism and discrimination. They didn't care that they dominated people, and, in some aspects, continue to dominate people today. White people think that they have always owned certain continents, such as North America, Australia, and New Zealand; however, these lands belonged to Aboriginal people before the white men took over. Aboriginal people will never have their land back and they will never have independence in their own countries. Regardless of whether white people originally owned land, they will still dominate over other peoples and races as well as oppress those people in their own land. Most countries and continents around the world are controlled and ruled by white people from the United States or Europe. They enslave other races and nationalities, controlling their economies. For instance, people can't work by their own rules and set their own prices because Europeans and Americans have most of the power in this world. White people have always ruled the world and continue to control most of the world to this day. No other race dominates in the way that whites do; nobody controls Caucasians, steals their rights, controls their resources, takes their land, or murders them without a legitimate reason. Only Europeans steal other lands and control other countries. Europeans and Americans control third world countries and their economies. White men don't want peace or equality; they want to maintain racism and discrimination throughout the world. They don't want people to have nationalistic pride in their country because they will kill people who support their own country. Caucasians are mainly interested in natural resources; if a country doesn't have any resources, then white people will leave them alone, but if a nation has valuable resources, then Caucasians will want to exploit the country for their resources. White people only care about their business and money and they don't care about people of other nations. Many European countries make third-world countries sign contracts so that these underdeveloped nations never become developed. Some of the countries that exploit impoverished nations include the following:

- Ireland	- France
- England	- Spain
- Netherlands	- Portugal
- Belgium	- Italy
- Luxembourg	- Malta
- Vatican	- Switzerland
- Austria	- Germany
- Iceland	- Sweden
- Norway	- Finland
- Denmark	- Poland
- Hungary	- Romania
- Lichtenstein	- Greece

China and the United States also control third-world countries as well as African nations. Although Europeans have a significant amount of power, the Americans have the most power in the world because they control other people's countries more often than Europeans. Americans and Europeans don't want third-world countries to experience success because these countries have resources that could take the power away from the white man. Especially in the case of Europe, white-dominated countries lack sufficient resources, explaining their tendency to steal from other nations. White men fool people or lie to them by promising them peace and a stronger economy. In reality, white people bring war to other lands, causing people to die or starve because they lack sufficient resources for sustaining their own food. When Europeans and Americans take over third world countries, people don't have food and water and they can't support their families. Caucasians won't allow other people to build and sell weapons but they can create and sell weapons to other countries. Caucasians cause many problems in the world, such as war, poverty, hunger, and discrimination; yet they blame other people for their problems. They don't like when they see that people of other races are intelligent or physically strong because they feel as if their power is threatened.

White people travel everywhere in the world and receive respect from the natives of those countries. Nobody will try to control white people in their country or make strict rules such as requiring a visa or having to follow strict immigration policies. Caucasians can live in another country for as long as they want and they can always travel back to their own country without any hassle. Many Caucasians live in other parts of the world, such as Caribbean Islands, African nations, Asia, and Latin America, without having their lives complicated.

Nobody forces white people to return to their countries or exhibits discrimination and racism against them. White people can have dual citizenships or break rules and laws in other countries and still live peacefully in these countries. Most people of other countries don't mind white people living in their nations as long as they respect the rules of the country. Governments of these countries don't harass Caucasians or stop them from receiving citizenship in another country. In contrast, most countries discriminate against blacks and take their opportunities away. Some examples of the world discrimination against blacks are as follows:

- Black people cannot travel anywhere they want in the world
- Blacks cannot go back and forth from one country to another
- Blacks can't live in other people's countries and can't have 2 or 3 citizenships
- Most other races are not welcome in foreign countries and don't get the respect that white people do
- Even if people of non-white races respect another country's rules and laws, these countries fail to provide them with the proper respect and deport them from the country for arbitrary reasons
- While white people are not contained in airports, people of other races are often detained in airports
- People of other races always need visas and yet white people don't require these documents
- White people don't have strict immigration rules but people of other races have to face harsh immigration policies

- White people don't have to face the same rules and laws as people of other races

Caucasians treat people of other races differently and impose arbitrary laws and policies on those people simply because they aren't white. White people treat others differently and insult people with racism, discrimination, and segregation. Many people of other races have experienced difficult lives and yet Caucasians continue to make these individuals suffer. People that immigrate to Europe, Australia, New Zealand, and North America will never gain acceptance from white people. The governments of these countries don't treat colored races with respect and deport immigrants for arbitrary reasons.

Governments have forced many young people to go to war and innocent soldiers have died in wars of other countries. Unlike older people, young people lack knowledge about politics and have no control over events in the world. In contrast, older individuals, especially white people, control the political structures of a country and the entire world. Although it seems as if Caucasians speak the truth, they lie to other governments and peoples in order to exploit them for their resources and economy. Caucasian people want to make other countries and citizens overreact in order to take advantage of those people. Some people prefer to hear what the white people have to say rather than the actual truth. When people speak the truth, the Caucasians, especially the ones in power, take offense and want to silence those that speak the truth. White men don't want to hear the truth because the truth reveals that they are selfish, greedy, jealous, and power-hungry. The world lives in a white supremacy, and Caucasians believe that people of other nations lack intelligence, yet this is not true. White people don't want to believe that people of other races are smart because they believe that intelligent people of other races will threaten their world domination. Specifically, in certain countries, white people fear intelligent people with strong bodies who know their own rights. Although white people don't like these individuals, they will still respect them and leave them alone. Caucasians particularly look for individuals of other races that appear weak and unintelligent so that they can take advantage of these people. Weak people lack intelligence and ability, so white men can easily express their dominance over these individuals. Specifically, white people fear Latinos, Arabs, and Asians, because people of these races are intelligent and difficult to dominate; however, whites don't fear blacks because they believe that black people are easy to control due to their weaknesses. However, some black men are physically strong and many black people are very intelligent. Most races live under the supremacy and rule of the white man despite the façade of independence and equality. Malcolm X was right when he stated that white people are like the devil. All other races, including blacks, Hispanics, Arabs, Asians, Natives, and Aboriginals are all under the control of white people. Not only do white people discriminate against blacks but other races, including Latinos, Arabs, Asians, Aboriginals, and brown people all exhibit hatred against black people. Only God can help black people.

Both ugly and beautiful places exist in every country throughout the world. For instance, ugly places can exist in North America, Australia, New Zealand, and Europe, while beautiful places exist in Africa. Caucasian people believe that Africa and its people only manifest ugliness, projecting Africans as homeless and hungry people that will eat anything to survive. However, white people don't understand that not all African individuals are in poverty. They impose their stereotypes and prejudices onto African individuals, generalizing the entire nation based on only some individuals in the poorer regions of the country. In fact, white people have poverty in their own countries, but they won't admit to these issues on their media networks. They don't want the rest of the world to know about their poverty because they're embarrassed by the situation and don't want to tarnish their image of wealth. On the other hand, white people want to take advantage of Africans and depict their nation in a negative way. White people don't want Africans to speak the truth about their situation so that they can continue to oppress them. Black people don't hate any other races and respect everyone regardless of their skin color. However, white people, and people of other races will continue to discriminate against blacks.

Security Guards

On Tuesday, March 4, 2014, a black man named Jason Williams was returning home from a meeting with a financial business group. On his way home, he went to the Safeway at Southgate Mall, in Edmonton, AB. Although it was 10 p.m. and the mall had been closed since 9 p.m., Jason crossed by the mall in order to avoid the cold, as it was approximately -30 degrees. After purchasing his groceries at Safeway, Jason remained inside for a few minutes in order to put on his winter outerwear, such as a hat and mittens. While Jason was gathering his belongings in preparation to leave, a young black security guard came quickly out of the security office door and informed Jason that the mall was closed. Jason replied to the security guard, informing the guard that he realized that the mall had been closed since 9 p.m. and that he was only arranging his stuff before leaving. Then, Jason put his gloves on and headed towards the exit. The security guard returned to his office and watched Jason through the window. He opened a window slightly and pointed his finger at Jason, repeatedly shouting at him to leave. Although Jason had already left the mall exit, the security guard ran out of his office towards Jason, who initially ignored the guard and stated that he didn't want any problems. The security guard didn't need to repeat his request so rudely, as Jason had already left the mall. Thus, the guard's actions constituted harassment because he had pointed at Jason rudely and threatened him. Jason hadn't done anything wrong, so the guard's actions were insulting and offensive.

Like police officers, security guards should respect people, especially if people obey them and display respectful behavior towards them. Most people know the rules of the mall and other public facilities, and the majority of individuals respect these laws and rules. While officials such as security guards and peace officers have certain policies and procedures that they have to follow, they should still perform their work in a respectful manner. Some of the inappropriate actions of security guards and officers include the following:

- Assaulting people
- Provoking people into a fight
- Discrimination or racist treatment
- Threatening people
- Accusing people of a violation without proof
- Screaming or yelling at people
- Rudeness, insulting or offending people

Peace officers and security guards should avoid this behavior, as it is against the law and they can lose their job for it. Generally, these employees will receive a few warnings before being terminated. In the United States, one security guard was charged and lost his job for murdering an 18-year old man in June 2013. The security guard pulled out his gun and shot the young man, who had no weapon with him. This action represented a major violation for several reasons: the guard had no reason to shoot the man, the guard shot to kill rather than disarm, and the man had no weapon. The guard had shot the young man because he and his friends had attempted to rob a business in the building; although the robber was in the wrong, the security guard also acted wrongly. Rather than shooting the man, he should have called his coworkers and the police to try to catch the robbers and arrest them. The guard could have waited for the police to arrive and arrest the men, or they could have taken the men to the police station. Regardless, the guard had options, and he didn't need to shoot the robber.

Security guards, peace officers and police should only shoot for self-defense. Since the robber didn't pose a threat to the guard, as the robber didn't possess a weapon, then the guard shouldn't have shot the robber. Guards and officers who shoot to kill rather than to defend are committing an illegal action. People want peace on earth; they want good laws and rules that protect everyone rather than the perpetuation of bad laws and rules. In order to ensure the establishment of good rules, society needs to change laws about the following aspects:

- government
- immigration policies
- use of police force
- military force
- unethical security guards and peace officers
- harsher sentences for kidnappers and criminals
- stricter laws for schoolteachers
- the elimination of terrorism
- harsher penalties for illegal people
- the elimination of racist organizations, such as the KKK
- harsher penalties for murder
- eliminate discrimination and racism
- tougher sentences for spousal abuse

These laws need to be improved so that all of the negative, illegal, and harmful aspects of society are eliminated and all immoral behavior in professionals and citizens is eradicated.

Disease Facts

HIV/AIDS can be acquired from having sex with someone who has HIV/AIDS. In addition to sexual transmission, HIV/AIDS can also be contracted through blood-to-blood contact or other tools, such as needles, razors or knives. In many cases, people acquire HIV/AIDS through accidents or if someone didn't tell them that they had HIV/AIDS. HIV/AIDS is a serious disease; while it resembles cancer in its degree of danger, it is stronger and manifests worse symptoms than cancer. In most cases, HIV/AIDS is fatal. Although people can receive treatment for HIV/AIDS and sometimes feel slightly better, most individuals don't survive the disease. Currently, HIV/AIDS has no cure despite the fact that researchers and scientists have been working hard to find a cure for the disease. To this date, no one has succeeded in finding a cure for HIV/AIDS. Since HIV/AIDS has no cure, people cannot survive this disease. People with HIV/AIDS generally die within 5-10 years due to the extensive damage to their bodies.

Unlike HIV/AIDS, cancer doesn't necessarily manifest obvious symptoms and its symptoms are less damaging than that of AIDS. Since HIV/AIDS is a dangerous, powerful, and lethal disease, people should avoid this condition by maintaining distance from people with HIV/AIDS. This way, people can protect their own bodies as well as preventing against the spread of HIV/AIDS. However, by staying away from people with HIV/AIDS, individuals are not necessarily trying to disrespect them or opposing them in any way. In contrast to people with HIV/AIDs, individuals with cancer are not contagious, so people don't need to avoid them.

Many older people believe that cancer lacks a cure; although cancer didn't have a cure in the past, today, most cancers have a cure. More than 80% of individuals can survive cancer and their bodies can be eliminated of this disease. However, a small percentage of people still die from cancer, as their prognosis depends upon their bodily condition, their genetics, and the severity of the cancer.

Regardless of whether or not an individual has faith in God, He can heal diseases. Many doctors lack complete knowledge in their jobs, so in some cases, they make mistakes. Unlike doctors, God knows everything about a person and their life. Oncologists and other physicians don't understand all of the facts about a person and their condition. For instance, if a person has an accident, the doctors cannot accurately predict if they will fully recover, while God has the answer. God can heal people so that they can walk again. Although it may take some time, God can eventually restore a person's functionality, and they can help by doing exercises to become completely healed. Similarly, God can heal people that have cancer. Oncologists lack the power to determine a person's destiny; they don't have the ability to determine if someone will live or die, as only God has this power. Doctors may have some knowledge, but they lack the ability to fully predict a person's future. Many oncologists fail to practice ethically; like the police, they abuse their power by failing to treat patients properly. For example, some oncologists and other physicians abuse their patients by forcing them to receive certain medication or treatment against their will.

Michael Jackson's doctor made a medication error, leading to Jackson's overdose and death. As a result, the doctor lost his job and went to jail. Bad doctors like Jackson's physician will be caught, resulting in the loss of their jobs and their imprisonment.

Despite the fact that some doctors are immoral, doctors and other scientists are not necessarily bad. God gave people the knowledge to learn about the way in which the world works and in the present and in the past. However, although God gave people the ability to understand some aspects of the world, He didn't give them the power to know everything like Him. God is the Supreme Being with power over all of his creation, so people shouldn't assume that they know more than God. While some scientific knowledge is true, other theories and assumptions have been proven false. For instance, the idea that humans originated from monkeys has been proven false, as God created humans and animals separately. While a monkey is an animal, a human is a totally different type of creation. In addition, the belief that men can become pregnant through a Caesarian Section birth or natural birth is completely false, as men lack the biological apparatus for developing a child, giving birth, and nourishing a child through breast milk. In contrast, women's bodies are designed to grow children inside of them and delivering children. Babies can only survive from their mothers by living inside of them and drinking their breast milk. Caesarian Section deliveries are not natural and should only be used if there is a problem with giving birth in the natural way. Most women don't like to give birth by a Caesarian Section, so doctors and scientists should respect their wishes.

Government Law

People need to follow the rules and laws of their country as well as those of all countries in the world. Before entering a country, people should learn the laws of the nation in which they intend to immigrate. Specifically, they should study about the country and read the signs that post rules and laws. In the Bible, God indicates that people who obey the leaders obey Him, while those who disobey the leaders ultimately disobey God. The same rules apply for any country in the world. People should obey God and the world's leaders because God is ultimately the authority of the leaders ruling the world. God is the ultimate and original authority that all men should obey.

The government should treat all people of a country equally regardless of their skin color, gender or religion. As long as people follow the laws and don't commit crimes, they should have respect and freedom. The government shouldn't discriminate amongst people unless those individuals disrespect the government or other authorities. If people make minor mistakes of which they are unaware, they shouldn't go to jail. On the other hand, if people intentionally break the law or commit major crimes such as theft or murder, they should receive punishment, such as a fine or a jail term. When people make unintentional and minor mistakes, the government should provide them with a warning and another opportunity to follow the law. However, sometimes the government doesn't provide a warning and puts people in jail without an explanation about the rule they broke. The government should forgive people for minor errors, especially when they don't understand the rules of the country. Since God demonstrates forgiveness, the government should also do the same. People should forgive others, because there are times when those individuals may need to be forgiven. Forgiveness is important because it keeps peace in society and eliminates violence and hatred. When you are forgiven for an error, you should not repeat the error, especially if you don't want problems with the government or with another person.

Problems occur when people know that something is bad or illegal and yet they commit that action. When people knowingly commit a crime, they should go to jail. The earliest form of rules and laws occur in the Bible, when God transmits The Ten Commandments through Moses. These rules set the precedent for the rules of all societies. As a result, people need to obey the rules of their parents, schools, jobs, and country. People should understand the general rules that apply everywhere. For example, people should know not to possess drugs, commit murder, perform terrorist acts, steal, assault, possess weapons, cheat. The foundation of these rules occurred in The Ten Commandments and are universally accepted and enforced.

In some countries, people encounter moral and ethical dilemmas when they have a friend who commits a crime. For example, if a person has a friend who steals, possesses drugs, or assaults someone, they may be liable if they knowingly allow their friend to commit a crime. In order to prove their innocence, people should tell their friend not to commit the crime or attempt to stop them from doing so. If the person committing the crime doesn't listen to their friend, the friend can inform the police or government about the situation in order to avoid being charged. This way, people can prove that they're innocent and avoid trouble. If the police or government find out about the crime, people can explain that they didn't commit the crime and that their friend is guilty. If the offender calls their friend a snitch or betrayer, they should stop associating with that friend. Someone can avoid trouble by refusing to hang out with criminals. The police can charge a person as an accomplice if they were present or participated in the crime. Although it doesn't seem fair to be charged as an accomplice, especially if a person didn't actually commit the crime, the law still operates in that way. For example, if a friend left drugs at your home, you should not be responsible for your friends' actions. The government should not be able to blame or accuse you and make generalizations; however, in cases of accomplices, they often find associates responsible for the crime. The police should be trained to recognize an individual's involvement in crime and to understand whether someone is guilty or innocent. Also, police should perform an investigation to accurately distinguish between guilty and innocent parties. Since offenders are innocent until proven guilty, then the police should have proof before arresting someone for a crime. If the police arrest someone without proof that they committed a crime, the police are committing an illegal action. Although the circumstances surrounding a crime can make it difficult to distinguish between guilty and innocent parties, the police are still responsible for fulfilling this duty. If someone is innocent while their friend is guilty, they shouldn't be arrested for a crime that they didn't commit.

In the case that a friend wants to involve someone in a crime, that person should refuse any involvement. For example, if a friend has stolen money and wants to hide it at another friend's house, the friend should refuse and tell the offender to hide the money somewhere else. Sometimes, people are afraid to refuse their friends' requests or they want to help their friends avoid apprehension. However, people that want to avoid trouble with the law should avoid any association with a crime. Although police shouldn't charge people if they are innocent, officers can make mistakes and charge innocent people for crimes they didn't commit.

In some cases, an offender may threaten their friend if the friend refuses to help the criminal or if the friend threatens to tell the police. As a result, one should avoid snitching on their friend; rather, they should simply refuse to help with any aspect of the crime. This way, a person can avoid problems with their friend and the police. If a friend tries to convince an innocent person to help in a crime and threatens or insults them, the person should not respond and should avoid associating with their friend in the future. Sometimes, it's difficult to escape a gang or drug-related community because the other members may threaten or try to kill a person; in this case, the person trying to escape their former lifestyle should seek a safe place. However, the best strategy is to avoid associating with a criminal so that the police and government don't become involved.

People that become involved with drugs and gangs often end up in some form of trouble. They will likely encounter conflict with the law or with others in their community. If a person is responsible for putting their friend in jail, the friend may come after them and try to kill them once they are released from prison. As a result, the best strategy involves avoiding any kind of crime or trouble. Although people may try to force others into criminal activity, people should know their rights and the moral code of the country. While some countries pardon crimes, other countries don't follow this policy.

Many countries have laws against distracted driving. For example, people should not use their phones to make calls or send text messages while driving. These individuals can be apprehended by the police and provided with a ticket or penalty. In some cases, police will provide individuals with a warning, in which case, the person should be careful not to repeat their mistake. People that violate driving laws, such as distracted driving, can end up causing a car accident that causes severe harm or death to themselves or someone else. Other rules of the road include speeding, use of alcohol or drugs, and driving while intoxicated. For speeding, individuals should watch their speedometer to ensure that they are not travelling in excess of the posted speed limit for the area. For example, if the speed limit is 60 km/h, you should not drive at 80 km/h. Also, people shouldn't drive if they have been using drugs or drinking prior to driving. If you are caught driving while intoxicated, you may end up losing your license, losing points, paying a heavy fine, going to jail, or having a criminal record.

People that are no longer intoxicated can drive themselves or someone else somewhere. In the case of drunk driving, people need to understand the law because they can save their life and the life of someone else by avoiding this behavior. Drunk driving represents a serious crime for which the law cannot provide multiple warnings or pardons due to the effect that this crime can have on individuals and society.

If people have a criminal record, it can last for the rest of their lives or interfere with their lives. If a person commits a crime two or three times despite the fact that they have been given a warning, then they are fully responsible for their crimes and thus their record. However, if someone only commits a crime, especially a minor offense, for the first time, they should receive a warning rather than a criminal record. Most people that receive a warning, especially when it clarifies their understanding of the law, ensure that they don't commit that offence again. Although the initial instance of a crime still constitutes a criminal offense, if the offense is minor, the offender should receive a warning. In this case, people should make sure that they never commit the offense again, as they are likely to receive a criminal record if they repeat the same crime. Depending on the country in which the crime has been committed, a criminal record can last for seven years or it can last for the rest of a person's life. However, in countries where a person's criminal record lasts for their entire life, the government should change this policy because a person should not have to suffer for their entire life because of one crime. If people with records follow the law for several years after committing the crime and live a respectable life by contributing to the community, the police should erase their criminal record so that the person can go back to living a normal life. They should be able to have references and part-ners, especially if they are innocent. All people should have access to a good lawyer, regardless of their financial means. People should be able to use their lawyer in order to remove their criminal record, especially if they have lived a good life. However, it is not easy to find a good lawyer or a reference to clear a criminal record. As a result, it is important to avoid a criminal record by avoiding confrontations with other peo-ple, even if that means fighting in self-defense. People should ignore those that bother them and avoid starting trouble. This will help to keep a clean criminal record.

One way to avoid crime involves having a good education, which enables one to obtain a respectable career and fit in with society. People should attend school and receive their high school diploma in order to get a good job and have a good life. Many people have dreams, especially to get married and have children.

Many countries used to have death penalties, including Canada, European nations, Australia, and New Zealand. However, these countries have abolished the death penalty and will likely never have it again. Even if people vote for the death penalty to return, it will never return. In Mexico, people convicted of murder will go to jail for a long time; however, if people commit repeat murders, the government will employ the death penalty. When people ignore warnings and commit repeat offenses, then they are responsible for their own sentence. Some countries believe that if someone commits murder, the government doesn't want that individual in society, so they put them in prison. If the government knew that the offender would commit murder again, they would never let them out of prison. In this case, there is no point to releasing someone or giving them a second chance. Repeat offenders should stay in prison for their entire lives.

On the other hand, many countries still have death penalties, including the United States, RDC, China, Thailand, Russia, Columbia, El Salvador, Venezuela, the Philippines, and North Korea. In China, convicted criminals are either executed by hanging or shooting. In the United States, they use the electric chair, execution by poison, or gas. Although the criminal can sometimes choose the type of death penalty in the United States, most of the time, the government will decide upon the execution method. In these countries, if someone commits a crime and threatens their innocent friend, the friend can go to the police without their knowledge; otherwise, the situation may become worse.

Prison life is much different from life outside of prison. In prison, money and other material entities don't matter. Prisoners don't pay tax whereas other people, such as doctors, teachers, and police officers, have to pay taxes. While many people complain about this reality, the tax money goes towards the prison employees, building costs, utilities, clothes, and food. People should realize that taxpayers still have better lives than prisoners because they can be with their families and build a good life. On the other hand, people in prison have to serve sentences for their crimes and cannot see their families very often.

Most prisoners prefer prison life to the death penalty. In Europe and Canada, the prison term for major offenses such as murder is between 25-30 years. In recent years, European countries have extended their life sentences from 10 years to 25 years, while Canada's maximum prison term is now 50 years. These harsh penalties exist to reflect the immoral nature of murder. Murder doesn't make sense because eventually, everyone will die, and there is no reason to take someone's life.

While murder represents a major offense, other thefts are more minor. However, some countries punish smaller crimes very severely. For instance, some nations punish theft by removing the hand of the thief. Although theft is wrong, the governments of these countries are too harsh in their use of justice. On the other hand, in Canada and Europe, thieves receive criminal records, and, if they continue stealing, they will have a criminal record for the rest of their lives. This type of punishment makes more sense than removing a criminal's hands. Since criminal records affect someone for their whole life, they cannot obtain education or a job. As a result, people should avoid committing theft.

Furthermore, people that have a reputation or a record as a thief lose the trust of others. As a result, individuals that want trust from others should avoid theft. Whether or not people have done wrong, the government can teach them about the difference between right and wrong, the laws of the country, and even the Gospel. However, people shouldn't be forced to change their lives because nobody has the power to tell another person how to live their life. The actions of the government sometimes seem as if they want to change people's lives or force them to do something. In this case, it appears as if they have forgotten that God is Almighty and that only He can change people's lives. People should be provided with the chance to stop their crimes and avoid repeating these mistakes in the past. If people stop their criminal actions and become a good person, God can still change their life and turn them into a good person.

Gang life and crime occurs mainly in the city, especially in areas where homeless people tend to live. While some people choose that lifestyle, most people feel forced into a life of crime. In this case, the government fails to care for these individuals, as many of them suffer discrimination due to their ethnic background, skin color, or religion. These individuals experience barriers in their education and employment life, as many of them fail to obtain their high school diploma. As a result, they cannot obtain a good career. The government should treat people equally and with respect in all countries. People that have been treated badly by the government experience difficulty in finding a job, which prevents them from supporting themselves and a family. In some cases, people have spouses and children, making it more difficult for them to support a family without a good job. As a result, many people have to resort to crime to survive. These people commit crimes such as theft, murder, and the sale of drugs or weapons. In most cases, these individuals are homeless and have lived in poverty due to discrimination.

These situations happen not because of individual people but because of the government. This type of government corruption occurs in all countries. In these instances, innocent men are killed and women, especially attractive women, experience rape and sexual assault by criminals or even by the police. Sometimes, there are problems with the police. While many police are good, there are also many bad officers who apprehend or mistreat innocent people. Because they are in a position of authority, police have the power to commit any action that they want, including putting an innocent person in jail. For instance, there have been cases where even if a person has their ID present, the police will still put them in jail. Many police also shoot people for no reason, which represents an illegal action. In many of these cases, police officers are committing these unlawful actions and abusing their power due to discrimination. The police cannot treat individuals badly because of their skin color, religion, culture, or ethnic background. However, they still exercise discrimination against many individuals, especially in the case of blacks. Black people experience the greatest amount of discrimination and abuse from police officers. In many cases, police officers intentionally harass and provoke black people into a fight so that they can arrest them. This type of abuse should not be tolerated.

In cases where the government and police officers treat people equally and provide them with rights and respect, these individuals should take advantage of this opportunity and avoid committing crimes. People that want to progress in life require high school diplomas as well as post-secondary education, such as university and college. However, people definitely require their high school diploma because it provides them with the opportunity for a respectable job and a reasonably good quality of life. Most people want spouses and children, so they need a good job in order to support their family. The majority of individuals want good jobs so that they don't have to work hard at a job that they hate, such as a manufacturing job, food service, or retail, which provide a lower salary. Thus, people should work hard to constantly improve their education and skills in order to get a well-paying job that they enjoy, which will make them happy.

People have many expenses in life, including

- Rent
- Gas
- Electricity
- Water
- Taxes
- Food/Beverages
- Clothes
- Personal Products – soap, shampoo, toothpaste

Since these expenses are quite numerous, people need to have good jobs in order to not only pay their basic expenses but also to save money, which allows people to plan for retirement and increase their social mobility. Also, people want to enjoy a little bit of their money by socializing and spending money on things that they like. As a result, people need good salaries.

However, people should manage their money wisely so that they don't spend too much money on things that they don't need and then have trouble paying their bills. Many people ask the government for money when they make foolish spending decisions. Even if they government gives them the money, they should learn from their mistake and avoid repeating the same bad habits. For example, many individuals in university and college need to borrow money from the government in order to support them while they attend post-secondary school. I believe that these people shouldn't have to pay the government back, especially if they respect the rules of the school, complete their education, and get a better job. However, at the same time, people shouldn't take advantage of the government's generosity. While the government should help people in some cases, people ultimately need to pay for their own lives. The government shouldn't support people unless they have a serious illness or disability. Everyone without an illness or disability should find employment to support themselves and their families. In good countries, the government has many ways of helping other people in need so that they can eventually find a job and support themselves. However, in bad countries, the government doesn't provide people with these opportunities, as they don't want people progressing in society. These governments want the rich people to stay rich and the poor people to stay poor; in other words, they prevent social mobility with their rules and their policies.

Most young people would prefer to obtain work rather than to borrow money and have to pay it back to a friend, family, or the government. There are many opportunities for people to make good money. For example, people can travel outside of the city in order to make more money in a camp. These camp settings provide jobs in many different areas, including food preparation, custodial work, cleaning, or industrial trades. People working in the camp can earn from $18-20/hr to start and their expenses are severely reduced because they have free food, utilities, and sometimes even rent. Many of these camps are paid by the government or the employer, which allows workers to save their money for other purposes or to accumulate long-term savings. As a result, camp workers can save more quickly to purchase a house and car or they can save for a long-term goal, such as opening one's own business. Many people opt to work in these camps because it provides them with large, short-term financial gains. On the other hand, other people who work at these camps can blow all of their savings once they return to the city, choosing to spend all of their money on restaurants, alcohol, drugs, women, gambling, and partying. People that choose to spend their money in this way should not receive support from the government when they realize that they can't afford their basic expenses. These individuals had the opportunity to save money for the future and instead wasted it on unnecessary expenses.

When I worked in a camp, some of my friends wasted their money on partying, and, although I advised them to save for the future, they didn't listen to me. Personally, I prefer to save my money rather than spending it. However, I don't like to brag about my money management and I don't judge individuals that waste their money. While I want to work to make good money, I also care about my health. I prefer to work in an area that utilizes my skills and experience yet represents a safe environment. Some jobs are hazardous, especially some of the industrial jobs in camps. Most people want to work in a safe environment and avoid things such as chemicals, factories, and heavy equipment, which can lead to diseases, disabilities, or death. People tend to focus too heavily on money and ignore important aspects such as safety; however, people should prioritize their wellbeing over money.

Canada is a country with many opportunities. While all provinces in the country provide good job opportunities, the best areas in which to work are currently the Prairie Provinces, such as Alberta, Saskatchewan, and Manitoba. Within Alberta, many cities have high employment, including Edmonton, Calgary, Fort McMurray, Red Deer, Sherwood Park, Stony Plain, and St. Albert. Since Alberta possesses oil resources, it has the best economy among all of the provinces. Individuals with their high school diplomas can find work in any Canadian province. Although people without diplomas can still obtain a job, they have fewer opportunities than individuals with their diplomas. Most people from Canada's east coast, such as Quebec and Ontario, are moving to the Prairie Provinces for better job opportunities. Since Western Canada currently has better employment than Eastern Canada, the Canadian government should ensure a more equal economy across the nation. Specifically, they should change their policies so that people can obtain good careers in all provinces, providing all Canadian residents with equal opportunities so that they can take care of their families. This way, people wouldn't have to move from one province to another in order to better support themselves and their families.

Many places in the world have democratic countries, including Canada, USA, Mexico, Greenland, Japan, European nations, Australia, and New Zealand. These countries have varying degrees of democracy, and among these continents and nations, Canada is one of the freest and most democratic nations. Although Canada is one of the best places to live because of its democratic system, it still has crime. However, many countries have bigger crime problems than Canada, including the United States and European nations. Some of these countries have issues with people illegally making and selling weapons or drugs. Countries have varying laws about these issues; for instance, Cuba, Japan, and Canada have strict rules against weapon production as well as the importing and exporting of guns and drugs, while the United States and some European countries have more relaxed rules about these issues.

The United States has many problems with major crimes, such as the mass shooting of innocent people. For example, some criminals initiate shooting sprees on schools, killing innocent teachers and students. People feel afraid because they never know if their acquaintances are friendly or potential criminals. Many mentally-unstable individuals overreact to minor or unintended insults, causing them to seriously hurt or kill someone because they feel offended by actions or words that they might misinterpret as offensive. In this case, people should be careful about what they say or do to others because their words or actions may be subject to misinterpretation. On the other hand, people shouldn't overact to a minor insult because the person who offended them may be looking for a fight or a problem, which could escalate into serious violence or death. By being careful about their words and actions, people can avoid a problem and stay out of trouble.

Many crimes happen because people have mental illnesses or problems, which result in intentional or unintentional violence as well as other offenses. Since people with mental illnesses need help, the government should intervene to provide these individuals with assistance so that they can overcome their disorder, thus reducing the amount of crime in a given society. The government shouldn't discriminate against people with mental illnesses because this prejudice is similar to racism and other forms of discrimination. If the government ensures the equal treatment of all individuals in society, then everyone will have equal employment opportunities, which will enable them to support themselves and avoid the necessity of crime. When people with mental illness commit crimes, they are usually sent to prison. I believe that mentally-ill individuals that commit murder should go to prison because they represent a threat to society. However, mentally-ill people who don't commit threatening crimes should not necessarily go to jail. For instance, one lady in Edmonton accidentally murdered her child by leaving him unattended in the bathtub, resulting in his drowning. She was accused of murder and she was sent to prison. Since this lady had a mental illness, she didn't realize the implications of her actions and should not have been sentenced to jail. I believe that people who intentionally murder their children should receive a prison sentence because the murder of one's own children is one of the worst wrongs; however, if someone didn't intend to kill their child, then they shouldn't be imprisoned. In this case, the police recklessly accused her of murder and failed to conduct a thorough investigation. When her husband attempted to explain the situation and defend her, the police refused to listen to him. She also had many references from people who knew her well, and they were all upset at the police because they believed that the police should not give her a life sentence in jail. She had a mental problem and needed help, so the government should have provided her with resources and services. She should not have been left alone to bathe her child without assistance.

While the United States claims to be a democratic country, they are not completely democratic because they don't treat people equally and discriminate on the basis of color. For example, the government and police treat black people more poorly than they treat people of other races. The law treats blacks more harshly when they commit murder, while they provide more lenient sentences for other races, such as Whites, Asians, Arabs, Hispanics, or Natives. Sometimes the police provide shorter prison sentences for whites in comparison to blacks. In fact, some people can escape criminal records by hiring a good lawyer who can free them from prison or influence their acquittal. Some lawyers find ways to circumvent the rules in order to win their cases. In contrast, if a black person kills someone, they will receive a life sentence for murder. Regardless of their financial status, black people are less likely to successfully manipulate a lawyer and judges are less likely to provide the criminal with a lenient sentence. This different treatment of blacks represents discrimination in spite of the American claim of democracy. While Canada and European Nations exhibit minor instances of discrimination, Americans are more blatant in their racism.

Discrimination and racism occur on a worldwide basis. For example, a black American who killed 12 innocent people is now in prison while a white person who murdered an innocent black boy was ruled as not guilty by the Supreme Court. In the case, a young black teenager went to the store to buy gum and pop. He didn't have any weapons or threaten Zimmerman in any way, but Zimmerman shot this boy for no apparent reason other than his skin color. When the police released Zimmerman on the basis of his claims for self-defense, the city protested, which the police subsequently stopped by killing five protesters. I believe that the police acted wrongly in this case because people have the right to protest; also, I believe that Zimmerman should have been convicted for his crime. The laws should be applied consistently to people regardless of their skin color. While individuals that murder for self-defense should be acquitted, I don't think that Zimmerman acted in self-defense because the black boy possessed no weapons. In the United States, guns are readily available in stores such as Wal-Mart, and innocent people, such as elementary school students, die as a result. The intentional murder of someone for reasons other than self-defense is always wrong, but the murder of innocent people and murder based on discrimination is even worse.

Both Canada and the United States have strict policies regarding entry into the country. While Canadians and Americans can enter into each other's countries more easily than people from other countries, they still have many rules about cross-border movement. For example, Canadians are not permitted to bring weapons into the United States, and Canadians with criminal records cannot cross the border into the United States. On the other hand, Canadians have more lenient policies about Americans entering the country, as many Americans have crossed the border to bring weapons and drugs into Canada. Canadians also buy weapons from the Americans or bring guns from the United States back into Canada in order to sell guns on the black market in Canada. In addition, the Canadian government has allowed American companies to enter Canada and exploit Canada's natural resources while causing environmental damage. These actions are wrong and should be addressed by both governments.

Other cities around the world, including those in Cuba, UK, China, Australia, New Zealand, and Japan, have tighter regulations controlling the cross-border movement of drugs and guns, with the exception of major cities in England, such as London.

Strong governments should eliminate the existence of several problems that lead to crime. These problems include the following:

- Mafias, such as those of Italians and Hispanics, and other gang activity
- Drug dealers and trafficking
- The production and sale of weapons, such as guns, knives, and bombs
- Terrorist attacks
- Illegal immigrants
- Thieves, liars, and kidnappers
- Sexual assault and rape, including pedophiles
- Murder
- Poverty
- Discrimination and racism

By stopping all of these factors, the government would increase the safety of a country, eliminating the injuries and deaths of innocent people. Furthermore, the government can eliminate issues such as poverty, gangs, and discrimination by treating everyone equally and providing all citizens with equal opportunities regardless of their race, religion, sex, orientation or ability level. If everyone has the same chances, all citizens can all obtain a good education and career. This way, issues such as gun control would be less relevant and people will oppose the possession of weapons. In countries such as Cuba, Japan, and European nations, the government provides individuals who attempt to commit crime with a warning. If they continue their actions, they end up in prison as a means of protecting the citizens and enforcing the laws. Since many other countries don't permit the manufacturing, possession, sale, or use of weapons, their countries are safer than Canada and the United States. President Barack Obama has a strong platform for eliminating crime and instilling peace within the country. In contrast, George Bush mandated violence by initiating wars with other countries and supporting the use of guns. Many people oppose Obama's ideologies because of his skin color, yet he mandates greater crime control than Bush. In fact, Obama only won his second term because of his healthcare plan, as his race has otherwise worked against him. The United States and some European countries continue to allow weapons and crime because they want to control the resources of third world countries. These superpowers believe that they can increase their profits through military action; however, they should find other ways of increasing their profits.

Assange and Snowden spoke out about the way in which the United States treats citizens, immigrants, and refugees. In particular, these politicians maintained that Americans treat people poorly and focus too heavily on militarization. As a result, their exploitation of third-world countries, especially their use of resources, perpetuates international inequality. In contrast, Canada is a peacemaking country with a good international reputation; while people from other countries dislike Americans, they welcome Canadians. Many Americans change their passport to Canadian and seek Canadian citizenship because they are afraid of trouble in other countries. Canada should refuse citizenship to Americans that live in the country for three years and then leave again. While Canada refuses immigrants from other countries, they let

Americans easily obtain passports and citizenship. This makes no sense and shows that the Canadian government favors the Americans and discriminates against people from other countries.

In some countries, the governments are involved with the mafia or other criminal organizations, but in Canada, this type of involvement is illegal. However, the Quebec government has been accused of being associated with a mafia. When Snowden was working for NSA, he exposed their files to the public, showing the corruption involved in the organization. Many citizens were happy that Snowden and Assange exposed the truth to the world. While some people found their actions reprehensible, I believe that they did the right thing by telling the truth. Unlike many others who perform controversial actions, these individuals didn't break any law. They are not criminals, thieves, or terrorists. They didn't worry about what the government thought of their actions because they considered the truth as the most important thing. For instance, they didn't consider questions such as:

- Are you going to charge me and arrest me?
- Are you going to kill me or poison me?
- Are you going to hate me and say bad things about me?
- Why do you hate me and treat me like the enemy?

People that reveal the truth are never committing a criminal action. Despite people's attempt to bury or conceal the truth, they can never hide it for long. The truth is always better and more permanent than a lie, because a lie will eventually become exposed. National authorities, such as the government and police, can abuse their power and commit crimes or tell lies; however, these actions are morally wrong and these people will eventually be revealed. People prefer to know the truth about things, so people that reveal the truth shouldn't be considered criminals. Some people desire truth so badly that they are willing to die for it. In this case, they aren't afraid of death, because they know that they were good people by seeking truth, and so they believe that they will go to heaven. People that have committed evil should apologize to God and ask for forgiveness; otherwise, they will go to hell, as recounted in the Bible.

During the time that he was charged by the government, Edward Snowden went to several countries, including Ecuador, Cuba, China, Norway, Sweden, Iceland, and Russia. He exposed the secrets of NSA to these different nations. Since the entire world knows about the corruption of NSA, this organization doesn't have any more secrets and will have difficulty in deceiving people again. While some people in other countries supported Snowden, others didn't support his actions. Snowden was born and raised in the United States; both of his parents were also American. Although he left the United States, he can't return to America because the government considers him as a dangerous person and will either kill him or sentence him to life in prison. At one time, he was stuck in Moscow at Russia's International Airport because the government had cancelled his American citizenship. In fact, the United States even grounded Ecuadorian planes because they wanted to catch him. I don't believe that the American government should have revoked his passport and citizenship because he exposed the truth about their corruption. Other countries, such as Bolivia and Venezuela, supported him and allowed him to seek sanctuary in their countries. In addition, the Russians also offered him protection because he had given them information about American corruption. Americans shouldn't control people's entry and exit into Embassies in different countries without asking the permission of that country. The government and police should be able to enter Embassies in the case that the person seeking sanctuary has committed a crime; however, in Snowden's case, they shouldn't be allowed to pursue him in that manner. Americans want citizens and other countries to follow their rules and yet they don't follow the rules of other nations.

Syria has a serious problem with their government. Specifically, their president attacks innocent people, especially women and children. The police and military in that country rape women and kill innocent children. The United States planned to declare war on Syria, while England and France agreed to go to war against Syria. However, these two countries backed out of the war. Although some people may point to a lack of resources or a fear of Arabs, these European nations likely quit because they disliked the idea of killing innocent women and children. Rather than declaring war and bombing innocent civilians, the Americans and their allies should arrest or kill the Syrian president for his immoral and corrupt actions governmental organizations consider the various circumstances of immigrants, their denial of refugees due to a lack of proper documentation interferes with human rights.

Individuals should stay in their own countries unless they are fleeing danger. However, many individuals in several countries feel threatened by race, religion, or political beliefs. This sense of discrimination is known as "persecution". Some persecuted refugees leave their own country in desperation and seek asylum in a new nation. People need to understand and follow the rules of immigration because these rules benefit all members of society.

Many immigrants want to get a new opportunity in another country. They want the chance to live in a new country without the fear of being deported and sent back home. Since verybody likes to travel to other countries, people should respect new immigrants and give them a chance to live in their new country. It is actually illegal to kick people out of a country and send them back home, so the government cannot deport immigrants without a valid reason, such as criminal activity. Immigrants that follow the law should be provided with the opportunity for a better life, education, and employment in a new country.

Some immigrants feel welcomed and accepted when they arrive in another country. These individuals may have relatives to help them adjust, sufficient funds to find a home, or a job to work. However, most countries don't want to accept criminals, illegal activities, drug dealers, or terrorists in their nation. Because of these fears, governments feel uncertain about accepting many immigrants, even refugees who flee their countries due to danger. As a result, refugees and other immigrants have to wait longer periods of time for a government's decision to accept them. They may have to return to their country or pay fees to acquire the correct documentation. This experience can be very frustrating for new immigrants, who often feel as if the government is mistreating them. Most of these immigrants came into the country for good reasons and the government should not deny their request. When these individuals are forced to leave their country due to war, poverty or persecution, they should not be deported because it could result in an attack.

Regardless of the reason for emigrating, most individuals will leave behind friends and family. Even if a person is moving to a new job or home, they may feel anxious about fitting in and adjusting to new ways of doing things. Every aspect of a new country may be different to the immigrants including the weather, language, culture, currency, and transportation system. For instance, the adjustment to trains, metros, trolleys, and buses and their routes to work, school or shopping could cause difficulties.

As immigrants attempt to adjust, their new school or workplace may seem strange, especially if they don't speak the language of the new country. New immigrants will take time to learn various systems, learn the language, and make friends. Some ways to increase their sense of belonging include taking part in activities that you enjoy and attempting new pursuits. Even adult experience difficulties in adjusting to a new country. For instance, they may encounter

Immigration Law

Many people travel from one country to another. They may want to go on vacation or visit relatives; however, they usually return home after one or two weeks. Sometimes, people travel to another country and move there. People who move permanently to another country are known as immigrants. There are many immigrants in all communities: at school, at work, or on the street. Immigrants can be children, teenagers, adults, or senior citizens. They can also come from any country or ethnic background. In any given community, someone from another country has moved onto a street or started attending school. For many people, one of their parents used to live in a different country.

This book explains the experience of moving to a new country and discusses the issues involved in this process. For centuries, people have travelled across the world to settle in other countries. This process is known as "migration." On the other hand, "emigration" means to leave one's own country to live in another nation. "Immigration" means to come to a new country to settle there. Countries such as North America, European nations, Australia, and New Zealand experience immigration because people from all over the world settle in these nations.

Some of the first immigrants fled danger or poverty to find a better life in another country. Later, others sought wealth and opportunities in newly-discovered countries such as North America, European nations, Australia, and New Zealand. Today, there are new countries to discover; however, people still emigrate all over the world. People with different skin colors, different religions, and different languages have different ways of life, which are known as cultures. Communities where people of different cultures live side-by-side are known as multicultural.

In Australia, Aborigines lived in that country long before the first immigrants settled. Aborigines are the "native" or "indigenous" people of Australia. The first immigrants who settled in the country were also known as "colonists." The European people controlled Australia, enforcing their rules and ways of life without respecting those of the Aborigines, the original peoples.

People decide to live in other countries for many reasons. Individuals may receive a job offer or want to make more money in another country. For example, a family may settle in a particular country if a family member already has a job in that country. Also, others may want to live in a country with a better climate, and decide to move somewhere warm, such as Australia, Latin America, or Southern Europe, including Spain, Portugal, Italy, and Greece. Furthermore, people may move to another nation to live with their relatives or family members.

Many people emigrate because of more serious concerns. Some people are forced to leave their own country because of war or fear for their safety. While some of these immigrants never return to their country, others visit occasionally. In other cases, a lack of resources, such as food, water, or medication, may influence people to find a greater quality of life in another country. The process of emigrating involves leaving friends, family, and other familiar aspects, such as culture, language, or climate. The prospect of emigrating may cause people to feel very anxious about living in an unfamiliar country. Although immigration can initially be overwhelming, new experiences often turn out to have positive results. For many people, emigrating is an exciting new start. It represents a chance to see and experience new things and to meet new people.

Sometimes, in countries with war conditions, people often have to leave their homes with very little warning due to the prospect of danger. They may have to leave their family and belongings behind without knowing where they are going and whether they will ever be able to return. Imagine what it would be like to leave home with no time to pack or say goodbye to friends and family. In addition, immigrants might not know where they are going, how they will travel, or what will happen when they arrive at their destination. People in this situation have to cope with great fear, danger, and uncertainty. The idea of arriving in a different country with an unfamiliar language and culture can represent a daunting prospect.

Over the past 60 years, travelling across the world has become much easier than it was in the past. As a result, increasing numbers of people have immigrated. In response to rising immigration, many countries have introduced rules stating who can and can't live in their country. However, this idea has been challenged because people should have a chance to follow the rules rather than being banned from the country. These immigration rules often affect a person's choices concerning whether to emigrate.

Specifically, people with special skills, such as doctors, are welcomed in many countries. However, several countries have the need for people to work less skilled jobs, such as cleaning or crop picking. The immigration rules for these workers are often more strict, and they may be refused entry by some countries. As a result, these rules make it difficult for unskilled workers to find a new home. To avoid the restrictions, some people enter a country illegally, putting themselves at great risk. They may hide for days in trucks or airplanes or travel in crowded or unsafe vehicles.

To enter a country, a person needs to possess the correct documentation, such as a passport and/or a visa, which confirms the right of entry. Without such documents, potential immigrants can be refused entry into their desired country and sent back to their original nation.

People without the correct documents face many difficulties in immigration. First, they may be refused entry and sent back to their home country or they may experience a long wait period while the authorities evaluate their documentation. These government actions can harm immigrants because the immigrants may be refugees fleeing danger in their own country. As a result, the government needs to understand their situation before denying them admittance into their desired country. A person who leaves his/her country due to unsafe conditions is known as a refugee. Refugees that seek safety or asylum in another country are considered "asylum seekers." Each person has a human right to seek protection in another country. Although governmental organizations consider the various circumstances of immigrants, their denial of refugees due to a lack of proper documentation interferes with human rights.

Individuals should stay in their own countries unless they are fleeing danger. However, many individuals in several countries feel threatened by race, religion, or political beliefs. This sense of discrimination is known as "persecution." Some persecuted refugees leave their own country in desperation and seek asylum in a new nation. People need to understand and follow the rules of immigration because these rules benefit all members of society.

Many immigrants want to get a new opportunity in another country. They want the chance to live in a new country without the fear of being deported and sent back home. Since everybody likes to travel to other countries, people should respect new immigrants and give them a chance to live in their new country. It is actually illegal to kick people out of a country and send them back home, so the government cannot deport immigrants without a valid reason, such as criminal activity. Immigrants that follow the law should be provided with the opportunity for a better life, education, and employment in a new country.

Some immigrants feel welcomed and accepted when they arrive in another country. These individuals may have relatives to help them adjust, sufficient funds to find a home, or a job to work. However, most countries don't want to accept criminals, illegal activities, drug dealers, or terrorists in their nation. Because of these fears, governments feel uncertain about accepting many immigrants, even refugees who flee their countries due to danger. As a result, refugees and other immigrants have to wait long periods of time for a government's decision to accept them. They may have to return to their country or pay fees to acquire the correct documentation. This experience can be very frustrating for new immigrants, who often feel as if the government is mistreating them. Most of these immigrants came into the country for good reasons and the government should not deny their request. When these individuals are forced to leave their country due to war, poverty, or persecution, they should not be deported because it could result in an attack.

Regardless of the reason for emigrating, most individuals will leave behind friends and family. Even if a person is moving to a new job or home, they may feel anxious about fitting in and adjusting to new ways of doing things. Every aspect of a new country may be different to the immigrants, including the weather, language, culture, currency, and transportation system. For instance, the adjustment to trains, metros, trolleys, and buses and their routes to work, school, or shopping could cause difficulties.

As immigrants attempt to adjust, their new school or workplace may seem strange, especially if they don't speak the language of the new country. New immigrants will take time to learn various systems, learn the language, and make friends. Some ways to increase their sense of belonging include taking part in activities that you enjoy and attempting new pursuits. Even adults experience difficulties in adjusting to a new country. For instance, they may encounter difficulties in finding a new job or meeting new people. This leads to isolation and loneliness, which makes it necessary for natives of the country to show understanding. When someone from another country arrives in a community, members should make a special effort to make him/her feel welcome. For instance, people could invite newcomers to join in their activities or offer help. Although people may not understand the language of newcomers, they can show kindness without using worlds. When a young person has moved to a new country, they may be influenced by the way other young people behave, which can lead to conflict in the home and other environments. Children should try to consider their parents' viewpoints and refrain from letting others put pressure on them. They should discuss their feelings with their family and come to an agreement on acceptable behavior.

When immigrants arrive in another country, they may feel unsure about their sense of belonging. Their new home will probably be very different from their old home. However, they can still participate in both their new and old countries and the nations' respective cultures. Some immigrants may live near other people that share the same country of origin, religion, or culture. While this proximity makes it easier for immigrants to feel at home, it can also make them more reluctant to get to know local people and their customs.

People should understand and respect the differences between their culture and the culture of their new home countries while also accepting the culture of new immigrants. Everyone should respect the values, beliefs, and cultures of everyone else, regardless of their country of origin and/or their current country of residence. Many immigrants feel part of both their country of origin and their country of residence. After living in a country for a certain amount of time, immigrants can apply to become a "citizen" of that country. Citizenship gives people rights shared by other citizens, such as the right to vote in that country's elections. Many citizens of a country can trace their family back to find people who arrived as immigrants. Permanent Residency is below the status of Citizenship, as Permanent Residents lack some of the rights of citizens, as only citizens are permitted to vote.

I had a friend that lived in Canada for 20 years. He was born in the United States and left America when he was 17 years old. However, his parents were from Vietnam and he came to Canada to get a better education and a better life. While in America, he lived a depressed life. He was not illegal or a criminal, as he never broke the law in any country.

As a result, he had dual citizenship to both Canada and the United States. In the past, it was easier for him to get his Citizenship Status, but today, it has become much more difficult to become a Canadian citizen.

Some people can become citizens of two or three countries as long as they respect the law and the government has accurate information about them. For example, my friend had citizenship in both Canada and the United States, so he was considered part of both countries. This allows him and others with dual citizenship to travel back and forth between nations, but he also has to pay taxes to both countries.

In one instance, my friend went to the United States Embassy because his American passport had been expired for the past eight years. Passports normally last for five years, and citizens are required to renew their passports every five years. If a person's passport expires, they still have the opportunity to renew their passport. Two months later, he returned to the United States. He didn't know that the government had changed their policies about passport expiration and renewal. The new policy specified that since he hadn't renewed his passport, he couldn't have dual citizenship in both Canada and the United States. Although he didn't have any criminal record, the government took away his right of dual citizenship and he spent two weeks in jail at a United States airport. Subsequently, he was sent to Vietnam despite the fact that his parents had emigrated from the United States. In addition, the Canadian government changed their policy regarding passports and dual citizenship, refusing to support him anymore.

The government shouldn't be able to change their policy and kick people out of the country, especially when they didn't break any laws. People that are part of two countries should have dual citizenship and the government shouldn't force them to give up one of their citizenships. As a result of government actions, my friend lost both American and Canadian citizenships. Consequently, he was forced into a dangerous place, which resulted in his death nine months later. My friend's tragedy results solely from governmental actions.

Many other immigrants are not properly informed about government policies regarding citizenship and immigration. Several immigrants have different backgrounds, such as African, Asian, or Latin American. Others are citizens of Europe or Australia and have lived in those countries for a long time. Finally, other immigrants have job experience in countries where they emigrated illegally by claiming refugee status. Although these individuals changed their names and identities, they never actually broke the law or committed any crimes. When these people immigrate, they can't tell the government anything about themselves because they are in danger of being deported back to their former countries. They also can't tell their friends or other acquaintances in case those people tell the government. New immigrants hate to live in secrecy about their status and constantly fear that someone will discover their identity and inform the government. They have to be careful not to let someone force them to talk about their private life. Even if someone is a close friend, they shouldn't force a person to discuss their past. In fact, the government shouldn't need to know about a person's history or private life as long as they are honest and respect the law.

Some people immigrate to North America in order to find better education, jobs, and lives than the ones they left behind in Europe or Australia. In their former countries, individuals may have inferior education, poor jobs, discrimination, or a low quality of life, which is the fault of that country's government. North America claims to treat people equally and doesn't discriminate based on skin color, religion, country, or culture, which attracts many immigrants who escape these conditions in other nations. To obtain Permanent Residency, new immigrants to North America need to wait only 3-5 years rather than the 8-20 years in other countries. However, while some people only wait for 3 years, others need to wait longer periods of time because the government wastes time. Since North America purports to treat everyone equally, all new immigrants should take the exact same time period to receive Permanent Residency or Citizenship. The governments of all countries should establish more consistency in this regard, perhaps mandating that once an immigrant has lived in that country for, say, three years, they should become part of the country and obtain a status like Permanent Resident or Citizen.

Individuals that leave Europe, Australia, Japan, China or New Zealand can return to the Embassy in their new country or can return to their previous country to rcncw their passport without explaining their private business. In these countries, the government gives individuals another chance with a friendly waning because their policy doesn't permit them to kick someone out of the country. Also, individuals with relatives in a certain country can renew their passport with the address of a family member. However, people with no relations may experience difficulty in renewing their passport because they lack a permanent address to which the passport will be mailed. For individuals temporarily residing in a hotel, the government can send their passport to this address. The easiest way to apply for and receive a passport renewal is online. The government will allow people to choose whether they want to receive information and documents by email or physical mail. Many people also prefer to pick up their passport in person, so that they can exchange their old, expired passport for their new one. People who choose to apply online can ask other people to help them with the process, so that they understand how to apply in the future. The application for a passport is similar to that for a job, work permit, or study permit. Although the application process is relatively simple, the government should provide people with second chances and warnings when forgetting to renew their passport. This will teach people about the rules concerning passports, ensuring that people follow the correct passport laws. People who understand the rules and fail to follow them will be in trouble with the government.

Countries in Europe, North America, Asia, Australia, and New Zealand should not rescind an individual's citizenship and deport them to their previous country for any reason, including their long absence from the country, their birth in a different country, their parents' birth or residence in another country, the death of their parents, or the existence of a criminal record. If the government cancels a person's citizenship, then they are discriminating against that person. Although the government has done this in the past, they should not be permitted to do so, and the laws should change. The government should not deport people to their former countries because these countries may entail danger or the deportee lacks experience with the other nation. If an individual has never resided in another country and lacks knowledge of their laws and customs, they may be in danger. Therefore, the government should not endanger people by sending them back to their countries without a valid reason.

Everyone should have the opportunity to apply for a new passport or renew their old one without any complications or difficulties. They shouldn't have to go through long waiting periods, interviews, or questioning. Even more so, they shouldn't be kicked out of the country regardless of their birth status and their length of time in or away from the country. Everyone immigrates to a country at a different period of their life, but they should all receive equal and fair treatment in their new country, which includes the right to keep their status. Although people with dual citizenships don't suffer as much when they lose their status in one country, they should still have the right to keep both citizenship statuses. People shouldn't be forced to choose between two citizenship statuses; rather, they should be permitted to keep both, even when one of their passports expires. The governments of all countries should allow people to renew expired passports at any time as long as they follow the laws of that country. People should have the right to retain their citizenship status and renew their passports without government interference. The government cannot infringe upon people's rights and take their citizenship away or make them choose between two or three citizenships. Immigration policies, especially in this regard, should remain constant over time.

In some cases, people have dual citizenship because their parents are from different countries. For example, their mother may be Mexican and their father may be from Poland. In other situations, people's parents may be from one country, but they may have lived in more than one nation. In these circumstances, people should not be forced to choose between countries and should be able to obtain and keep citizenships from both countries. In the same way that citizens have to respect the laws of a country without committing crime, the government should also respect the status of people within that country. Since discrimination represents a crime in many countries, then the government should not discriminate against citizens and revoke their statuses for any particular reason. Based on these rules, all branches of government, including immigration, embassies, social services, and counselors, should follow these laws and refrain from discriminating for any reason. Discriminatory actions not only include deportation, but they also include creating additional complications, such as extra steps, interviews, required information, and wait periods in order to keep or obtain a rightful status.

Individuals with good lawyers can defend a person who feels as if their rights, including citizenship rights, have been violated. However, good lawyers are difficult to obtain and cost a significant amount of money. Since many new immigrants lack the necessary funds for a lawyer, they will experience difficulty in fighting the government's decision to revoke their citizenship. Also, some lawyers lack the skills and experience to successfully defend their clients or they will simply take the client's money and put limited effort into the case. Another difficulty is that some defendants are not clear about their circumstances, and, as a result, the lawyer will either lose the case or refuse to take on the client because the lawyer may believe that the government is right in revoking their citizenship. Lawyers have a responsibility to help their clients. In order to make sure that the lawyer is responsible, individuals should obtain his/her card, verify his/her employment, and take voice recordings and/or photos of the lawyer without his/her knowledge. This way, the defendant has proof about the lawyer's status and can ensure that this person can help them in their case.

The Embassy, City Council, social services, and any other branch of government all have a responsibility to help individuals and advocate for them in cases of discrimination or other issues. If individuals in these employments refuse or fail to assist someone, they will lose their job. Individuals have the right to report these employees if they fail to perform their duties. These employees cannot discriminate because it's against the law.

Alonzo Bernardo Martinez is an American-Mexican born in Los Angeles, California, USA. His mother was Irish, Scottish, and American, while his father was Mexican. He grew up in the United States and spent his whole life in the US. As an educated person, Alonzo completed high school, college, and university. As a result, he had a good job and his life was very successful. In addition, Alonzo followed the law and had no criminal record. He met his wife, Miranda Apalo Aguiera, at the University of California in Los Angeles, CA. Like Alonzo, Miranda had a strong educational background and followed the law. They had two daughters aged two and four. Miranda married Alonzo for love rather than as a means of obtaining a Green Card or American Citizenship. Prior to marrying Alonzo, Miranda lived in the United States for three years. She had full Mexican citizenship without a history of illegal immigration. She wanted an American Citizenship or Permanent Residency status, but the government didn't allow her the opportunity to have dual citizenship. They also failed to provide her with a warning, and, after six months, they kicked her out of the country, forcing her to return to Mexico. She had to leave her husband behind, but she ended up taking her two children. Alonzo wasn't allowed to contact his wife and children. He was also forced to sell all of his belongings, including his house, and find another place to live. Otherwise, the government would force him to go to jail. In this case, no plausible reason exists for the government to kick Miranda out of the country and force Alonzo to move. Alonso was extremely upset and went to various government offices to seek justice, but nobody was able to help him. During this time, the United States government threatened him twice. He couldn't sleep at night because he feared that the government would harm him in some way. If Alonzo and his parents were both born in Mexico, then Alonzo would also be deported back to his country along with his wife, and their children would have to stay in America. In this case, who would take care of the children?

Some individuals apply for a visa that allows them temporary residence in a foreign country. This period may range from three weeks to three years. The application process for a visa can entail several difficulties. Also, once the visa has expired, they need to return to their original country. If someone with an expired visa remains in a country for too long, the government may become upset and they may be refused reentry into that country, so they need to exercise caution. The government shouldn't kick immigrants or newcomers out of a country. However, people that want to temporarily or permanently reside in another country should be aware that they must follow the rules of that country rather than only the laws of the host nation. Similar to a passport, visas can be renewed and travellers can return to their own country. Foreign countries contain embassies representing most countries, enabling travellers to resolve discrepancies concerning their international documentation. People can consult such embassies to apply for or renew an expired visa or passport. In addition, embassies can allow people to apply for a status such as Permanent Residency or Citizenship. Individuals that plan on living or working in a particular country for a long period of time should apply for a status, as it proves that they belong in the country and protects them from deportation.

Most people prefer to obtain passports rather than visas. A passport enables individuals to travel to any country while a visa restricts a person to visiting or temporarily living in only a certain country. These documents provide individuals with a sense of comfort, as they allow individuals to live in peace and comfort without feeling threatened that the government may question their presence in a particular nation. Many countries issue passports that don't require additional visas: European nations, Israel, Canada, USA, Mexico, New Zealand, Japan, South Africa, and Australia.

Individuals that immigrate to a certain country for the purposes of marriage cannot have their citizenship revoked by the government upon divorce. If the government tries to deport an individual because their marriage to someone failed, then the government is committing a crime. Individuals need to know their rights and defend themselves against this action. In some cases, the government may deport a person after divorce because they changed their name and/or identity, which may cause the government to question the person. However, individuals may change their names in a new country because they escaped their former nation for such reasons as discrimination, war, or poverty. In these cases, the government of the former country, rather than the individual, is at fault. Since these individuals are not responsible for such circumstances, they should not be deported from their country.

Many countries, including European nations, China, Japan, North America, New Zealand, and Australia, have erected security mechanisms at their borders. These checkpoints occur in all travel spaces, including roads, railroads, and airports. In particular, International Airports have various security features that control incoming and outgoing people and cargo. The government has authorized security personnel to use strict methods of control. Newcomers, former immigrants, and former citizens are all affected by this government mandate. These rules exist due to terrorist, criminal, and drug activities that occur on an international level, ultimately affecting innocent immigrants. Since these criminals don't follow the rules, governments don't want them in their country. Security can control people to make sure that they don't possess any weapons, such as guns, bombs, or knives, or illegal drugs. If the security officers catch people with these items, then they will put them in jail. They will make the offender explain why he/she was carrying drugs or weapons and to inform them that they are breaking the law by possessing those items. However, some security officers confiscate materials other than the illegal items. Security should only take away weapons or drugs and leave the offender with their other belongings, since these items are legal and some of them, such as passports, are important. The officer shouldn't check the person's belongings, including the name and identity on their passports or the number of passports, because these items are not the officer's business as long as the person isn't breaking the law. Rather, the security person should explain the law and provide the offender with a warning instead of automatically sending them to jail or deporting them from the country. If the person can follow the law once they have been warned, then the government, police, and security should leave them alone. Everyone should be trusted and treated fairly unless they are a proven criminal, such as a drug dealer or terrorist.

Although the government and security agencies should give people chances, once they clearly break the rules after at least one warning or lie to the government, then they shouldn't be trusted. At that point, the offender should be put in jail with a harsh enough term that will guarantee that they never break the rules again.

Unfortunately, international airports cannot trust people anymore because many illegal activities happen at airports and security has no way of separating the criminals from the innocent people. Thus, all travellers are subject to the same security measures, and security officers must perform the duties assigned to them. However, innocent people, including immigrants and newcomers, suffer because of the actions of drug dealers, criminals, and terrorists. It doesn't seem fair that innocent civilians should face the same security checks as criminals. In fact, many civilians complain because of the tight and invasive security procedures at airports. Some security personnel even abuse their power, attacking people who are innocent. Officers or government employees that beat or shoot an innocent individual on the basis of their race or other factor are committing a crime. In particular, it is illegal to touch a woman in an invasive way. These officers will lose their job, become charged, and even spend time in prison.

People travelling through airports can take two passports, and if necessary, these passports can have different names. In this case, one passport can be used and the other can be put in the safe, but travellers can also keep both passports on their person. However, these people need to exercise caution because they want to avoid possible questioning from security. Many people don't feel safe traveling through international airports because they face too many strict controls, which causes them to fear airports. Airports should not exercise harsh control over everyone, because not all individuals are criminals. Governments and security officers should not assume that individuals of certain colors or religious denominations are criminals or terrorists. These attitudes cause particular populations to fear airports and to travel through other means, such as railways or boats. For instance, some people prefer to travel directly from Canada to Europe while avoiding the United States, which has security-heavy airports. Similarly, other people like to fly directly from Canada to Europe or vice-versa in order to avoid the strict control in the United States.

People who travel by ship can avoid the strict control measures of road borders and airports. In the port, immigrants or other travelers don't have to worry because ports don't have the strong security features of an airport. This is because far fewer people travel by boat than by plane. People who want to travel directly from one country to another shouldn't listen to those that insist on the lack of a direct route, because the vast majority of routes are direct and don't require a connection through the United States or United Kingdom. Personally, I prefer to travel on a world international ship; however, future innovations to boat travel should make ships that are both safer and faster.

Newcomers have every right to travel in their new country regardless of their reasons for moving. In particular, residents of the country should treat immigrants with respect and welcome them into the nation. Unfortunately, however, some people treat immigrants unfairly and unkindly. When individuals treat someone poorly or differently because they are from a different, culture, country, or race, they are committing "racism." Even immigrants who dislike other immigrants from the same country because they have a different race, religion, or culture for are still racist. I know of previous immigrants to a certain country that like some immigrants and dislike other immigrants because of their former country, culture, race or religion. These people should consider that they were once immigrants just like the newcomers that they dislike. In particular, refugees are victims or racism. Thus, it is wrong to treat a person differently because that person comes from another country. Racism involves any action that is intended to hurt, offend, or disadvantage someone because of their skin color, culture, religion, or race. Racism is never acceptable and shouldn't be ignored. Individuals that have experienced or witnessed racist actions should tell a grownup they trust. However, not all adults will help because even some adults are racist.

In one case, a family moved from one country to another. The father was a doctor in his previous country; however, because he didn't have the correct documentation and/or degrees to practice as a doctor in the new country, he could only obtain work packing boxes. As a result, some people made cruel comments about the family; however, the doctor knew that they had a right to be in the new country because they worked hard. He ignored the mean comments and chose friends who accepted him for who he was. Immigrants can be deported if they break the rules of the country and commit crimes, but most immigrants are innocent and don't commit crimes. Individuals that deport immigrants from the country on the basis of their origin are committing racism or discrimination, which are both against the law. The government is responsible for making laws upon which the citizens agree, and these laws should make people happy. Countries that make poor laws and have unhappy citizens are bad nations in which no one wants to live.

Individuals that committed offenses as minors should not be charged or discriminated against as adults. For example, once a person becomes 18 years old, the government can't consider them as a criminal if they already served jail time as a teenager. In the case that a minor may have stolen something in a store and was apprehended by security, they shouldn't serve jail time because there is no evidence that they stole anything and they weren't arrested on charges. However, individuals that are above the age of 18 and committed serious crimes such as theft, drug trafficking/possession, and murder should go to jail and have a criminal record. Anyone without a criminal record as a youth or adult shouldn't be arrested and serve jail time for a crime of which they are innocent. For citizenship, the same rules should apply. Regardless of a person's citizenship status, they should still possess the ability to apply for or renew their passports without having to serve jail time or getting a criminal record. As long as there is no evidence that a person broke the law in a particular country, they should not be deported or forced to serve jail time. The government should not have the right to cancel a person's passport or rescind their status because of their prolonged absence from a country. Since people often leave their country for an extended period of time, passports should last for more than 5-10 years. If passports were valid for 15-20 years, people would have greater freedom in their ability to travel without the fear of being apprehended for an invalid passport. This change would eliminate the stress in people's lives, allowing them to extend their absence from a country without a penalty. When considering the length of time for passports, the government should also exercise leniency in allowing people to renew their passports without penalty, especially in the case that they have no criminal record. In their policies, the government shouldn't discriminate according to race, color, culture, religion, gender, age, or ability level. Since each person's circumstances are different, the government should consider the situation of each individual in assessing their eligibility for passport application and/or renewal. The government should reduce their level of control over passport issues by increasing the length of passports, considering individual circumstances, and eliminating needless penalties and fines.

Many people express a natural fear of immigrants, especially since these individuals and their ways of life are unfamiliar. When large numbers of immigrants arrive in a country, local residents may experience difficulty in accepting these immigrants. As a result, these people may make racist comments or blame problems on immigrants. For instance, some people believe that immigrants take jobs away from the country's other citizens. This belief lacks a valid foundation, especially since immigrants accept undesirable and low-paying jobs that most people refuse to do. On the other hand, many immigrants also fill important vacancies. This type of thought represents a fixed idea or "stereotype" of immigrants. Stereotypes are one-sided generalizations about a group of people. While in some cases stereotypes are helpful, stereotypes about immigrants distort reality because they fail to consider the uniqueness of each individual as well as their strengths and weaknesses. Due to their stereotyped beliefs, racist individuals often refuse to make a genuine effort to learn about the culture and religion of new immigrants. They also refuse to acknowledge the positive benefits that immigrants bring to a nation or community. For instance, immigrants help the economy, fill job vacancies, increase the pool of skilled workers, and add cultural and artistic contributions to society. By forcing immigrants to leave the country, people not only exercise discrimination but also harm the country's economy and culture. Society can change racist stereotypes by showing understanding and awareness as well as making a genuine effort to get to know immigrants and their culture.

Airports and airlines restrict individuals from transporting certain items. As a result, people travelling by plane need to know what they can take and what they need to leave at home. Airlines permit packed luggage and a carry-on, the latter of which cannot contain liquids and gels over a certain size. In addition, airports have limitations pertaining to food and drink items in the baggage. As a result, people must pack these items in their luggage. Otherwise, security personnel will remove these items from carry-on luggage and confiscate them. In order to avoid losing these items or being subject to further scrutiny, individuals need to learn airport regulations pertaining to acceptable carry-on items. Due to incidents of terrorism, security measures have tightened and some security companies and officers exercise strict control over people carrying restricted items. As a result, security officers may refuse to give people a chance to explain themselves and will impose harsher penalties for carrying unacceptable items. They may put people through a lot of trouble and even perform invasive searches. There have even been cases where security officers have abused their power and stripped young females; however, this behavior is unacceptable and unnecessary, even given the increased regulations.

The difference between individuals gives life variety and makes it exciting. Without such variety, the world would be a very dull place. This diversity is achieved by the presence of people from different cultures. Various languages, foods, fashions, and games come from all different parts of the world. Thus, immigrants have contributed to the variety of choices in life. Everyone who comes to live in a particular nation can contribute to the community both financially and culturally, sharing the richness of his/her culture. We can all learn from one another. When children join a school or move onto a street, children should get to know them. For instance, people can introduce immigrants to rules, routines, customs, and activities that the newcomer might not be familiar with. In return, locals can learn from immigrants and find out about different ways of life. For example, people may learn new games, taste different foods, or make new friends. Most people don't realize that in addition to people, food also migrates! Without people travelling and settling throughout the world, countries wouldn't be exposed to as many foods.

The government policies and citizens of a country tend to divide people; however, people should learn to live together peacefully. Racism causes people to become divided against each other according to race, causing problems within communities. Ultimately, racism stems from fear, especially when people lack understanding of other cultures. With understanding and awareness, both immigrants and locals can live together in peace and friendship. It's important to treat others with respect and understanding, especially when people want others to treat them the same way. Although individuals may disagree with the political and religious views of others, people still need to respect the beliefs of immigrants. Everyone should have pride in their beliefs and opinions as well as their country of origin; in addition, people should accept and respect others despite any differences.

Shaida is going to Bangladesh to see her aunt and grandmother. She really wants to show her family pictures of her friends and explain the way of life in the new country. Her teacher, Mrs. Smith, asked her to keep a diary, so Shaida can show her classmates about her trip.

When I have moved to this country, then I will try to join in with as many local activities as possible. Be aware that there may be different ways of doing things. I would tell my classmates and friends about my culture. You can tell a parent or teacher if you are being bullied. If someone I know has moved to this country, then I will involve them in activities and make an effort to talk to them. I can find out about their culture and remember that they may have terrifying experiences that they may not feel comfortable discussing. Also, I need to stay out of trouble.

Many people travel from one country to another. They may want to go on vacation or visit relatives; however, they usually return home after one or two weeks. Sometimes, people travel to another country and move there. People who move permanently to another country are known as immigrants. If you look around, at school, at work, or on the street, there are many immigrants. Immigrants can be children, teenagers, adults, or senior citizens. They can also come from any country or ethnic background. Perhaps someone from another country has moved onto your street or started attending your school. Maybe one of your parents used to live in a different country.

This book explains the experience of moving to a new country and discusses the issues involved in this process. For centuries, people have travelled across the world to settle in other countries. This process is known as "migration." On the other hand, "emigration" means to leave one's own country to live in another nation. "Immigration" means to come to a new country to settle there. Countries such as North

America, Europe, Australia, and New Zealand experience immigration because people from all over the world settle in these nations.

Some of the first immigrants fled danger or poverty to find a better life in another country. Later, others sought wealth and opportunities in newly-discovered countries such as North America, Europe, Australia, and New Zealand. Today, there are new countries to discover; however, people still emigrate all over the world. People with different skin colors, different religions, and different languages have different ways of life, which are known as cultures. Communities where people of different cultures live side-by-side are known as multicultural.

Did you know that Aborigines lived in Australia long before the first immigrants settled there? Aborigines are the "native" or "indigenous" people of Australia. The first immigrants who settled in the country were also known as "colonists." The European people controlled Australia, enforcing their rules and ways of life without respecting those of the Aborigines, the original peoples.

People decide to live in other countries for many reasons. Individuals may receive a job offer or want to make more money in another country. For example, a family may settle in a particular country if a family member already has a job in that country. Also, others may want to live in a country with a better climate, and decide to move somewhere warm, such as Australia, Latin America, or Southern Europe, including Spain, Portugal, Italy, and Greece. Furthermore, people may move to another nation to live with their relatives or family members.

Many people emigrate because of more serious concerns. Some people are forced to leave their own country because of war or fear for their safety. While some of these immigrants never return to their country, others can visit occasionally. In other cases, a lack of resources, such as food, water, or medication, may influence people to find a greater quality of life in another country. The process of emigrating involves leaving your friends, your family, and other familiar aspects, such as culture, language, or climate. The prospect of emigrating may cause you to feel very anxious about living in an unfamiliar country. Although immigration can initially be overwhelming, new experiences often turn out to have positive results. For many people, emigrating is an exciting new start. It represents a chance to see and experience new things and to meet new people.

Sometimes, in countries with war conditions, people often have to leave their homes with very warning due to the prospect of danger. They may have to leave their family and belongings behind without knowing where they are going and whether they will ever be able to return. Imagine what it would be like to leave your home with no time to pack or say goodbye to your friends and family. In addition, you might not know where you are going, how you will travel, or what will happen when you arrive at your destination. People in this situation have to cope with great fear, danger, and uncertainty. The idea of arriving in a different country with an unfamiliar language and culture can represent a daunting prospect.

Over the past 60 years, travelling across the world has become much easier than it was in the past. As a result, increasing numbers of people have immigrated. In response to rising immigration, many countries have introduced rules stating who can and can't live in their country. However, this idea has been challenged because should have a chance to follow the rules rather than being banned from the country. These immigration rules often affect a person's choices concerning whether to emigrate.

Specifically, people with special skills, such as doctors, are welcomed in many countries. However, many countries have the need for people to work less skilled jobs, such as cleaning or crop picking. The immigration rules for these workers are often more strict, and they may be refused entry by some countries. As a result, these rules make it difficult for unskilled workers to find a new home. To avoid the restrictions, some people enter a country illegally, putting themselves at great risk. They may hide for days in trucks or airplanes or travel in crowded or unsafe vehicles.

To enter a country, a person needs to possess the correct documentation, such as a passport and/or a visa, which confirms the right of entry. Without such documents, potential immigrants can be refused entry into their desired country and sent back to their original nation.

People without the correct documents face many difficulties in immigration. First, they may be refused entry and sent back to their home country or they may experience a long wait period while the authorities evaluate their documentation. These government actions can harm immigrants because they may be refugees fleeing danger in their own country. As a result, the government needs to understand their situation before denying them admittance into their desired country. A person who leaves his/her country due to unsafe conditions is known as a refugee. Refugees that seek safety or asylum in another country are considered "asylum seekers." Each person has a human right to seek protection in another country. Although governmental organizations consider the various circumstances of immigrants, their denial of refugees due to a lack of proper documentation interferes with human rights.

Individuals should stay in their own countries unless they are fleeing danger. However, many individuals in several countries feel threatened by race, religion, or political beliefs. This sense of discrimination is known as "persecution." Some persecuted refugees leave their own country in desperation and seek asylum in a new nation. People need to understand and follow the rules of immigration because these rules benefit all members of society.

Many immigrants want to get a new opportunity in another country. They want the chance to live in a new country without the fear of being deported and sent back home. Since everybody likes to travel to other countries, they should respect new immigrants and give them a chance to live in their new country. It is actually illegal to kick people out of a country and send them back home, so the government cannot deport immigrants without a valid reason, such as criminal activity. Immigrants that follow the law should be provided with the opportunity for a better life, education, and employment in a new country.

Some immigrants feel welcomed and accepted when they arrive in another country. These individuals may have relatives to help them adjust, sufficient funds to find a home, or a job to work. However, most countries don't want to accept criminals, illegal activities, drug dealers, or terrorists in their nation. Because of these fears, governments feel uncertain about accepting many immigrants, even refugees who flee their countries due to danger. As a result, refugees and other immigrants have to wait long periods of time for a government's decision to accept them. They may have to return to their country or pay fees to acquire the correct documentation. This experience can be very frustrating for new immigrants, who often feel as if the government is mistreating them. Most of these immigrants came into the country for good reasons and the government should not deny their request. When these individuals are forced to leave their country due to war, poverty, or persecution, they should not be deported because it could result in an attack.

Regardless of the reason for emigrating, most individuals will leave behind friends and family. Even if a person is moving to a new job or home, they may feel anxious about fitting in and adjusting to new ways of doing things. Every aspect of a new country may be different to the immigrants, including the weather, language, culture, currency, and transportation system. For instance, the adjustment to trains, metros, trolleys, and buses and their routes to work, school, or shopping could cause difficulties.

As immigrants attempt to adjust, their new school or workplace may seem strange, especially if they don't speak the language of the new country. New immigrants will take time to learn various systems, learn the language, and make friends. Some ways to increase your sense of belonging include taking part in activities that you enjoy and attempting new pursuits. Even adults experience difficulties in adjusting to a new country. For instance, they may encounter difficulties in finding a new job or meeting new people. This leads to isolation and loneliness, which makes it necessary for natives of the country to show understanding. If someone from another country has recently arrived in your area or school, it's important to make a special effort to make him/her feel welcome. You could invite them to join in with your activities or offer your help. Although you may not understand their language, you can show kindness without using worlds.

Think about it: when a young person has moved to a new country, they may be influenced by the way other young people behave, which can lead to conflict in the home and other environments. Children should try to consider their parents' viewpoints and refrain from letting others put pressure on them. They should discuss their feelings with their family and come to an agreement on acceptable behavior.

When immigrants arrive in another country, they may feel unsure about their sense of belonging. Their new home will probably be very different from their old home. However, they can still participate in both their new and old countries and their respective cultures. Some immigrants may live near other people that share the same country of origin, religion, or culture. While this proximity makes it easier for immigrants to feel at home, it can also make them more reluctant to get to know other local people and their customs.

People should understand and respect the differences between their culture and the culture of their new home countries while also accepting the culture of new immigrants. Everyone should respect the values, beliefs, and cultures of everyone else, regardless of their country of origin and/or their current country of residence. Many immigrants feel part of both their country of origin and their country of residence. Did you know that after living in a country for a certain amount of time that immigrants can apply to become a "citizen" of that country? Citizenship gives people rights shared by other citizens, such as the right to vote in that country's elections. Many citizens of a country can trace their family back to find people who arrived as immigrants. Permanent Residency is below the status of Citizenship, as Permanent Residents lack some of the rights of citizens, as only citizens are permitted to vote.

I had a friend that lived in Canada for 20 years. He was born in the United States and left America when he was 17 years old. However, his parents were from Vietnam and he came to Canada to get a better education and a better life. While in America, he lived a depressed life. He was not illegal or a criminal, as he never broke the law in any country. As a result, he had dual citizenship to both Canada and the United States. In the past, it was easier for him to get his Citizenship Status, but today, it has become much more difficult to become a Canadian citizen.

Police Force Laws

If the world was perfect and there was no crime, police wouldn't need to carry guns. However, since the world is not perfect and most countries have substantial crimes, police require weapons in order to control crime.

Although police carry guns, there are several rules that govern their use of these weapons. For instance, police can only shoot if their lives are in very serious danger or if they feel as if they will be attacked. Also, if someone tries to attack a police officer or an innocent person, the police can use their guns for self-defense or to defend the victim. In the case that a police officer believes that an innocent person will be attacked, they can shoot at the attacker. However, police cannot use their guns and shoot innocent people if no crime or threat of a crime has occurred.

The following situations represent instances of police abuse:

- shooting to murder an innocent person
- beating someone unconscious
- hurting prisoners, as prisoners are already in captivity
- verbally assaulting someone, including insulting them or arguing with them
- abusing power to hurt someone
- aggressiveness

- sexual assault and rape against innocent women
- use of Taser to murder people
- chasing innocent people
- hitting innocent people with a car
- relentlessly pursuing an innocent person
- arresting people without a warrant or without proof
- discrimination and racism resulting from citizenship status, nationality, race, religion, or skin color
- harassment
- provoking a fight with an innocent person or trying to cause trouble

In the above scenarios, police officers are exhibiting illegal behavior that will cause them to lose their job and perhaps even become permanently banned from the police force. Especially in cases where police officers receive continual warnings, their engagement in such behavior should result in consequences.

Although police may use force against criminals or suspects, they shouldn't start a fight with these individuals; rather, they should only use force against criminals if the offenders begin trying to attack the officer. Even in these cases, police should avoid shooting or murdering the criminal; they should only use sufficient force to subdue their attacker. Police are trained to use self-defense in a professional way that avoids killing unless absolutely necessary.

Police seem to find many excuses for wanting to murder other individuals. For instance, they often have a problem with people because of their relatives or family members. Even if the family members have committed a crime, police should not harass their relatives. Also, police seem to want to kill people that argue with them or disobey them, even in the case that these individuals do not represent a major threat. Among the cases where people run away from the police, some situations involve a dangerous and armed individual, but, in other cases, these individuals do not carry weapons or they are not threats to hurt the police or other people. Police are justified in shooting when the person fleeing carries weapons, but when a person is unarmed, the police should not shoot them. In this case, the police can pursue them and use a Taser with only sufficient force to subdue them.

Police should not want to kill someone simply because that person is connected to a criminal or suspect. In several instances, police have murdered or attempted to murder individuals because of their connection with other people, such as

- spouses or family members
- neighbors
- teachers
- managers, employees coworkers
- supervisors
- counsellors
- children or teenagers
- government workers
- lawyers or judges

In addition, the police also tend to commit illegal actions for the following reasons:

- murder people on the basis of their skin color, culture, religion, citizenship status or nationality
- inquire into a person's private business or private life

- cheat in law assessments
- act jealously because people have an attractive partner or spouse, leading them to separate the individual from their partner while also cheating on their own partners
- abuse their authority and take away an individual's human rights despite laws and freedoms in that particular country
- murder or arrest someone because they are exercising their right to protest against the government
- arrest or murder someone because that person discovered the truth about something

Although people realize that they have mistakenly broken the law and apologize to the police, the police may still treat them badly. Conversely, when some police officers realize that they have made a mistake and mistreated a person, they will apologize and refrain from repeating their mistake again. However, many police officers don't care and continue to mistreat citizens.

Not only do municipal police officers abuse their authority but other police and military also mistreat people. For instance, sheriffs, military personnel, provincial police, and peace officers all have the tendency to abuse their power and citizens. Despite their position, all police and military officers that mistreat people break the law and should lose their jobs. The abuse of police force occurs at many levels and in most countries. In several cases, one or two police officers set bad examples and their colleagues or subordinates will imitate them and learn poor police behavior. Although many police are good, the police that abuse their power stand out, causing people to stereotype and generalize police as power-hungry individuals. Unfortunately, the few police officers that abuse their authority negatively affect their co-workers and bring shame to their organization.

Although some people may blame the actions of all police on one officer, individuals should not blame innocent officers for their actions; rather, they should only blame the specific officer that abused them. Police are prohibited from murdering innocent citizens or from using his/her colleagues against an individual. If people report the police officer that abused them, the officer that harmed them can still get fired. However, if a person who committed a crime reports police abuse, the police and government will still pursue that individual despite the fact that a single officer may have lost his/her job. The criminal that committed an offense should go to prison and the police officer who abused their authority should have a criminal record. Once a person is imprisoned, they lose their opportunity to have friends, partners/spouses, and employment. Regardless of a person's financial status, they can try to bribe their lawyer to freedom and remove their criminal record; however, most criminals, both police and regular citizens, will spend their life in prison and have their passport cancelled. In the case of the police, the police officer is responsible for his/her own imprisonment because they abused their authority and committed a crime against an innocent person. Although the officer's fate can depend upon the situation, in most cases, if the police commit a wrong action, they will lose their jobs and become banned from the police force. Police shouldn't be treated differently than regular citizens, especially when the commit crimes. If police break the rules, they should have the same punishment as regular citizens and the law should not make exceptions for them simply because they are police or military.

The law should apply consistently to all citizens of a country, regardless of their profession or status. If the police don't want to lose their jobs, they shouldn't commit wrong actions. Police shouldn't think that they can abuse their power simply because they are in a position of authority. They shouldn't believe that nobody has authority over them and that the government will allow them to commit crimes or hurt innocent people. Some police officers become offended when people criticize or even apprehend them for committing offenses. They will continue to commit crimes even if people inform them of their abuse; in these cases, some police will even kill or harm people to silence them.

Not only do the police break the law by killing innocent people, but they also sexually assault women. In particular, some officers strip-search females under the pretense of searching for illegal weapons. Police can also rape and sexually assault women in both public and private places, including offices and prisons. Officers may even purposely embarrass people by assaulting them in public places, where the offending officer as well as his/her colleagues can make fun of and insult the victim.

Furthermore, people should be able to assert their rights without the fear of retribution from the police or government. When innocent people inform the police of their rights, the police continue to brutalize or assault people that resist or state their rights. In fact, police have even attacked people for performing innocent actions such as kissing their spouses, laughing, or dancing. People that follow the law should have the right to live their life freely without worrying about police brutality.

Another instance of police assault occurs when people act in their defense against police brutality. Sometimes, police murder or attack people that defend themselves against provocation. For example, if the police swear at someone for no reason and the person swears back in defense or gives the police a bad attitude, police have been known to murder those people. Even when the police don't actually murder or harm someone, sometimes they can threaten to hurt a person for not immediately complying with commands. For instance, police can say: "I'm going to kill you if you don't put your hands up!" Or, they can continue holding a gun to someone even if that person has not committed any crime.

Many police also exhibit discrimination against people as a result of their race, nationality, color, sex, religion, orientation or ability level. In some countries, individuals can bribe police for forgiveness by paying them money. This behavior is wrong because people should follow the law and police should not allow people to break the law for their personal profit. Police are responsible for ensuring that people follow the law and the failure to do so means that they are not doing their job properly. In most countries, such as Canada, individuals cannot bribe the police. As a result, police should explain that individuals have broken the law and allow them a second chance to correct their mistake; however, police generally disregard explanations, believing that people are making excuses for their crimes. Even worse, police exacerbate the problem by brutalizing people, causing the offenders to retaliate and leading to further conflict between police and citizens.

While some police are helpful, others do not help citizens who ask for assistance. Police should be available to help people if they have followed the law and need assistance. When people approach the police, some officers may believe that the individual seeking help is trying to disrespect the police, resulting in the police harassing the person. However, many people need police help for different reasons; they may have been beaten or victimized in another way, such as theft. Several types of theft can occur, such as robbery of the house, car, belongings, money, and private information. Victims of theft are not responsible for the crime that happened to them, especially in cases where they didn't share their personal information or belongings with the thief. In the case of monetary theft, people should be able to call banks and explain their situation without harassment or difficult questioning. Banks usually ask people difficult questions which can be stressful and difficult to remember, especially during a traumatic situation like theft. Banks should also have cameras and mirrors so that they can identify people that conduct transactions. If banks allow thefts to occur, they should be taken to court for irresponsible business conduct. The stolen money is your money, so it shouldn't be able to disappear into the hands of a thief and the bank should pay you back. Otherwise, people should be able to complain and report the crime, especially if they know the full names of the employees. In this case, the employees that allowed the theft to occur should lose their jobs and the bank should replace your lost money as well as provide you with new cards and passwords. Similarly, lawyers and judges cannot free people who are criminals by accepting bribes from their clients. The law should be applied equally in all cases, and criminals should go to jail regardless of their financial status. Lawyers and judges that demonstrate corrupt behavior by accepting bribes should lose their jobs and go to jail.

In one scenario involving identity theft, a man named Jacob gave an employee named Mrs. Webbit his file number on July 9, 2010. That same day, he found a police booklet about restitution for victims of crime in his mailbox. On July 5, 2010, Jacob spoke with Mrs. Martin, who claimed that he was responsible for an identity theft despite his innocence. In this situation, the bank was responsible for the supposed identity theft. When employees suspect suspicious transactions, they should contact their head office, which will then close the customer's account until the matter has been resolved. During this time period, several large transactions occurred on Jacob's account, and the bank didn't take any action to resolve the matter. The bank knew that someone was stealing the money out of Jacob's account and yet they didn't act, thus putting Jacob at a greater risk. In this case, the police are responsible for requesting the bank to provide video tapes of the situation; however, the police refused to help Jacob, even when a picture of the thief had been obtained. Jacob sought help from several organizations, including the bank, police, legal aid, Legal Service Center, Student Legal Center, Law Enforcement Review Board, Alberta Ombudsman, Alberta Solicitor General, and Public Security. However, none of these organizations were willing to help him. Jacob wanted justice; if he had committed the theft, then he would expect to suffer arrest and imprisonment. Since Jacob was innocent and had not committed the theft, he expected the thief who took his backpack, wallet, bankcard, and money to get charged. Jacob felt abandoned and poorly treated because he deserved help and justice, yet he hadn't received any support. The police should help people like Jacob, who are victims of crime.

Some people are not afraid of the police. For example, some larger men have played sports or competitive training and are larger and stronger than police officers. When people are attacked by the police, they can fight with the police in order to defend themselves. If people are larger and stronger, police will have more difficulty in attempting to harass them. However, people shouldn't start fights with the police because they will be charged for assaulting an officer and may even encounter other problems, such as police harassment and assault. Many of the police officers believe that their police status provides them with an advantage over other citizens because of their power and authority; however, the police should not have extra privileges over other citizens. If police don't stop abusing their power and treating people badly, citizens may eventually rebel against the police and start a war. This war will harm innocent police officers, who do their job properly and don't abuse their authority. As a result, only the police that abuse their power should suffer punishment. People that understand the law will eventually seek revenge on abusive police officers and murder them because of the innocent people that they have wronged. When abusive officers get harmed or die, it's their own fault because they have treated other people badly. In fact, the Bible says that bad people are reserved to die.

People should treat others the way that they expect or desire to be treated. Police officers that take the lives of innocent people should die because that's how they treated other people. The police are not above the rest of humanity and their status doesn't grant them immunity from the law. Accordingly, they shouldn't interfere with people's business unless it concerns the law or current investigations.

The following ten stories provide examples of police interference in people's lives:

1. Four women from Africa were working for the custodial company Bee Clean. The manager made a

mistake and neglected to arrange the pails in the janitor room. One of the African women, the Angolan, showed up at 5:30 p.m. and began doing her work immediately. Three other employees, two women from Ethiopia and one woman from Eritrea, showed up late to work. The Angolan woman was unknowingly using the supplies allocated for one of the Ethiopian women. When the Ethiopian woman discovered that the Angolan woman was using her supplies, she began yelling at her and verbally abusing her. In response, the Angolan woman asked her to stop yelling and to explain the situation to her nicely. The Ethiopian woman refused to stop screaming despite the fact that the Angolan woman was innocent and hadn't actually done anything wrong. Then, the Ethiopian lady started to physically attack the Angolan woman, and the other two women joined in, scratching her, pushing her, and beating her. The three women almost killed the Angolan woman before other employees intervened. Specifically, one Spanish co-worker from El-Salvador and the Spanish manager tried to stop the fight. Other people and some students also heard the noise from the fighting. The surveillance camera recorded the situation and the security guard had video access for showing the police. The security guard called the police, who showed up almost immediately. The two police officers, one male and one female, requested the employees to explain the situation to them. The innocent lady explained the truth to the officers. Normally, the police would arrest the three suspects, especially since they committed the major criminal offense of assault. However, the two police abandoned the victim and refused to serve justice. The police were likely racist because all four women were black and African. As a result, she suffered humiliation from people on the street, who made fun of her and her injuries. She also had to spend two days in the hospital and seek legal assistance for her injuries, which she couldn't afford. The lawyer asked her to use her manager as a reference; however, when she asked the manager to provide a reference, he refused to help her and did not provide compensation for her injuries. Although the manager fired the other three employees, he didn't treat her fairly, so she quit her job. If a White or Hispanic person was attacked by a Black person, the police would arrest the Black person. On the other hand, if a Black person was attacked by a White or Hispanic individual, the police would not arrest the offender. This scenario provides an example of racism, which shouldn't exist in Canada. However, despite the Canadian laws opposing racism and discrimination, these phenomena occur everywhere in the world. Police constantly exhibit racism and discrimination against people by favoring certain groups of people over others. The victimized Bee Clean woman found a new job catering for six months, but the same thing happened to her: she was harassed, assaulted, and scratched by a racist Spanish lady from Columbia. The police once again showed up and refused to help her in any way. She felt angry because the police were racist and abandoned her.

After she went to the hospital, she was fired from her job. All of these events happened to her because of her skin color. In her third job, as a custodian for a meat company, she was accidentally hit in the face by a mop from another woman. Another custodian, an East Indian lady, was mopping the floor when the Angolan lady came downstairs to collect the garbage. The East Indian lady, neglecting to look around to check the safety of the situation, accidentally came up quickly with the mop and hit the Angolan lady in the face. The Angolan lady incurred another major injury and was rushed to the hospital by ambulance. The manager refused to pay compensation for her injuries and did not fire the East Indian worker that had accidentally hit her in the face. As a result, the Angolan lady quit her third job; although the doctor and the government had allowed her to receive EI, she still experienced significant turmoil resulting from three accidents due to her status as a black person.

2.   Sammy Yatim was born in Syria in 1995. He moved to Toronto, Canada with his parents and sisters for an education and for a better life. In 2008, when he was 13 years old, Sammy had established himself as an excellent teenager who had never committed a crime. Many people knew him and liked him in the Toronto community. Many of his friends, family members, and acquaintances stated that he was a hard worker at school and also worked in a restaurant during the summer time when he was 18. At the restaurant, he worked the night shift from late night until the early morning. One day

on the streetcar, he was carrying a knife that he used for work. He had been alone on the streetcar, minding his own business, when the streetcar driver saw his knife and called the police. Ten police officers showed up and Sammy approached them with respect. However, the police were brutal and disrespectful towards Sammy. One of the police officers, James Bernardo Forcillo, yelled at Sammy three times to drop the knife. However, Sammy didn't listen and put the knife back in his pocket. Then, Forcillo started to shoot Sammy, who fell down immediately and died. The police continued to shoot him and even tasered him twice. Another officer came by the front door of the streetcar and kicked him hard on his legs, and another officer came through the back door of the streetcar and kicked him three times in the head. While shooting Sammy once would have sufficed, these police officers continued shooting him, kicking him, and tasering him even though he was already dead. The police shot Yatim nine times in total and tasered him two or three times. The police shouldn't have killed Sammy; rather, they should have tasered him with enough force to subdue him before arresting him. However, since Sammy hadn't committed a crime, he shouldn't spend any time in prison; rather, he should have been released. It wasn't fair that several police ganged up on Sammy; one or two would have been sufficient to subdue him and remove the knife. Since the police had behaved inappropriately, the three that attacked Sammy were charged. This had been the second time that

James Bernardo Forcillo had killed a person. He should have lost his job and gone to prison after the first shooting. His behavior is not acceptable, especially since it resulted in the death of an innocent 18 year old boy.

3. Erik Sarvy was a black man who was walking to school one day. Since he was late for school, he crossed the street and began running. The police stopped him for no reason, other than the fact that he was a black person running, so they had assumed that he had committed a crime. Normally, the police shouldn't be able to control people or ask for their government documents without reason. However, the police asked for Erik's documentation to check his citizenship status. Erik was an African Canadian citizen who was born in Toronto. Erik was part of the country and hadn't committed any crimes; however, the police stopped him and harassed him, eventually provoking him into a fight. As soon as Erik retaliated, an officer named David Caven, grabbed a gun and shot Erik five times. Erik, an innocent man, died in March 2010. David Caven, along with James Forcillo, had murdered two citizens. As a result, David Caven lost his job and was charged with murder, spending the rest of his life in prison. These two police officers are like the police in other countries, such as Spain and U.S.A, who commit racism and discrimination against citizens.

4. Robin Willem had been in a youth center from 2006 to 2012. The people and employees who knew Robin said that he was a good person and

not a trouble maker. The children and their parents liked him because he worked well with children and played with them. Everybody trusted Robin and nobody had to tell him the rules because he knew all of the policies and procedures of the center. When he asked to go into the kitchen, nobody harassed him; all of the employees and manager respected him. Since Robin grew up in the youth center, he would find it difficult to leave, especially since he was a volunteer and many of his friends were there. However, when the youth center hired all new employees and a new manager, the new supervisor didn't know Robin very well. Robin explained that he had spent a long time at the youth center; however, the employees didn't listen to him or treat him like an adult, although he was over 18. They put him in the same category as the little children and treated him as a youth, constantly reminding him of the rules. The new manager and employees decided that he should leave the building and never return, not even to visit his friends. This decision occurred because of his skin color and age, which made Robin very angry. When he tried to come back and visit, the new employees harassed him despite the fact that he wasn't a criminal. The employees called the police, and two officers showed up. Without even checking the problem, the police arrested Robin without any evidence or proof. The police brutalized him and arrested him.

5. In 2012, the police killed a man because that man was robbing a bank in Southwest Edmonton.

Although the man committed the serious crime of robbery, he shouldn't have been shot by the police officer. The police could have tasered the suspect or used minimal force in order to stop him and subdue him, especially since the thief didn't possess a gun. In many cases, the police kill someone without telling the truth about why they murdered that individual or refusing to admit that they made a mistake. Police shouldn't shoot people unless it is absolutely required, and they shouldn't lie about their reasons for shooting or their mistakes. There have also been situations where police have arrested, beat, or murdered people for assuming that the person mistreated their dog or child. In some of these cases, the person was only administering light discipline to their dog or child as a means of controlling their behavior. Some parents and dog owners need better education on how to treat children and dogs, but they don't deserve to die.

6. In the United States in 2008, an older African American lady experienced racist treatment from a White Lady, who was a neighbor of the Black lady. The White lady called the police because of an apparent problem with the Black lady. The police asked the White lady about the situation, and she explained that the African American lady's granddaughter, a little girl, had woken her up with noise. The police immediately arrested the Black lady without asking for her side of the story or without having proof of any kind. The granddaughter was asking what had happened; when she saw that her grandmother had been arrested, she came out

of her bedroom and asked the police why they arrested her grandmother and telling them to leave her grandmother alone. The police began yelling at the little girl, and one officer grabbed a gun and shot her in the face, killing her at the age of 7. The grandmother, as well as her entire family, was upset with the police. The White lady had to attend Supreme Court and the police lost his job and was assigned to life in prison. Although the police may have insisted that his actions were accidental, it is highly unlikely that the shooting was an accident. In the United States, the police murder many black people, especially if they see that black people have something in their hand or pocket and assume that it's a gun. Most times, people just have something innocent on their person, such as a phone, keys, or a chocolate bar. Rather than overreacting, the police should check the person's belongings to determine whether or not they have a gun. Even if a black person has no criminal record and has a bulge in their hand or pocket, the police may shoot them. However, if the person is white, the police will not shoot them because they have the same skin color as the officer. The police should not exhibit racist behavior, especially because in Canada, racism is against the law and police officers should protect the law rather than break it. In these cases, the police abuse their authority and power. They should be able to differentiate between a cell phone and a gun as well as check more carefully.

7. In Los Angeles, California, USA, a woman was in a clothing store with her children. One of the

employees in the store was harassing her because she was spending too long to find a suit, which she needed for a job interview the next day. The woman had even asked the employee for help on at least two occasions; however, the employee had ignored her. Although the woman was innocent, the employee forced her to leave the store and called the police. When they arrived, the police asked the employee to explain the problem and she lied about the customer's actions. Although the manager was not in the store and the surveillance camera showed that the customer was innocent, the police chose to believe the employee. During this time, the customer had been quiet and respectful toward the police; however, the police accused her of a crime and beat her up in front of the employee, manager, and security guards. The customer was beaten so badly that she had to stay in the hospital for almost three months and nearly died. She also lost the respect of her children because of the situation; since she was divorced, she would have a hard time in getting her children back. The two police officers that beat her were charged and lost their jobs, and the store manager had fired the employee that lied about the customer.

Although many Americans believe that Arabs and Muslims are terrorists, the police need to stop generalizing people because they need proof in order to arrest someone. Anybody of any color, race, or religion can be a terrorist, even a white person. As adults, people should know the difference between right and wrong, and stereotyping represents a wrong action. People shouldn't allow another person to lie to them or brainwash them. Adults should be fairly intelligent unless they have a mental disability.

In March or April of 2013, terrorists attacked a group of twelve people in Boston during the Boston Marathon. Two of the terrorists were brothers from Bosnia, and there was also a mother, father, and two children. They had immigrated to the United States and had been American citizens for six years. Although the group of twelve almost died, they survived with injuries, and several children died. There was also a terrorist attack in New York on September 11, 2001, where many innocent people died. In Kenya in 2013, many people died from a terrorist attack, including two innocent Canadians. Terrorism results in the death of many innocent people and also hurts their loved ones, such as families and friends. After the Boston attack, the two Bosnian brothers were charged and attacked by the police. The oldest was shot because he had a weapon had had tried to attack other people, including the police. In this case, the police shot the terrorist in self-defense while also defending the other people. If the terrorist was innocent, the police officer would have lost his job; however, because the terrorist had killed several people and was threatening more individuals, he represented a serious threat and should have been killed in this case. The younger of the two brothers went to jail and the mother was complaining that her sons were killed, injured or imprisoned.

In this case, the police performed their duties correctly; however, in many cases, they treat people badly. The police need to follow their job duties and obey the law. When police harm innocent people, they are not following the law or rules of their job. However, the police don't care about obeying the rules because of their authority and power. The police believe that due to their status, they are better than the rest of the citizens and don't need to follow the laws. Some police even believe that the law can be bought and sold through corruption and bribery. However, this belief represents a major wrong, because police are not politicians and they should not abuse their power. The police seem unable to turn against their aggressive and immoral leaders and colleagues but instead murder or hurt their good colleagues. In addition, the police collaborate with bad leaders and bring corruption to society. The citizens pay for the police services, so police should follow the law and perform good actions.

Terrorists should attack he politicians, government, police and soldiers, since these individuals have a lot of money and power as well as tend to abuse their authority. In countries all around the world, the leaders such as police, military and government exploit their power to control people, resulting in murder and corruption. However, the government, military, and police that follow the law and treat people well shouldn't be attacked. Terrorists need to direct their attacks away from innocent civilians and towards central powers that exercise corruption. Since many terrorists operate as suicide terrorists, it seems redundant that they put themselves in danger in order to hurt innocent people rather than bad people. While I believe that terrorists, if they operate at all, should target corrupt powers rather than innocent civilians, I still think that terrorism is a bad activity and terrorists should be punished and stopped.

8. Hendrik Lema was a young man that immigrated to Zurich, Switzerland with his parents and siblings when he was five years old. He went on vacation to Nigeria in order to visit his grandparents, but when he returned, to Switzerland on October 20, 2011, his passport had expired two days before his return. He had to renew his passport, since he was a Swiss citizen and had lived in that country for a long time. Although Hendrick hadn't committed any crime, he was apprehended by authorities in the Zurich International Airport. The authorities treated him as if he was a criminal; they called the police and three officers showed up to deal with him. The police confiscated his recently-expired passport and other identification documents. Hendrik became angry at the police and security, and one officer responded by drawing his gun and shooting Hendrick because he was a black man. Hendrick died from the gunshot wounds, and the police and security guards involved in the incident were charged. As a result of this incident, many Nigerians protested against the murder and against the racism in Switzerland.

In Germany, two black men were killed by the police because they were accused of running away from the police. The German police demonstrated racism by killing black people without a legitimate reason. Among all European countries, Germans demonstrate the greatest amount of racism, while Americans are the most racist of all North American countries. Other European countries, such as Spain, England, and France, have racist police officers that discriminate against immigrants and kill them despite the fact that the laws in these countries oppose racism. However, in addition to committing murder and racism, police also take away people's passports and ID without giving these documents back. This action represents theft, which is worse for police than regular citizens because police are supposed to obey the law.

9. In the Netherlands, on August 20, 2004, a black lady named Jasmina had emigrated from Suriname to the Netherlands. As a single mother, she and her three children had lived in the Netherlands for thirteen years and had Dutch citizenship. Her passport had expired, but she managed to renew her passport as well as those of her children. Jasmina had experienced difficulty with Jessica, her 16-year old daughter, whose friends were a bad influence on her and taught her to commit wrong actions. While good friends teach people to respect the rules and treat their parents well, Jessica's friends disrespected their parents, so they influenced Jessica to behave in a similar fashion. One day, Jessica wanted to go out late at night, but Jasmina wouldn't let her

leave the house because it was dangerous in their area, especially for girls, many of whom had been kidnapped. Although Jessica's mother was trying to protect her, Jessica disrespected her mother and tried to argue with her. Her two brothers tried to persuade Jessica to stop arguing with her mother, but Jessica continued arguing with her mother and even got angry at her brothers. She used bad language with both her mother and her older brother. At this point, Jasmina was very upset with Jessica for her rude behavior and began hitting her as discipline. Jessica ran away from her mother, running into her mother's room and trying to escape from the balcony. Their apartment was on the 7th floor, and Jessica tried to jump from their balcony onto her neighbour's balcony, which was on the 6th floor. Jessica missed her jump and screamed for help. A Dutch lady heard Jessica screaming and called the police. When the police showed up, the Dutch lady gave a false report, claiming that Jessica's mother had beat Jessica. Jessica didn't have any injuries and her mother had only hit her for discipline, so the mother shouldn't be arrested. The Dutch lady didn't have any evidence or proof against Jessica's mother; she only disliked Jasmina because she was black. In the Netherlands, if the police have no evidence or proof, they can't arrest someone. If someone calls the police and gives a false report because they lack awareness of the situation, the police are not at fault; however, if the police begin brutalizing and arresting someone, then they are at fault. Although Jasmina wasn't guilty of any crime, the police were aggressive as soon as they came. The police almost broke the door down until the oldest son opened it. When the police entered, they didn't know the nature of the problem and didn't bother asking Jasmina. Rather, they brutalized her and arrested her immediately, taking her straight to jail without even allowing her to wear her shoes. The police also embarrassed Jasmina, with two male and one female officer making fun of her. Although other citizens were laughing at her, the police should know better and shouldn't disrespect Jasmina. The police disbelieved Jasmina and they also disregarded the report of the Columbian woman, who gave a positive report of Jasmina. The police officers believed the Dutch lady's report that Jasmina had hit her daughter repeatedly with a stick. They wouldn't listen to Jasmina and they refused to tell her who had reported her. Jasmina had to spend the night in jail, and in the morning, she explained her situation to the police supervisor. The supervisor discovered that she was innocent of the crime for which she had been charged and that the officers who apprehended her had exhibited racist behavior. As a result, the supervisor talked with the officers and informed them that their behavior was inappropriate and illegal as well as warning them that they would lose their job if they repeated this mistake. Although the officers refused to apologize to her, Jasmina left the prison and returned home. Two weeks later, Jasmina had the same problem with her daughter, and she called the police, using the Columbian neighbor as a witness. This time, the police didn't want to do anything about the situation because they had gotten in trouble during the previous occasion.

In Amsterdam, one black man named Nick was a customer in a snack bar and tried to buy a sandwich and pop. Nick had been to this shop many times and had never experienced a problem with the employees nor was he a criminal. Since Nick had many friends and acquaintances in this area, he had a positive reputation with most people. However, this time, a Dutch lady served two Moroccan and Dutch customers their food while Nick waited a long time to order his meal. Since Nick had felt neglected, he mentioned the poor service to the employee, who tried to kick him and refused to serve him his meal. She called the police, and when the police arrived, they shot him twelve times at point blank range, killing him instantly. The five policemen also tasered him five times. The officers were of Dutch, Indonesian, Pilipino, and Moroccan, who were racist against Nick because he was black.

In addition to being racist, some police are also sexist, especially against single women with children. In particular, police will make inappropriate comments and verbally abuse these women with sexual remarks. If the women gently protest to this treatment, the police will swear at these women or will even beat them. This treatment is against the law because it's considered sexual harassment. However, famous cases of male police officers sexually harassing women in Holland have occurred in 2005, 20009, and 2012. When Nick died, the police officers that shot him lost their jobs and ended up in prison. Nick's sisters were upset and the entire city of Amsterdam protested against the criminal police.

10. In 2005, after terrorists had hijacked the metro in England, an innocent black Brazilian man was waiting for the subway. The police should have controlled the area properly in order to make sure that nobody had any bombs or weapons. The black Brazilian didn't have any weapons and had been waiting for a long time for the subway. He was in a hurry to get to work and didn't want to be late. He ran to catch a subway that was arriving, but the police assumed that he was running away from them and that he was a criminal. Consequently, the police shot the Brazilian man because of his color. The British police are racist, mainly against black people. Police harass and murder black people in countries such as France, Holland, Germany, Switzerland, Ireland, Scandinavia, Austria, Australia, New Zealand, Spain, Portugal, Italy, Greece, China, Japan, and Thailand.

In 2004, Congolese people that were Dutch citizens immigrated to London, England. These individuals were attending the wedding of a family member, and they spent five days in London. Before they returned to Holland, they were busy and forgot to obtain cash. Since the traffic was busy and they were in a hurry, he didn't park his car very well at the bank. The police saw him step out of his car and go to the bank machine and return to his car a few minutes later.

The police saw that his sister-in-law wasn't the driver of the car and didn't talk nicely to her. Since she didn't know how to speak English very well, the police harassed her and yelled at her to move the car. The police were swearing at her and insulting her with racial slurs because she failed to understand their commands. The police shouldn't swear at people and exhibit racism against individuals simply because they can't understand English.

Although British police officers exhibit racism, Canadian and American police are more racist. In Alberta, one man accidentally drove through a red light. When the police stopped him, he politely apologized for his actions. However, the police pushed him to the ground and punched him in the face continually. The man went to the hospital for his injuries, and the RCMP officer lost his job and was charged for his actions. In the United States, a black Spanish man from Cuba was killed by an FBI officer, who was charged and lost his job.

In many cases, police officers try to cut the throats of people who swallow drugs as a means of avoiding arrest. People shouldn't be using or trafficking drugs, which represents a criminal offense and will result in a jail term. However, police shouldn't beat or kill people that they suspect are using or trafficking drugs. Regular citizens and police officers can only kill someone in self-defense, which occurs only when another person has threatened their lives or the lives of a friend, spouse, or family member. In these situations, people shouldn't go to jail; however, when people murder other individuals for reasons other than self-defense, they should be arrested and go to prison.

Police and regular citizens shouldn't kill someone unless that person is a criminal. Murder is a major criminal offense that usually results in long prison sentences and a permanent criminal record. In the case of wild dangerous animals, humans can kill these animals to defend themselves or their children. Although self-defense represents an acceptable scenario in which to murder an individual, many police exploit this defense and claim that a person represented a threat when, in reality, the person was harmless and innocent. Many police like to start trouble with people or provoke people to act badly, disobey them, or resist so that they can beat or murder that person and claim self-defense. However, this behavior is wrong and police that practice these actions should lose their jobs and go to jail.

Many of the police don't know or don't care about the laws that are in the Bible. When they have their own children, they need to follow laws and rules to set a good example for their children. Parents should establish laws for children, and children should obey those laws. However, even when children disobey their parents, the parents shouldn't mistreat, beat, disrespect, or abuse their children. Also, older children, especially teenagers and adolescents, shouldn't abuse or hit their parents. In particular, parents and children shouldn't murder one another and they should respect one another. However, children should have significant respect for their parents because their parents brought them into the world, raised them, and provided for them. Siblings should also respect one another and treat each other well. Although parents should treat their children with respect and avoid beating them, parents should be able to discipline their children for disobedience or bad behavior. The police shouldn't arrest parents for administering discipline to their child, but parents should also try to avoid hitting their children. Police and social workers are not allowed to take a person's children or grandchildren away because they administer light discipline for disobedience. Similarly, if people lose their children or grandchildren by lack of attention, they shouldn't have their children taken away. Although the government has currently established this law, they should change it because nobody likes bad policy. Instead, I think that they government should change the law to provide one warning to parents or grandparents that neglect their children.

I also think that the government should only take a person's children or grandchildren away if they cannot afford to care for them or if they set bad examples for their children. Some children learn bad things from their parents, so, in this case, the children should be taken away from their parents. However, other people learn inappropriate behavior from other sources, such as friends. Most parents try to teach their children about the difference between right and wrong, but a few parents fail in this regard.

Although only adults can go to jail, children and teenagers can also commit a crime; however, youth suffer a lesser sentence and punishment than adults. The same level of responsibility cannot be assigned to children and adolescents for their crimes, as shown in the following examples:

- an eight year-old child murdered another child of the same generation or age, such as a twelve year-old
- a twelve year-old or fourteen year-old child that murders another child in the same generation of age or who is two or three years younger or older than the victim.

Although children are considered minors, the law has zero tolerance for child crimes, especially since their behavior will continue or get worse when the reach adulthood, as is the case in places such as Northern Alberta, US, and European countries. In many cases, the police treat child crime too lightly and don't want to deal with it. The police should deal more harshly with child crime and put the children in a type of jail or camp that teaches them proper behavior and punishes them for their crime. These camps should be strict and enforce discipline on the children. For example, in Northern Alberta, a 14 year-old murdered a 12 year-old child, an eight year-old murdered two children, 7 and 14. Also, a nine year-old boy threatened a six year-old girl and a seven year-old boy. The government needs to address the issue of child murder more seriously than current policy dictates. In some cases, the parents are at fault, and they should teach children better discipline; however, at other times, the parents are innocent and did their best to raise the children properly. Parents should not go to jail for their children's crimes, and the police should not harass the parents if their children committed a crime. A few examples below illustrate cases where parents were blamed for their child's crimes:

- A Turkish man was held responsible and imprisoned for murdering a police officer that harassed his mother and siblings. He was recently released from jail and has gotten his criminal record cleared. The government found that he was not guilty because a police officer had accused his mother of abusing him, but she was found innocent. The police officer had also stripped, beat, and raped his sister in jail. The Turkish man had taken revenge and killed the police officer, who was later found guilty.

- All bad leaders, especially police, military, and leaders deserve to die, especially in the case that they have killed innocent people. In London, France, Holland, United States, and Canada, police officers and soldiers were killed because they had attacked innocent people. These individuals died on their breaks or after they had left the job.
- Innocent police officers, armies, people and national leaders should not be killed if they haven't committed a crime or have only committed a minor crime. People that revenge others are showing that they deserve respect and they shouldn't be mistreated. Similarly, adults and children need to respect one another. For example, a black man was upstairs and police were downstairs for their lunch; the black man shot three police officers because they had murdered his sisters and brothers. He revenged them, showing that it was their fault that they died rather than the black man's fault.

Bad police, armies, and government represent the enemy of all humankind. They make bad rules and laws as well as distort the existing laws to serve their own purposes. As a result, the world should have more democracy and rights. Current legislation should be challenged so that humans have better laws, especially since most people are not criminals and will not break the laws. People will continue to follow the rules and laws, but the governments need to find a solution for making civilians happy and having peace on earth. People are sick and tired of issues such as corruption, murder, racism, discrimination, and inequality resulting from bad government, police, and military. Terrorists or other individuals seeking revenge shouldn't seek vengeance unless a crime has been committed or an injustice has occurred. In Canada, nobody, even the police, can interfere with a person's rights or arrest them for stop them from protesting over legitimate issues. For example, if a person calls a police officer a racist, the officer has no right to arrest or beat the person, especially if the police officer was in the wrong and did discriminate against that individual.

If a white person disrespected a black police officer, the officer would usually give the white person a warning. If the white person disregards the warning and continues to insult the black police officer or emit racial slurs and the black officer becomes angry and hits the white person out of anger, the white person would be responsible because he disregarded the warning and continued using racist language. The black police officer shouldn't lose his job simply because of his skin color. The situation should be exactly the same in the case of a black person insulting a white police officer; the white person should not lose his job but should get suspended without pay or transferred to a different location. However, in reality, the black officer would lose his job and suffer negative repercussions from his white manager and colleagues while the white officer would not suffer any consequences. This example shows the racism evident in society and needs to change.

People differ regarding their perception of racism in society; while some people believe that discrimination represents a serious problem, other people don't see the extent of racism in society. Some people don't believe that the police are racist because the police have never done anything wrong to them. However, when police officers insult or victimize those people, they will regret their previous opinion and change their mind. The examples that I have provided throughout this chapter show that these incidents really happened and that many police officers exhibit discrimination against black people and people of other races. Although these cases have occurred in the past, they are still happening today in all parts of the world and they will likely continue to happen in the future. People need to know and understand their rights and the government needs to curtail brutal police and military. Police need to understand and follow the laws of their countries in order to avoid harming people. Some officers believe that their power and authority allows them to treat people poorly; however, police are equal to everyone else and have no right to abuse people. Many people have lost family members or loved ones because of police brutality. Police officers that murder innocent people should lose their lives either by the government or by civilians taking revenge. People don't live forever, so there is no point to taking someone's life and it is also illegal.

Good police officers, military personnel, and leaders should populate this earth. These individuals will ensure that good laws and rules are made to provide equal rights, freedoms, and democracy in every country. People can't live without rules, laws, and law enforcers because otherwise, there would be no protection against criminals and crimes. Police officers are responsible for helping people, resolving problems, stopping crime, and enforcing order in society. However, this job doesn't involve insulting, beating, or killing innocent people, especially during demonstrations and protests. These behaviors are prohibited and illegal, and police officers should lose their job for acting in this way. Good police perform their job properly and respect people. Accordingly, people should respect good police, especially since the job of a police officer is a difficult one.

Part of the job of a police officer involves checking people to ensure that they aren't criminals or breaking the law. When police officers catch someone performing a minor crime, such as drug use, they should provide the person with a warning before arresting them or giving them a criminal record. However, if the person shows repeated difficulty in following the law or commits a major crime such as murder, they should be arrested and put in jail. Part of a police officer's job is to protect and free innocent people and to put criminals into jail. In the same way that police shouldn't disrespect citizens, civilians shouldn't disrespect police by performing actions such as swearing, arguing, or hitting police. If people disrespect police officers, the police will become angry and may beat those people, which, in this case, is the fault of the person rather than the officer, especially if the officer warned the person about their disobedience and their behavior continued. If an investigation found that the police attacked a person in self-defense, the officer will not be guilty but the person that disrespected the officer will be guilty, so they will be arrested and put in jail. People should conduct themselves properly around the police in the following ways:

- Respect the police because of their authority
- Change your behavior so that you accord them the proper respect
- Obey and follow their instructions properly
- Perform the actions that the police request and avoid acting in ways that they warned against
- Show your ID if but only if the police officer asks for it
- Monitor your words carefully when speaking to an officer

- You have the right to ask the police to repeat their instructions if you don't understand them
- Your conversation with the police should be short and you should only respond to questions that are asked to you rather than asking them questions
- If you feel that the police harass you or discriminate against you, you shouldn't overreact for minor issues unless the harassment is of a severe nature
- Don't use foul language with the police
- Don't begin yelling at the police or try to start a fight with the police

People that aggravate the police will increase the officers' determination to harass them, arrest them, or assault them, even when such behavior is not warranted or necessarily within police jurisdiction. Even if a person feels as if the police have done wrong to them or their friends/family members, they should not respond in a negative way because the situation will become worse for them. Rather than reacting impulsively, people should use their smarts to deal with the situation in a different way. For instance, people may be able to subtly record the situation, taking note of the officer's name and behavior, and reporting the situation it to the authorities, such as police chiefs or government. This way, a person will have proof of the officer's mistreatment and can support their claim. People that feel they have been mistreated by the police can approach a lawyer, the police supervisor, or a government branch. If the officer had committed a minor breach or violation, the police officer will likely receive a warning from the police chief. If they don't correct their behavior or if their violation is more serious, such as murder, they will lose their job and go to jail. People shouldn't feel guilty in the case that a police officer loses their job, because the police officer deserved their fate by insulting and harassing people.

For instance, one lady in the United States killed her husband because he had abused her for a long time. Her husband controlled her to the extent that he threatened her if she told anyone about the way in which he treated her, so she couldn't report the abuse. After tolerating the abuse for a long time, the lady finally shot her husband in his sleep. However, this crime was not her fault because she didn't want to kill her husband; she only wanted to end the abuse. As a result of the murder, she went to jail and couldn't see her four children anymore. After many years, she was released from prison. She had a good reputation among her family, neighbors, and lawyers. The government had discovered that she was not guilty because she had acted in self-defense. As a result, she was released from prison and had her criminal record erased. Some of the police officers don't like lawyers because lawyers know the law well and they can defend people's rights, especially against police abuse.

In another case, James Gibenson murdered his stepfather in Los Angeles, California, USA. Gibenson had killed his stepfather as a way of protecting his mother from abuse. For many years, the stepfather had disrespected, controlled, and abused James and his mother. One night, James was sleeping downstairs in the basement because he had an exam at school the following morning. While he had been trying to sleep, James heard noise from his parents and went to investigate the problem. The stepfather had started a fight with the mother and had begun to attack her. When he saw the problem, he tried to separate his parents, which caused the stepfather to become defensive and attack James. Gibenson told his father that he treated the mother poorly, but the stepfather ignored James and started to swear at him. The mother started to go upstairs to avoid the confrontation and the father followed her, catching her and starting to beat her. The stepfather beat her so badly that she almost died. In response, James grabbed a gun and shot his stepfather twice in order to save his mother's life. In this case, the stepfather was guilty and deserved to die, while James and his mother were innocent. Although James was arrested, he was quickly released from prison because the government found him not guilty and declared that he had acted in self-defense. Gibenson also had good references from his neighbors, friends, and lawyers, so his criminal record was revoked. As a result, James can have good access to education, work, and personal relationships.

Life Experience

I have African-Jamaican Ancestry. I have lived here in Canada for ten years. Although I have completed my high school and college degrees, I need to attend NAIT in order to take a course in welding or plumbing. I believe that a new diploma will enable me to secure a better job and a good life. I plan to open my own business in the future and have a successful life like other people. Like everyone else, I have my own dreams and my own goals. I am good in some courses but struggle in other subjects, such as math, language arts, and essay writing. I am working with a tutor in order to obtain help in areas that I experience difficulty and don't understand. However, I practice and work hard without giving up until I understand something. In the beginning, nothing is easy and it takes a while to understand. The level of difficulty depends on the individual course as well as the job. People need to be serious about their schoolwork and their jobs. However, people shouldn't take these aspects so seriously that they insult other people. Although misunderstandings occur, people shouldn't become angry towards other people or insult them. We shouldn't tell people that they aren't listening to us because these individuals may lack understanding or have difficulties. Instead of becoming angry or feeling insulted, we should explain things to these people and train or teach them properly so that they understand. The provision of adequate training allows people to perform their job effectively so that they can feel more comfortable. Every human being possesses uniqueness, so we can't judge people at school or work because God created people's nature and we need to respect that. In your education or career, you will know your strengths and weaknesses as well as have experience that allows you to perform well. People should respect you as long as you don't break any rules at school or work. During my education or career, I'm allowed to ask a question if I don't understand something. This enables me to avoid mistakes and problems while learning how to do something properly. Bosses or teachers shouldn't take offense when students or employees ask questions because people need to learn. However, if I understand the material or work, then I don't need to ask questions because I know my job. I don't like when people yell at me: "pay attention!" If this happens to you, you won't like this person or you don't want someone that constantly tells you what to do or what not to do. People shouldn't tolerate other people who boss them around like this. Managers, supervisors, and coworkers should treat people with respect in order to develop good workers and teams. If the company can treat me properly, I will stay with the company; however, if they treat me poorly, I have the right to leave the organization. Before I leave a firm, though, I would find another job, even at a temporary agency in order to ensure that I have enough money to pay my rent and save money. People need to be prepared before quitting their job because it can be difficult to find a new job. Once I get a new position, I can leave my company. When looking for a new job, you need to find a company that will treat you properly. While some companies can treat their employees poorly, other firms will treat you badly and even exercise discrimination against you.

I have one sister and two younger brothers. I used to fight a lot with my siblings, especially my sister. Since I was the oldest of all siblings, I was stronger than my sister and brothers. My sister used to be cruel to me by insulting me and disrespecting me. Her treatment of me was horrible, as I felt embarrassed in public. Although I made mistakes, I never mistreated my siblings; I always treated them equally and with respect. Although my younger brother was also mean to me, my sister treated me more badly. I told my sister her that I wasn't her boyfriend, fiancé, or husband. I asked her to treat me with the same respect that I gave her. I also told her that I needed more respect from her because I was older than her. My second youngest brother was upset because he believed that my sister shouldn't treat her older brother with disrespect. He mentioned that if my sister mistreated me in front of my future girlfriend or wife, my partner would also learn to treat me in the same manner. Also, my brother's future partner may also treat me with disrespect after watching my sister. Therefore, my brother believed that I needed to stop my sister from disrespecting me so that others could also learn to respect me. Many people have similar issues in their families with their siblings or their cousins. In fact, my male cousin was also mean to me in the past. For three years, I haven't talked to my sister or cousins. After my sister and cousin came to my place, they offered an apology because my second youngest brother had talked to them and influenced them to change their ways. He had told them that they had done wrong to me in the past and owed me an apology. When they apologized, I also told them that I was sorry if I had made a mistake or done anything to offend them. I believe that family members should apologize to and forgive one another in order to solve problems within the family and to make peace. While it is important to forgive your cousin, your siblings are more important, and we should eliminate hatred against our siblings. Although family members may have done something wrong against you in the past, you should forget past mistakes and try to forgive them.

Currently, I don't have any hatred or animosity against my siblings and I have forgiven everything that my sister has done. While most people forgive their siblings, some people hold grudges against their family members, but I believe that continuing to hate your family is wrong. Despite our previous issues, I still communicate with my brothers, my sister, and my cousin. I no longer fight with my siblings, especially my sister. Since my sister is female, I need to make sure that I give her the proper respect. My siblings and I are all adults, so we know the difference between right and wrong. I would never tolerate a man attacking my mother, my sister, my two younger brothers, or my cousins because I will become angry with that person and I will attack him in order to defend my family. If I fight someone in self-defense or to defend my family, I will not get in trouble because I am not at fault. I would never attack anyone's family, so nobody has the right to attack mine.

When I was younger, I used to fight with girls; however, now that I am an adult, I don't do that anymore. Regardless of whether I am strong or not, I know how to defend myself. Even if some people think that I am dumb or stupid, I still have the skills to use self-defense. I don't attack or fight with women; I will only fight with men, and, even then, I will only attack men in self-defense. I don't like fighting, so I prefer not to start a fight; however, if someone attacks my family or I, I have to fight back. I become angry when men attack or try to kill a woman, so I will attack the woman's assailant in order to defend her.

For example, in the early 1940s, Anna Frank, a Dutch-German Jewish woman, had an older sister who mistreated her when they were children. Her older sister disrespected her when they were in public and embarrassed her in front of other people. Many other people disrespected Anna Frank because of the example that her older sister set. When Anna Frank became an adult, she turned against her own sister and developed hatred towards her for the way that she had treated her as a child. Anna did not allow her older sister, Jessica, to visit Anna's family, which included her husband and two children. Anna's grudge against her sister was wrong, because Anna should have forgiven her sister. Although people can hold grudges against non-family members, they should always forgive; however, it's much worse to hold a grudge against a family member than a non-family member. Your sister, brother and cousin are more important than other people outside of your family. In particular, if your sibling apologizes to you, you should always forgive them. Family members should love one another rather than have hatred towards each other and hold grudges. Love keeps peace among family members and ensures that no violence occurs within the family. Hatred doesn't get you anywhere, so people should forget the wrongs that others did against them in the past. I don't want anyone else to experience the situation that happened to Anna and Jessica. We should all show love to our siblings and refrain from being disrespectful or holding grudges. When siblings are young, they shouldn't fight with each other, but even if they do fight, they should forgive one another as adults. When you and your siblings grow up, you should respect each other without any hatred or grudges.

In Anna's case, her husband told her to refrain from holding a grudge against Jessica and hating her forever simply because Jessica had wronged her in the past. Although your siblings may have hurt you in the past and caused emotional pain to you, they are still your brother or sister and you should forgive them. Your brother and sister have a character and they can't change their own personality. They will always be your sister or brother. Only God can change the situation and improve the character of the brother or sister and improve the relationship that you have with them. Also, Anna could have forgiven Jessica and forgotten their childhood incident and Jessica should have apologized and asked her sister for forgiveness.

I'm going to tell you about myself. I have the following characteristics:

- I'm not a bad person
- I'm not a hypocrite
- I'm don't discriminate or have racism
- I'm disrespectful and suspicious of others
- I'm not a terrorist
- I'm not a criminal
- I'm not involved in politics or religion
- I'm not against police, soldiers, or the government
- I'm not against any civilian
- I'm not an illegal person or lawbreaker
- I have never committed a crime and I have never broken the law of any country
- I have never kidnapped or raped young girls and I have never sexually assaulted adult women
- I don't have a criminal record and I have never been arrested or in prison

- I never had a problem with the police, government, soldiers, peace officers, security guards, civilians, immigrants, or locals of any country
- I have never been in trouble with men or women
- I believe that a person's skin color doesn't matter. For example, I don't care if a person is black, white, Arab, Asian, Latin/Hispanic, or Aboriginal
- I believe that a person's religion doesn't matter. For example, I don't care if a person is Christian, Jewish, Muslim or Buddhist

I will never have a problem with someone if they are a good and moral person. I care more about personal character than I do about color, race, or religion. Also, I treat everyone equally and with respect. I am not a troublemaker and I try to avoid problems with other people. I believe that people need to become acquainted with each other in order to establish trust. However, you can't trust bad people; you can only trust good people.

I enjoy having conversations with people and I like to make friends with new people. I don't force anyone to like me and I don't necessarily want to become friends with everyone that I meet. However, I want to gain the respect of everyone I meet and provide other people with the respect that they deserve. The following list provides details about the way in which I interact with people:

- I know how to respect people and the importance of respect
- I know how to deal with people's problems and how to solve problems

- I don't react badly over small problems unless the problem continues or becomes worse
- I try to avoid creating problems with people and I avoid talking excessively. I exercise caution in avoiding speaking too much or saying the wrong things
- I always speak the truth unless falsehoods are necessary in order to avoid major problems, such as the risk of death.
- I don't judge other people, insult people, or make trouble with other individuals
- I forgive other people when they apologize to me. I also expect other people to forgive me if I apologize for making a mistake or doing wrong to them
- I'm a nice person and I respect people, but I don't let people take advantage of me. When people insult me, act cruelly towards me, or hate m, I will still forgive them but I won't trust them anymore and I won't spent time with them as a friend
- I would never play games or take advantage of people who are nice to me. People that are nice don't deserve other people to act cruelly towards them. I believe that people should never play games or take advantage of others. Although people should be serious most of the time, we shouldn't insult others or hold grudges against them.

Currently, I am a student. As an employee, I work and pay tax in Canada. When I declare my taxes, I am honest with the government. In the future, I would like to have a beautiful wife and children. I don't care about my wife's ethnic origin or skin color, although I prefer Spanish and Latino women because, in my opinion, these women are the most beautiful women in the world. I have seen beautiful women of other ethnic backgrounds; however, I believe that Latino or Spanish women are the most desirable because they can cook, clean, and take care of the house and children. These women are hard workers like Asian and African women. Although I appreciate women that work hard, I don't think of women as slaves. I believe that men should help women in their cleaning, cooking, and childrearing duties. In the past, men mistreated women and expected them to do all of the work; however, I respect women and treat them well. As a result, I'm looking for a woman that has a good character and can respect my family and I. In return, I will respect her and her family.

One of my major concerns involves illness. In particular, I am worried about contracting HIV/AIDS, because people with this disease can become sick and die early. I believe that people should wait until marriage to have sex because it will increase their chances of avoiding sexually transmitted infections. Before having sex with someone, people should know the other person very well and have knowledge of their health conditions. The law should mandate that two people perform blood tests to see if they are healthy before having sex. This way, people can learn if their boyfriend or girlfriend has HIV/AIDS or another disease before deciding to sleep with that person. People have the right to ask a potential sexual partner if they have any diseases; I am not trying to insult or offend this person and they shouldn't feel as if I don't trust them. I am only trying to protect my own health and body. All countries, such as North America, Europe, Australia, New Zealand, Asia, and South Africa should have laws for protecting people against sexually transmitted infections. These laws would not intend to insult or offend people but to protect people. Since many people are afraid of disease and death, these laws would help to prevent these issues.

Here are some more of my personality characteristics:

- I'm not a shy person
- I like to talk with people
- I'm not scared of people and I don't think that other people fear me
- I'm a positive person that has an optimistic outlook on life
- If someone is a good person, then you can hang out with that person and talk to them
- It's important to become acquainted with people before talking to them, because you don't want to give the wrong information to bad people
- People can talk to other people, but individuals shouldn't discuss too many personal details or opinions with other people. People that share too much information may create problems with other individuals

When people talk too much or share too many personal details and opinions, they may cause problems with other people. On the other hand, people that don't share as much information with other people will have fewer problems. We should avoid talking too much in order to prevent problems with other people, especially if we want to live a long and comfortable life. Instead of talking, we should listen to other people and provide them with advice to solve their problems. There are many bad people around, and if we say the wrong things, we may jeopardize our safety. If you listen to my advice, you will be safe, but don't blame or judge me if you don't listen and get into trouble with someone. People have no right to judge other people; only God can judge us. If we obey God and love Him, then he will judge us in a positive way rather than in a negative way. God loves everybody, and we should all love God in return. God doesn't judge anybody negatively unless they sin against him. In this case, you need to repent.

Brutal Police

I stand against discrimination, racism, and police brutality. In many countries, such as Netherlands, Belgium, Germany, UK, Italy, Switzerland, Austria, Cyprus, Greece, Australia, South Africa, and especially the United States, many of the countries' laws prohibit black people from the following aspects:

- A better education
- Good jobs or the ability to open their own business
- The ability to progress through life and enjoy social mobility
- The ability to borrow loans from banks and other institutions
- The ability to protest if they feel that they are being oppressed or marginalized in some aspect of life
- The capacity to enjoy their rights and freedoms
- The ability to achieve justice for former wrongdoings
- The right to have their complaints heard from government and society
- Help from lawyers and police officers

Because of their skin color, blacks are deprived of many basic rights, freedoms and opportunities that other members of society enjoy. All other races and religions, such as Arabs, Moroccans, Turks, Jews, Asians, Latinos, Aboriginals,

Indians, and especially whites, have more chances and opportunities than black people. Black people have difficult lives because they receive unequal treatment from other races and religions that hate blacks and want to kill them. These people will never like blacks solely because of their skin color. As a black person, this makes me angry and offended because this discriminatory and racist treatment makes me feel like an animal rather than a human being. However, we are human beings, just like everyone else on this earth. I don't understand why whites and other races treat us differently and why they discriminate against us with attitudes of racism and hatred.

Regardless of whether or not a black person committed a crime, they will still receive unequal treatment from the police. Specifically, the police will stop or arrest black people and ask for their ID. Many police will murder black people for no reason while they would never act like this with whites or other races. I feel pain and anger for people of my race. Unfortunately, racism is not new in society. Most of the police force is white, which accounts for their discrimination against black residents. Data gathered by the Missouri Attorney General's Office shows racial profiling against blacks. This profiling accounts for the level of distrust between the police force and the town population. Police have become increasingly militarized, especially against protesters. Police use tear gas and rubber bullets against black people in addition to calling them animals and other insulting terms. Police wouldn't behave this way against other races, such as whites, Arabs, Jews, Moroccans, Turks, Asians, and Latinos. For example, Germany is the first and most racist country in Europe. After Germany, Netherlands, United Kingdom, and France round out the top five racist European countries. In the Netherlands, Amsterdam, Rotterdam, and Gouda involved protests concerning the treatment of black people. Specifically, black people wore shirts that read: "Black Pete is racist" and complained in the media. Many black people provided their opinions and protested against racism in the Netherlands. However, the Netherlands police arrested many protesters and killed two blacks. In particular, the police strangled one man and beat up a black female, who subsequently died from her injuries in the hospital. This woman, a 24 year-old Dutch resident, left two young children under the age of four. The two police that assaulted her were charged and imprisoned for 40 years or life. This incident occurred in November 2014.

Throughout 2011 to 2014, Dutch and German police killed and assassinated many black citizens. In fact, police sometimes saw a black person on the street and decided to kill them. However, this police conduct is wrong and immoral. The European governments wouldn't take any action to stop racism, discrimination, and police brutality, while the population, mostly composed of white citizens, failed to protest against this treatment of black residents. This lack of protest from European citizens results from the fact that white citizens have hatred and hold grudges against black European citizens. Consequently, European police continue to attack and kill blacks, so blacks will never have justice in countries like the Netherlands and Germany. When I hear about these incidents, I become angry because the government serves as an accomplice to police brutality against blacks. While many white police are racist against blacks, many black police all over the world refuse to take action against this racist mentality. I want to ask these black police the following questions:

- Why can't you revenge white racism?
- Why do you refuse to listen to your own brothers and sisters?
- Why do black people kill members of their own race?

These black police officers are embarrassing themselves and their entire race. White people are using blacks for their police force and exploiting them to kill members of their own race yet black officers fail to realize this reality. In the meantime, white police still hate black police and will mistreat them and all members of their race. If black people declare their rights in European nations as well as in the United States, police officers will still kill blacks for protesting.

I understand that Saint Nicholas and Black Pete are part of the tradition in Dutch nations, as they are used for holidays and birthday parties. Although I respect this heritage and don't have an issue with these traditions, the existence of these historical figures shouldn't mean that blacks have to endure racism in these countries. For example, white people that celebrate these traditions will paint their faces black, wear black wigs, and wear red lipstick. The black protesters speak the truth about the racism inherent in these traditions and their protests demonstrate their true feelings about discrimination. Thus, when Dutch police stop, arrest, assault, or kill black protesters, they are perpetuating the discrimination against blacks.

A few years ago, in the French cities of Paris, Strasbourg, and Rouen, the police took away the rights of black protesters as well as attacking them. They constantly shoot and kill black people without any valid reason or limitations. In fact, the French police even attacked pregnant women and children because they were protesting against racism. In East Germany, one black newcomer from the African country of Burundi was attacked and killed by white German citizens because of his skin color. He died in the hospital as a result of his injuries. The police force and government refused to provide him with justice. In addition, the police and government shot many other black people in Germany. In Belgium one Congolese woman was married to a Belgian man, and the couple had two children, one of which was a 27 year-old daughter. This woman had come from work and needed to use a restaurant bathroom for two minutes before leaving for home. A Hispanic woman and a white woman, both of who were employees in the restaurant, came into the restroom and began harassing her simply because she was a black woman. They asked her why she took so long in the bathroom. The Congolese woman replied that she had only taken two minutes in the restroom. However, the two employees began arguing with her and started to physically attack her. The Congolese woman had to fight back in self-defense, and, during this time, someone had called the police. When the two policemen arrived at the restaurant, a few of the witnesses argued that the Congolese woman was innocent; however, the Belgian police refused to listen to the witnesses. The police didn't arrest the two employees, the Hispanic from El Salvador and the Belgian Flemish lady, and they refused to allow the Congolese woman to explain the situation or defend herself. Since the police had no evidence and blatantly refused to listen to the witnesses, they clearly exhibited racism and discrimination. The police accused, abused, and arrested the Congolese woman, pointing their guns at her as if she was a criminal. The Congolese woman spent a night in jail and lost her job two weeks later. When she tried to obtain justice against the two women and the police officers, her lawyer and the government refused to listen to her although she spent $10,000 in legal fees. Although the Congolese woman was a citizen of Belgium, she could not obtain justice because she was black.

In Cyprus, a black man from the Ivory Coast was a student and employee who encountered racism. He paid his taxes, followed the law, and stayed out of trouble with everyone, including citizens, immigrants, police, and government. He had no criminal record and had a legal status in Cyprus. One day, the police stopped this man from the Ivory Coast and asked for his ID. Although he complied with the officers and showed his ID, the police still retained him, harassed him, and discriminated against him because he was a black man. Subsequently, the police attacked this man and broke his leg; although the man was in obvious pain, the police continued to attack him. They called his employers and lied about his behavior. The witnesses were upset by the officers' behavior, as discrimination and racism were illegal in Cyprus. People believed that everyone should receive equal treatment regardless of color, race, and religion. The man couldn't trust the Cyprus police to take him to the hospital because the police often claimed to take victims to the hospital and yet ended up taking them to secret places so that they could continue beating or even kill them. Since racism is illegal, police that brutalize blacks are secretive; otherwise, they will get in trouble or lose their jobs. In this case, witnesses called the ambulance and took the victim to the hospital, where he stayed for two months. Later, the police officer that brutalized him was charged and held liable for his actions. When the Ivory Coast man came out of the hospital, he reported the officer and complained about his behavior. Initially, the government refused to listen to his complaint because he was black. However, since this time, the police officer was arrested and sentenced to prison for life. The Ivory Coast man was an innocent person and God will avenge the police officer that hurt him.

Jewish citizens and police harbor racist attitudes against African Immigrants and deport them out of Israel. Specifically, police officers in Jerusalem have stopped and killed many blacks because of their skin color. In the UK, a man named John was driving home from work when seven policemen stopped him for no apparent reason. The police harassed him and detained him although he hadn't done anything wrong. In addition, Ukraine also has a lot of racism because white citizens oppose black immigrants from Africa and attack them. When blacks fight back against citizens that attack them, the racist police arrest blacks. However, the police should arrest the white people who started the fight and who discriminated against the blacks. News reports show that 15 policewomen and 20 policemen were charged for shooting and killing black people because of their skin color.

In France, the police accused a man from Pakistan of being a terrorist; however, he and his family were innocent. The Pakistani man had returned from playing golf, but the police who stopped him thought that he had a weapon or bomb in his jacket. However, when the police searched him, they only discovered a golf club. The Pakistani man shouldn't have hidden golf equipment in his jacket because this type of behavior attracts attention from the police. The government have had issues with terrorist attacks, so they will exercise suspicion against people that may seem as criminals. Many objects, such as wooden and metal balls or sticks, may be mistaken for weapons. The police should provide a warning to people that carry these objects so that they can avoid suspicion and problems in the future. If someone is carrying a suspicious object, they haven't necessarily broken the law, so the police shouldn't automatically arrest them or make assumptions that they or their family are criminals or terrorists. The police and government shouldn't generalize and put all individuals of a certain race or skin color into one group. This generalization leads to assumptions that all people of a certain race are criminals, which leads to consequences such as arresting or deporting innocent citizens. The Pakistani man in this example came to France for his educational opportunities in order to improve his life. He had lived in France for two years with his entire family. The government shouldn't send him back to his country because he made a small mistake. In my experience, I have learned that people can only be deported out of a country if they committed a criminal or terrorist act as well as if they broke the law in a serious way. In such cases, people deserve to deportation. However, if you are innocent and followed the law, the police and government have no right to deport you. When the government deports innocent citizens, they are exhibiting racism and discrimination, especially if they deport someone without a criminal record or who only made a small mistake. In order to avoid deportation, I suggest that people take the following precautions:

- Avoid problems with citizens, government, and police
- Avoid committing any kind of crime or terrorist act

- Avoid possessing any suspicious substance, such as wooden or metal balls or sticks
- Avoid possessing weapons, such as knives, guns, bombs, and fireworks
- Avoid possessing drugs, such as marijuana, cocaine, and heroin

However, individuals that commit a crime or break a law can be legally deported from a country and sent back to his/her former nation. However, even if one person has committed a crime, their family may be innocent unless the police or government has proof. Even if one person of a certain race committed a crime, the police can't generalize among all members of the same race. For instance, some police profile Muslims or Arabs, especially if they have a moustache or beard. These stereotypes show racism and discrimination, which represents an immoral mindset. Many people will protest and complain against racism and discrimination from police and the government. In the case of the Pakistani golfer, the police should have given him a warning for carrying a golf club in a concealed manner. Rather, the government deported him and his entire family from France to Pakistan. Similarly, Canada, US and UK should follow the same course of action by providing warnings instead of automatically deporting people.

GPS is a good tool for helping drivers to navigate around a city or town, especially when they lack familiarity with its routes and directions. However, people should not always depend on GPS because drivers should know where they are going and follow signs in order to confirm their directions. Because GPS is a relatively new technology, it can make errors and provide people with wrong directions, especially in newly developed areas. People that rely too heavily on GPS may get into accidents or cross the border illegally, which will cause them to get into trouble with the police. As a result, people shouldn't depend entirely on GPS, and, when they use GPS, they should ensure that the use the latest version of the technology in order to avoid mistakes. For example, my friend, a Nigerian, has lived in Canada for a long time, so he is a Canadian citizen. He moved from Montreal to Edmonton and uses GPS in order to navigate around Edmonton. However, he is too dependent on GPS and doesn't follow the signs. One time, GPS took him in the wrong direction into New York, USA. As a result, the police stopped him and checked to make sure that he didn't have any drugs or weapons. He wasn't carrying any illegal items and he showed the police his ID and passport. Luckily, the police allowed him to return to Canada without any complications or issues. While Canadian citizens can travel around Canada and even cross into the United States without any major trouble, people that aren't Canadian citizens need to exercise caution in accidentally crossing the US border. Specifically, they should ensure that they pay attention to road signs rather than relying entirely on GPS. If you take a wrong turn and accidentally cross the border into the United States, you may get into trouble with the American or Canadian police and government. As a result, you may become deported out of Canada and sent back to your country. Some of the precautions that people need to take include:

- Avoid accidentally crossing the border from one country to another nation. Any small mistake or misinterpretation by the police could lead to major trouble

- Comply with police requests to show your ID and to search your person, vehicle, and belongings

However, the government police should still provide people with warnings. They shouldn't automatically deport someone from their country or arrest them for small mistakes or accidents. Although police can deport people for breaking major laws or committing crimes, they cannot deport innocent people. The police are allowed to search people and vehicles to provide safety against drug dealers, criminals, and terrorists. However, the police cannot insult people or discriminate against them because of their skin color or other features. In order to safeguard against misunderstandings, people should know the rules and laws as well as pay attention to their safety and security. The government can find better ways to make profit than selling weapons and bombs. In order to prevent terrorism and crime, the government should take away people's weapons and bombs. Instead of deporting innocent people, the government should focus their efforts more strongly on preventing terrorism and crime. Governments should avoid causing problems, such as stealing other countries' resources, creating wars with other countries, and trying to control other nations. Rather, governments should make and sustain peace both within their own nations and with the governments of other countries. By making peace, governments can avoid major problems, such as crimes, terrorism, and war. I don't have negative opinions or protests against the government, but I want them to exercise wisdom and to avoid building weapons and bombs for using against other countries. In the past, the American and European governments have created weapons, which I think is wrong, because it endangers the citizens of all countries.

People that tell the truth shouldn't be arrested, imprisoned or deported. The governments and police of various nations can't hide the truth forever. Jesus Christ was hated for speaking the truth and other individuals that protest against the government will also experience the same hatred. God should punish the police and governments that hurt innocent people for speaking the truth.

African Americans are Victims of Brutal Police

The following stories all provide examples showing that African Americans are victims of brutal police.

1. A black man was in a store attempting to make a purchase. He spent a long time in the store without committing a crime or theft. However, one of the store employees, an older white woman, harassed the black man by discriminating against him and arguing with him. She told him that he had to leave the store and threatened to call the police. When the police arrived, they treated the man badly by arresting him despite the fact that he was innocent of any crime. When the black man protested his arrest, one of the policemen grabbed his gun and shot the black man five times. In this instance, an innocent, 24-year old man died because of his skin color. The policeman was charged with murder and lost his job ten days later. He was sentenced to 30 years in jail, and many individuals were upset with his actions.

2. In Phoenix, one black man named Bribson worked as a drug dealer because he couldn't obtain food for his wife and daughters in a legitimate manner.

The government knew about his situation; he was a good person and had not committed any crimes. On Tuesday December 2, 2014, the police stopped him for no apparent reason, as he was not carrying a gun. When he stepped out of his car, the white policeman grabbed a gun and shot him twice. As a result, Bribson died at the age of 34, leaving his wife and young children to fend for themselves. The entire city was horrified by this instance of racism and opposed the policeman's actions. However, Rumain Bribson did not receive justice for his death. Two weeks later, the white policeman who had shot Bribson lost his job. In addition, he was charged with murder and sentenced to life in prison.

3. A twelve-year old black boy was shot by a white policeman because the police officer thought that the boy had a real gun when he was only holding a toy gun. A young boy of this age is small and innocent, so the police officer had no right to shoot him. The police officer was much bigger and stronger than the boy, so the officer should not have felt threatened, especially because the boy held a toy rather than a gun. Furthermore, the boy was innocent because he had not committed any crime. Instead of asking the boy nicely to put down his toy gun, the officer shot him, which was completely unnecessary. If the officer had respectfully asked the boy to put down his toy, the boy would have respected the officer's wishes, thus showing that the policeman's actions were completely inappropriate. In this case, the white officer was charged

with committing a criminal offense against the black child. The policeman lost his job and is now in prison for his actions.

4. In the 1970s, many blacks in South Africa were killed by white policemen for attempting to declare their rights. At this point, South Africa was a racist country that provided whites with more privileges, freedoms, and rights than black people. Many black men and women, including a man named Steve Biko, were killed by white police officers for fighting for their people's rights. In addition, the police raped attractive black women and got away with it. If the situation was reversed and a black man had raped a white woman, he would be charged or killed by the police for his actions.

5. A man named Eric Garner died at the age of 43 while being arrested by the police in Staten Island, New York on July 17, 2014. Eric used to be a drug dealer and had spent time in prison. However, he had gotten his criminal record erased and had earned the government's complete trust. Other than drug trafficking, Eric had never committed any crime. At this point, Eric had quit using drugs and had obtained a job to feed his wife and children. Eric had many references and witnesses that could attest to his hard work ethic and responsibility. The police also knew that Eric was clean, so that they couldn't make an excuse for following him and harassing him. One day, Eric was stopped and harassed by six white policemen. When the police officers stopped him, Eric didn't threaten the police or have a weapon. However, they arrested

Eric, put him in a chokehold, and threw him to the ground. Even though Eric protested that he couldn't breathe, the police refused to listen to him. They kept strangling him until he died. All six officers were charged, especially the young one who had killed Eric. The officers lost their jobs and Eric's friends and family members were very upset at him. Although racism in the United States was bad in the 1960s, it has gotten worse in recent years.

6. In 1999, one white police officer had shot a black man six times. This incident occurred in Texas, close to the Mexican border. The black man did not have a gun, and the policeman had shot him only because the man was black. As a result, the police officer was charged with murder and sentenced to prison, where he still remains. In this case, the black man was robbing a store and had run away from the officer. Although the black man shouldn't have tried to steal or run away from the police, the officer should have simply arrested him without killing him.

7. A young white policeman was found guilty for racism, harassment, and aggression against a black driver. When he had stopped a black man for apparently no reason, the driver had still shown respect to the police officer. He had no illegal items in his possession, such as drugs or weapons. When the police asked him for his ID, he had to reach back into his car to retrieve it from his backpack. However, the police officers became aggressive, pointing their guns on the black man and yell-

ing at him. Then, one officer shot him five times. When the man, who had a broken leg, lay on the ground after being shot, the police continued to brutalize him. Four more police officers showed up and all five police arrested him. When the police officers searched his car, they didn't find anything illegal; however, one of the police officers robbed the black man of his possessions. In addition, the black man had to go the hospital for his leg. He had almost died because of a racist white officer. After three weeks, the police officer lost his job and obtained a criminal record for assaulting the black man. Another innocent, homeless black man was arrested, harassed and assaulted by the police. Specifically, the police put him in a chokehold, tasered him, and beat him up to the point of bleeding badly and eventually dying of his wounds. In this incident, six police officers had assaulted one black man. Many citizens were upset with the police. Four white and two Hispanic police officers were charged with a criminal offense, went to court, and both policeman lost their jobs. The officers are still in prison, but they may receive the death penalty because they murdered an innocent American citizen. They deserve to die for their actions, especially because they were racist.

8. In California, the California Highway Patrol (CHP) police were caught on camera for assaulting a black woman, who had both children and grandchildren. A person had filmed the incident with their own cellphone when they were in their car. The video footage went viral on the Internet and

was published on television and YouTube videos. This footage provides indisputable proof that the black woman was completely innocent. The incident occurred when the woman parked her car on the side of the highway to get out for some fresh air. She didn't walk on the road or commit any other crimes. She walked on the grass by the side of the road and was on her way back to the car when the police arrived. The police officer began yelling at her, and, in response, she respectfully asked him why he stopped her and yelled at her. In response, the officer continued to scream at her and failed to acknowledge her question. At this point, she walked slowly away from the police officer in order to avoid a problem. One of the officers chased after her, pushed her, and threw her to the ground. Then, he sat on her and began punching her in the face. In order to defend herself, she attempted to put her hand over her face to block the punches. The officer continued hitting her on the head and pulled her hair. Even though her face was bleeding, the police still continued to attack her. The woman barely survived the attack and needed to go the hospital for her injuries. Male police officers should never hit a woman, especially an innocent woman who had done nothing wrong. It is illegal for a male citizen to physically attack a woman, especially his wife, girlfriend, fiancé, or mother. Police officers should not be exempt from the law. This incident represented a case of both racism and physical assault. The woman's daughters and sons were upset with the police; they reported him and took him to court. They spent a total of $3000 for their mother's justice. Three weeks later, the police officer was charged and lost his job. He is still in prison and will receive the death penalty because the woman has many witnesses and references. In another incident, two black men were arrested by the police because they attended a white church in Huntsville, Alabama. One member of the church, a white lady, and the pastor, called the police, who arrested the man. The Bible disapproves of racism and does not allow police or church officials to threaten people and evict them from the church.

9. Joseph Megan was a muscular, African American man that came from a poor family. Joseph had never committed any crime and had a good reputation in his community. The government and his neighbors agreed that he was an ethical and moral man. Joseph never encountered any problems with people or the law. A rich, white woman with a private business hired Joseph as landscaper. She paid him a good salary and he worked hard for her. His duties involved cutting grass, cleaning up leaves, shoveling snow, and picking up garbage. He also worked as a guard to protect the neighbors and kids in the rich neighborhood. One day, Joseph was out walking with his white girlfriend, when the police stopped him. Joseph hadn't done anything wrong or committed any crime, but the two policemen and one policewoman continued harassing him. Joseph's boss and his girlfriend were angry with the police and defended him. The police refused to listen and kept questioning the women about whether he was

a kidnapper, robber, thief or drug dealer. Although the police eventually left him alone, this incident still constituted an example of racism.

10. In California, Oscar Grant died five years ago at the age of 23, leaving behind his beautiful Hispanic girlfriend and daughter. Oscar was an innocent man; he didn't carry a gun and had never committed a crime. One day in 2009, Oscar was on his way home from work. While on the subway, Oscar noticed a bunch of people that were fighting and arguing. The police arrived at the Fruitvale Station; however, the suspects had run away before the police showed up. The officers that arrived consisted of one white and one Hispanic police officer. They accused Oscar of starting the fight that occurred earlier. They yelled at him, threatened him, and even pointed their guns at him. They screamed, "get out of the Metro!" Although Oscar was innocent and obeyed the police orders to leave the train, one officer brutalized him, throwing him on the ground and arresting him. Another policeman grabbed his gun and shot Oscar, who died at Fruitvale Station. The officer, a young man named Bart Johannes Mesherle, lied and said that the shooting was an accident. He claimed that he was grabbing a taser, when, in reality, he was grabbing a gun and shooting an innocent black man. Mesherle had worked in the police force for a long time, so he knew the difference between a gun and a taser. He also claimed that in his attempt to grab a taser, he was defending his coworkers. This statement represented another lie, as Mesherle clearly

knew what he was doing. After Oscar's death, his family and friends as well as the entire community were upset with the police. The police officers were charged and suspended from their jobs, while Bart Mesherle was fired, arrested, and sentenced to prison because he had shot and killed a black man. He deserved to lose his job and spend his life in prison because of his racist actions.

11. On August 9, 2014, Michael Brown was an innocent man that had not committed any crime, including theft or robbery. However, a police officer named Darren Wilson created a lie that Brown and his best friend had stolen cigarettes from a store. The entire community knew Michael Brown, who was innocent and had many good references. In fact, his best friend served as a witness for him. Even if someone was a robber or thief, police officers can arrest him without shooting him unless the thief has a gun. In this incident, Michael Brown and his friend did not have guns. Although the officer needed to defend himself, he could have used a taser rather than a gun. Furthermore, if police need to shoot a person in self-defense, they should shoot them in the legs in order to temporarily disable rather than kill them. When both of a person's legs have been shot, they cannot run away and they become harmless. In the case of Michael Brown, Michael had not gun; however, the police stopped Michael and his friend without providing a warning or explanation. The police officer, Darren Wilson, claimed that he was defending himself, but he was actually a racist liar. For no

good reason, he grabbed his gun and shot Michael Brown five times and killed him. Brown died at the age of 18. As a result of this incident, the entire city of Ferguson, especially the black population, were upset with the police and wanted justice for Michael Brown. For the past several months, the community of Ferguson has been protesting, but the racist government did not provide the blacks with justice. Although Darren Wilson should have lost his job and been arrested, it didn't happen. As a result, the black population of Ferguson, Missouri rebelled by robbing and burning police buildings, offices, and cars. Some people even attacked police officers, swearing at them, pushing them, and hitting them, threatening them, and throwing stones at them. Police officers continually mistreat and discriminate against African Americans and the government deports these individuals for no apparent reason. In Edmonton, AB, residents gathered at Churchill Square to protest against the police brutality in Ferguson. Brown's family hired a very expensive lawyer, which cost $60,000, for justice for their son. Darren Wilson will likely lose his job as well as become arrested and sentenced to prison for life.

Although police brutality in Canada is not as bad as that in the United States, Canada still has some incidents involving racist police officers victimizing black citizens. For example, an RCMP officer named Smithers was looking for a theft suspect. Irene Joseph, an elderly woman, was talking with a young man without being aware that he was accused of theft. Although the public knew that Irene was innocent and didn't have a gun, the police arrived and directly accused Irene of theft without asking her any questions. The police didn't have any proof or evidence that Irene had committed theft. When Smithers, the RCMP officer, asked Irene about the identity of the person she had been talking to, Irene truthfully answered that she wasn't acquainted with the man and didn't know his name. However, Smithers overreacted and accused Irene of being an accomplice to theft because she refused to reveal his identity. The police should not have accused Irene of a crime because they lacked evidence that she had done anything wrong. Although she may have seen something related to the theft, it is most likely that she didn't know anything. Since the law states that people are innocent until proven guilty, the police should not have accused Irene without knowing anything. In addition, the police should not have felt threatened by Irene, because, as an elderly woman, she lacks the ability to harm anyone. This incident raises several questions:

- Why did the police ask her about her private life?
- Why did the police ask her for her ID, address, and full name
- Why did Officer Smithers grab Irene in a brutal and aggressive way, throw her on the ground near slippery ice, injure her legs, and then put her in handcuffs? Irene Joseph was an elderly woman and they should not have used this amount of force against her.

Smithers was caught on a public surveillance camera, which proves his guilt. In December 2014, he was arrested and lost his job because he used excessive force against an elderly woman.

Similarly, in Edmonton, AB, an EPS Officer was caught on a surveillance camera and lost his job for shooting and killing a ten year-old child. The officer had shot the child 13 times because the child possessed a toy water pistol that the police believed was a real gun. However, the police are lying about this incident, because they should be able to distinguish a toy water gun from a real gun. After spending six months in prison, the officer was sent back to Germany.

In Montreal, Quebec, one lady caught police brutality on her phone. She filmed the police on her cellphone from a distance. In this incident, two beautiful young women were arrested by two police officers. The officers ordered these women to go into the police car. The police gave them alcohol to make them drunk and then they proceeded to sexually assault the young women. Because the police knew that the women would refuse to have sex with them, they used their power and authority to get them intoxicated and then strip them naked and rape them against their will. This action represents an abuse of authority and an illegal crime. As a result, the police officers lost their jobs and have been sentenced to life in prison. The two young women are not at fault because they are innocent. The police officers are 100% guilty and deserve their punishment.

If police brutality continues to exist, people will become angry and resist their authority. They may start a revolution against the police and government, especially in response to their racist actions of discriminating against people, deporting immigrants back to their countries, and mistreat citizens of the country. Since people don't want this type of behavior to continue, they may start a major war against the authorities. We hope that a large-scale revolution against the police doesn't happen because it will create a lot of problems in life. The war will involve many countries, including Canada, USA, China, Japan, Australia, New Zealand, and South Africa. If the police continue to mistreat and kill innocent civilians as a misuse of their power and authority, officers will think that they can act in any way that they deem appropriate. People will eventually rebel against the police, which may lead to a major revolution. In this war, people will threaten and use violence against the police. If people see police in the street, they will kill the police. The police will not be able to arrest people because the citizens will kill the police secretly, so that the police can't bring proof and evidence against them. Many corrupt and immoral police officers are putting their own lives at risk as well as that of their coworkers. The majority of police officers lack morality and don't know how to perform their job properly.

For example, in Indiana and other places in the United States, people voted for a new law. This law allowed people to shoot and kill criminals in self-defense. In addition, innocent women can defend themselves against abusive partners. However, the law should allow people to kill police when they use unnecessary force against innocent people. In the future, the US and Europe will have a war between the police and citizens, especially regarding the victimization of black people from police brutality. The job of police is to protect people, stop criminals, free innocent people, solve crimes, and help people with problems. In doing their job, police shouldn't insult, assault, discriminate, attack, or assault innocent people. People don't want police that abuse their authority and power because these actions are illegal and police that act this way should lose their jobs. The police can only shoot in self-defense and should never start shooting against an innocent person. Because we still need the police to protect us, we want good police that do their jobs properly. Citizens shouldn't murder police officers and the police shouldn't kill people because murder is against the law. The law should apply equally to all citizens.

Citizens should obey police officers. For example, if the police ask to see your ID, you should show it to them without questions. Regardless of whether you want to show your ID, you need to obey the police without reacting badly towards them. Specifically, you shouldn't yell, swear, or hit the police officer. If you act this way towards the police, you will definitely have a problem with them because they may arrest you, beat you, or even kill you. By answering the officer's questions and acting politely and respectfully towards the police, you will lead the police to believe in your innocence and avoid causing further problems. However, the law allows you to complain to the police chief or the government about the police or take the officer's picture without allowing him to know. By capturing inappropriate police behavior on camera, you can prove your innocence and the officer's guilt. In this case, the officer can receive a warning before he/she loses his/her job. If police officers continue to abuse their authority, they should lose their jobs.

In the future, public surveillance cameras and people with cellphones should film criminals, terrorists, and brutal police. However, these people need to exercise caution so that the police lack awareness and proof that their actions are being filmed. As technology progresses, the ability to detect police brutality on film may become increasingly difficult. When police commit wrongs against innocent civilians, people can publish their videos in newspapers as well as on television and the Internet. These videos will provide proof that the police were wrong and discriminated against the victim. As a result, the officers will get in trouble with the government and lose their jobs. While people can use cameras to protect themselves against police or government corruption, they shouldn't use these devices to illegally spy on people's private lives. Although people should respect good police, they should not trust bad police or brutal officers.

I suggest that people don't call the police unless they have an emergency. By calling the police for small problems, citizens might make the police angry, which will cause problems for them. People should try to solve small problems on their own without calling the police. Although a good policeman may come to help you, you might also get a bad officer who may use brutality against you, even shooting or killing you for no good reason. While police that arrest or assault someone without proof can lose their job and go to jail, the arrested officer may want revenge on the person that reported them. For instance, one black man named Moby, who lived in Winnipeg, Manitoba, had let his car license expire. He had already purchased his license renewal, which normally took two weeks to arrive. After two months, he still hadn't received his renewal, so he went to the registry to discuss his situation and try to solve his problem. One of the employees, Jessica Williams, was rude to him and discriminated against him. Although Moby showed his receipt, she refused to help him. He tried to talk to some of her coworkers, but Jessica had already told her colleagues not to help him. The registry employees committed an illegal action by refusing to help Moby. They could have easily helped Moby to get his license renewed without making complaints and causing problems; however, they discriminated against him because he was a black man. Jessica Williams, an older white woman, called the police on Moby because Moby had become upset with the employees' refusal to serve him. However, when the police arrived, Moby had calmed down. Although Moby was innocent and had a right to complain, the police treated him with brutality when they arrived. They attacked him, shot him 11 times, and killed him. One month later, when the people of Winnipeg were upset with the police and Jessica Williams, two city officers, one Japanese Canadian and Canadian white man, were charged for the murder of the innocent black man. They lost their jobs and were sentenced to life in prison. This incident shows that police can't arrest or shoot innocent people because these actions are against the law. Police should obtain proof or evidence against some-one before accusing them of crime. If they do receive proof that a person has committed a crime, then they can arrest that person; however, they have no reason to use excessive force or brutality against someone. The police are prohib-ited from using force against an innocent citizen unless the person is a serious criminal or attacks the officer. In addition to the arrest of the two policemen, Jessica Williams was also found guilty and lost her job at the registry. She was par-tially responsible for Moby's death because she had called the police and lied about him, resulting in his death.

In the East Coast of Canada, a similar situation occurred when one older man committed the same crime as Jessica; he called the police against an innocent man. This man, a hunter, was innocent because he had his hunting license and was hunting animals for his source of food. Since he had a license, his pursuits were legal. The hunter lacked awareness that he had one police officer behind him and another officer above him in a helicopter. Both officers opened fire, shooting him 20 times and killing him. The hunter's mother was upset because she had to bury her own son. The two officers were charged and lost their jobs. In addition, they were sentenced to life in prison. Although Canada provides life sentences, other countries have the death penalty for police officers that murder innocent civilians.

Another case of brutality involves a famous South African sprinter, Oscar Pistorius, and his beautiful girlfriend, Reeva Steencamp. In this case, Oscar shot his girlfriend, claiming that he believed she was an intruder. However Reeva was innocent and didn't have a weapon. Although I try not to get involved in other people's business, I don't understand how Oscar thought that his own girlfriend was an intruder. Obviously, Oscar had some kind of problem with his girlfriend, and he shot her. I don't know why he couldn't solve the problem in a non-violent way. The entire neighborhood witnessed this incident; they testified that while she was already screaming, Oscar continued shooting her. Although Oscar had a disability, he was not blind or deaf, so he shouldn't have lied and made an excuse about why he killed her. Although Oscar was a famous athlctc, hc shouldn't spend any less time in prison or have a more lenient sentence. Like anyone else, rich and famous people should spend their entire lives in prison for murder without having the opportunity to bribe the government, lawyers, or judges. In the past, the government followed the previous policy of treating everyone fairly; however, today, the government seems to provide rich criminals with the opportunity to bribe their way out of sentences. By providing preferential treatment to the rich, the government will cause people to rebel against them, possibly leading to a revolution. The law is the law, so it shouldn't matter if someone is rich or poor; everyone who breaks the law, regardless of his/her socioeconomic status, should go to jail. The same law should apply for police; police officers that break the law should have to serve the appropriate sentence. In the case of Oscar Pistorius, the Judge, Mrs. Thokozite Masipa, allowed Oscar to bribe her to provide him with his freedom. In normal circumstances, Oscar Pistorius should go to prison and spend his entire life in jail. Although Mrs. Masipa makes good money, she opposed justice in order to gain extra money and allow a criminal to go free. The government should not allow judges, police officers, or lawyers to accept bribes from criminals. Although the government eventually realized that Oscar Pistorius was guilty, they should never have allowed him to be judged as innocent in the first place.

Organ Donation

Hi. I have a Scottish and Irish background. In this chapter, I'm going to share my opinion about the realities of organ donation. People have the option of donating their organs to other people after they die. However, organ donation is only an option, and people don't have to donate their organs. Since we live in a democratic country, people have personal choice, and no person or institution, including the government, police, or private company, can force people to do what they want. Personally, I believe that organ donation is not right for me. When donating organs, certain donor characteristics, such as skin color, nationality, religion, and culture, do not matter. Although people may look different on the outside, all of the major organs inside of our bodies are the same. We are still human beings with the same vital parts, so people shouldn't discriminate in the case of organ donation. Specifically, people shouldn't refuse an organ because the donor had a different skin color. Although God created different skin colors, He didn't create the racism and discrimination that exists in this world. White people and others created negative attitudes towards people of different skin colors, which ultimately led to racism and discrimination. Even if God made all human beings have one skin color, discrimination would still exist in this world. People would find other ways of discriminating against their fellow human beings. For example, countries may discriminate against individuals on the basis of their nationality. If a Canadian person wanted to play football in the United States or an American wanted to play hockey in Canada, the governments of their countries may not let them cross the border into the other country. Similarly, the Spanish government may order the police to arrest a Portuguese person attempting to enter Spain and send the person back to Portugal. These examples, although fictional rather than real, demonstrate the extent to which humans will go to show discrimination and hatred against one another. I don't understand why people discriminate against one another and judge other people. For instance, if the police pull a gun on you, you should just calm down without overreacting or becoming stubborn and refusing to follow police directions. When the police order someone to put their hands up, they should obey the police and cooperate with them. Otherwise, corrupt police may brutalize and injure anyone that shows the least bit of resistance. However, the police are not legally permitted to point a gun at someone, even if they refuse to put their hands up, unless the police have proof that the individual has committed a crime. Even though you may feel as if the police are acting inappropriately in pointing their guns at you, you should still cooperate with them to avoid further trouble. This will convince the police of your innocence. If the police still insist on pointing their gun at you, you can politely tell them of your innocence and respectfully request that they don't shoot. This way, officers with bad intentions may feel persuaded to refrain from shooting you. For example, you can say: "Please don't kill me. I'm innocent and I haven't done anything wrong. Please tell me what I have done. I am sorry and I won't repeat my actions because I don't want any more trouble." In order to save your own life, you need to show the police respect and deference. The police may have accidentally suspected you because you fit the description of the criminal despite your innocence. Although the police are prohibited from taking an innocent person's life, your resistance may increase their suspicions towards you, resulting in increased trouble. Before arresting you, the police need to find the true source in order to receive legitimate proof. They should not use brutality against you if you are innocent.

Another problem that could occur with organ donation involves the issue of identity theft. In communicating with some public companies, you need to read all instructions carefully and ensure that you don't provide more informa-tion than necessary. You shouldn't leave too much personal information in the company's hands because they can use it against you to commit a crime, such as identity theft. In addition, many companies pose as legitimate organizations and will illegally manipulate you into signing contracts that bind you to certain rules. You should always ask if you are uncertain. Afterwards, you may regret your decision, espe-cially if you end up donating organs when you don't intend to do so. If you accidentally sign a contract that you didn't intend to, companies can come after you and hurt you or even kill you for your lack of cooperation. These people can kill you in many ways, including shooting or through a car accident. If you agree to donate your organs upon your death, these unethical companies may cause your death in order to receive the organ more quickly, thus increasing their profit. Companies that seek organ donors need to realize that God can heal people that have a disease, especially if He intends to keep that person alive. I don't understand why people seek organ donations, because all organs are the same and they don't need specific organs from specific people. Therefore, people should be able to choose if they want to donate their organs.

Another problem with organ donation is that it just represents another way to earn profit. When people die, the insides of their body don't work, so people shouldn't take their bodies apart to use their organs for other people. Most companies that solicit people to donate their organs are operating against the law. If these companies get caught, their businesses will be shut down and they will spend their whole lives in jail.

I advise my friends to protect themselves against corrupt companies that only want to take their organs for profit. Specifically, I suggest that they never sign any papers that involve requests to donate their organs. Due to the existence of these unethical companies, people that complete applications and sign their names are putting themselves at serious risk. In order to avoid these companies, people should just avoid offering or agreeing to donate their organs. Many companies are deceitful, so the best solution involves staying away from all companies that solicit organ donations. It's difficult to tell which companies are good and which ones are bad.

Some of the unethical organ donation companies collaborate with corrupt police officers. In these cases, the companies will send the police to kill the people that signed up to donate their organs. In this arrangement, the companies pay the police to kill people and the company receives money from the organ donor upon his/her untimely death. The police officers that join with unethical donor companies will never admit to their involvement in the collaboration, because their actions are illegal and they will lose their jobs. When police officers have collaborated with illegal donor companies, they will find excuses to provoke and shoot innocent people. For example, police officers working for organ donors will find the person that signed the papers and start harassing them for a fabricated and unrelated problem. Then, the person will become angry because they believe in their innocence. This will lead to a major confrontation between the police officer and the organ donor, leading the police officer to brutalize or shoot the person. The police involved in this situation are acting illegally because they should never shoot an innocent person regardless of the situation. If they are caught, they will lose their jobs and go to prison. In addition, the donation company will still get charged for the criminal offense because they hired the police to kill innocent people for their organs. When the company tries to hire the police to kill innocent people, the police should arrest the fake donor company for operating illegally and refuse to help the company.

In most cases, the victims of organ donation companies are black people. The police rarely agree to help these companies seek the organs of whites, Hispanics, or other races. The illegal donation companies must believe that black people have the highest quality of organs inside of their body in order to mainly target blacks. However, all healthy people, regardless of their color, have the same quality of organs inside of their bodies. As a result, the donor companies and police officers that target black people for their organs are racist. The government needs to pay attention to these actions and catch the unethical companies responsible for their illegal actions and discrimination. These organizations operate across the world, including countries such as Canada, USA, European nations, China, Japan, Australia, New Zealand, Latin America, and South Africa. In the United States, the Republican government bribes policemen and soldiers to kill black people for their organs as well as for other reasons. In fact, governments, police, and companies may use organ donation as an excuse to murder more innocent black individuals. The Republican government, military, and police the most guilty parties because they have money and power, so they have greater control over the murder of innocent black people. This behavior shows that racism still exists in the United States. If these actions continue into the future, a type of Civil War may be fought again in order to end racism and discrimination against blacks. Black people are angry about the treatment they have been receiving, and, as a result, they may rebel against the government, shooting and killing police officers and soldiers. If this rebellion occurs, the fault will lie with the government and police rather than the civilians. The government, police, and military have refused to provide blacks with equal rights, freedoms, and respect. In 2014, many black people were killed by the police and military, which will increase their hatred towards the government. Furthermore, some Americans, especially Republicans, despise the fact that Barack Obama, a black person, is the president. These people believe that only whites should rule America, thus showing racism and discrimination. Although I believe that Barack Obama is a good person and one of the best presidents, some people disagree for racist reasons.

Homage for Ms. Marie Misamu

I want to thank Ms. Marie Misamu and her entire family. She knew how to sing, dance, and act. She had talent that God had given her. Ms. Marie knew how to make excellent gospel music. Although there are many good Congolese musicians that compose gospel and world music, Ms. Marie Misamu was one of the best. She was a true gospel singer with a beautiful voice. Barbara Kanam is the second best Congolese female singer. Ms. Kanam is a beautiful woman, but Ms. Marie was more beautiful and talented than even Barbara Kanam in my opinion. In reality, Marie Misamu was the best singer than I had ever heard in my life. She was a star in the Congo and generally famous throughout the entire world.

I am not just praising Ms. Maric Misamu bccausc shc has recently died. When Marie was alive, I loved her music and passion so much. Although I was not initially a fan of hers, the more I listened to her music, the more I enjoyed her talent. Marie Misamu will remain forever in my heart. I will never forget her because she was everything for me. Marie was not only inspirational to Congolese, but people throughout the world also loved her. Although Marie is dead, she will remain forever in her fans' hearts.

Ms. Marie was a true Christian. She was a very respectful and passionate woman. She was never a troublemaker and never bothered or disrespected other people. The whole world loved her. She was a beautiful woman, similar to the beauty of Spanish women, and her beauty was acknowledged throughout the world. Ms. Marie didn't care about people's religion. She didn't care whether someone was a Christian, Muslim, Hindu, or Buddha. In fact, she didn't care if someone had no religion at all. She never judged people or forced people to commit to Christianity. She believed that a person could decide what religion they wanted to commit to. For this reason, I have strong respect for Marie Misamu. I believe that she was a true servant of God and spoke more truth than others.

Marie associated with people of many different ethnicities; however, these associations did not make her a sinner. Nobody believed that she was a sinner. She stayed out of trouble and avoided bad people. She knew that white and black people did not always like each other, but she tried to avoid making trouble. The important was that she knew her mission. God gave her the mission to teach people about ethics and Gospel, so that people could become closer to God. She didn't force people to convert to a certain religion. She only wanted to spread the word of God and pray for people. Although not all ethnic groups became Christians, many people in Congo became Christians because of Marie's work, songs, and preaching. She really educated her population, similar to the way in which Jesus Christ conducted his teachings. Marie never judged, hurt, or insulted anyone. She never did anything wrong to anyone. She did not use discrimination or racism against anyone. She didn't care about tribe, country, nation, or skin color. She supported everyone throughout the world, not only in the Congo, her native country, but also throughout the entire world. She never worked for the government, police, or military in her country or in any other nation. She mostly supported the citizens of her country. Marie helped many people, including disadvantaged groups like the poor. She was a very nice person and very respectful towards others. Everyone in the Congo and throughout the entire world loved her. Even though Marie passed away, nobody will ever replace her. Although other people may copy her style or appearance, such as her face, hair, or lips, nobody can ever become like her. Marie was much better and more beautiful, so nobody can replace her. Only her daughter, Ruth, may replace her, because Ruth has similar experience to her mother. Ruth has the opportunity to carry on her mother's responsibilities and job in music.

It is very sad and painful that Marie has passed away. We will really miss her. She was everything for me. She was the best female gospel singer in the entire world. Personally, I am a Christian, similar to Marie. Although I love and respect Marie, I do not idolize her. I do not think of her like a God. The one true Christian God commanded that we are not allowed to idolize and worship any human being. We are only allowed to worship Him and his son, Jesus Christ. Although we cannot worship regular people, we can still love them and respect them as long as they love and respect us. Nobody is my God; only Jesus Christ is my God. I am honest with my Heavenly Father. I will ask forgiveness for my sins when I am wrong and he will still forgive me. I can't play games with God or blame Him for my mistakes. I know that Jesus loves us and we love Jesus.

Although Marie died in January 2016, I am still sad, upset and hurt by her death. When Marie was alive, I loved her very much and I still love her. She is still in my heart and she will stay forever in my heart. Marie was a big star in the gospel music industry, similar to the way in which MJ,

Aalyia, Bob Marley, and 2 Pac were great stars. I still respect Marie and I will never forget her. Sometimes when I sleep at night, I think about her and cry in silent, so nobody can see or hear that I'm sad. When I heard of Marie's death, I was in so much shock. I was too emotional and sad in public and at work. I couldn't talk properly with my friends and family because I had a broken heart. I couldn't eat, drink, or sleep properly. It was very painful for me that a young woman at the age of 41 died way too early. She should have had lots of time left on this earth. I ask myself why this beautiful, young woman died too early. She was like a queen or a princess. She was like my true sister, my aunt, or my best friend. I thought of her as a friend or a family member. I loved her a lot and she was everything to me.

All of us are going to die one day and there is nothing that we can do about it. We won't stay forever in this world. Marie is already gone but everyone else currently alive has stayed on this earth. Her gospel life and her death teach us how to prepare ourselves for the next world. We need to stop our sins and ask forgiveness from God. He will forgive us if we don't repeat our sins again. We will go to heaven if we repent our sins because Jesus Christ loves us and we love him. God needs us to come back to him before we are going to die. Although some people's bodies can become resurrected, most people's bodies do not become resurrected. Although our bodies will die, our spirits will live forever if we repent our sins and believe in Jesus Christ. Our sister, Ms. Marie Misamu, is now in heaven with Jesus Christ because she was his true servant on this earth. Marie's soul rests in peace. We love Marie so much and loved her when she was alive. We will see her later and meet her together with Jesus Christ in heaven.

I want to tell people the whole truth about what happened with Marie and how she passed away. I don't want to create any controversy, judge anybody, or offend anyone. I am not here to criticize, threaten, use violence, or insult anyone. I only want to tell people the whole truth about Marie. Ms. Marie was born in 1974 and passed away in 2016.

What bothers me is that right now, Congolese Gospel music has nothing to do with Jesus Christ. The music is now about negative things, such as the following:

- Hatred
- Insulting people
- Controversy
- Making trouble
- Hypocrisy
- Dishonesty
- Theft
- Selfishness
- Lying
- Judgement
- Imitation
- Crime
- Jealousy

In fact, today's gospel music involves people singing about committing crimes and murdering innocent people. True Christianity is not about hatred or murdering people. People that have these behaviors and thoughts are not true Christians. God doesn't like people who hate or hurt others. Pastors and AMCC musicians should provide positive examples and correct their behavior before other people should listen to them and before they can teach the gospel to others. People that become a Christian can change their life as well as the lives of others. I am continually asking myself the following questions:

- Why do musicians and pastors make people angry and continue their hypocrisy?
- Why do musicians and pastors continue to talk negatively about other people?
- Why do the pastors and AMCC musicians not open their heart to people?
- Why do these individuals never provide the service that people ask for?
- Why are these individuals focused on politics and making money?
- Why do they judge other people?
- Why do they lie to people and confuse people about God's true gospel?

I understand that musicians and pastors need to earn money because they have spouses and children that they need to support. However, these people could have their own job or business apart from their gospel work. Gospel workers that earn money are pretending to be Christian because they don't understand anything about the gospel or gospel music. I don't understand how these people say that they respect the law of their countries but they don't respect the law of Jesus Christ. God gave us the gospel, gospel music, and the church. We can never spread his Word for profit. Gospel singers and pastors can feed themselves and their families but they need to consider the welfare of other Congolese citizens that are suffering. The pastors and gospel musicians should tell the truth rather than focusing on the selfish concerns of business and personal profit. These individuals don't care about others; they only care about themselves. In the Bible, Jesus said that other people would use his name and fool people into believing that they support Jesus when in reality, they only care about themselves.

Mrs. Marie Misamu had never done anything wrong to her gospel music colleagues. She never opposed her fellow musicians, discussed them in a negative way, or judged them. In fact, Marie never intended to offend them and she always forgave them without hatred. While Marie's colleagues were part of the AMCC, she was never part of this organization. The musicians in the AMCC never allowed her into the AMCC because they didn't like her or respect her despite the fact that Marie showed them love and respect. All of the AMCC musicians pretended that they were Christian; however, these musicians were not truly Christian. After the death of Marie Misamu, the AMCC musicians told falsehoods and demonstrated hypocrisy, showing that they never liked her. Marie had many enemies, including Mr. Patrice Ngoy Musoko, Mr. Jose Nzita, Mr. Matou Samuel, Mr. Aime Nkano, Ms. Esther Ekawa, Mrs. Esther Malela, Pasteur Mukuna, Pasteur Mtumbo, Pasteur Sony Kafuta, Mr. Mike Kalambay, Mr. Mbuta Kamoko, Mr. Thomas Lokofe, General Kanyama, Pastuer Kiziamina, Mr. Kakienza, Mr. Moise Mbuyi, Mr. Christian, Alice Ali and L'or Mbongo. These individuals were among her biggest enemies and played a major role in Marie Misamu's death. If these people did something wrong, they will not tell the truth; they will always make false claims and defend themselves. These people will continue to commit their crimes by putting poison in people's food and drink when they meet someone by inviting them over or visiting them at their place. Their innocent victims never know what's going on or what will happen to them. All of these AMCC musicians that I named cannot be trusted because they are criminals and murderers, including Congolese gospel musicians, pastors, generals, and military police. These people killed Marie Misamu with poison. I don't need to prove this situation because the Internet and television have already shown proof. The criminals will deny their actions because they are ashamed. People already know exactly what happened surrounding Marie's death. When people asked the AMCC musicians for a favour, they made excuses and denied their service; this is not right.

The following people were the enemies of Ms. Marie Misamu:

- Patrice Ngoy Musoko
- Jose Nzita
- Aime Nkano
- Pasteur Mutombo
- Pasteur Sony Kafuta
- Mike Kalambay
- Moses Mbuyi
- Thomas Lokofe
- Pasteur Kakienza
- Mrs. Olangi
- L'or Mbongo
- Esther Ekawa
- Esther Malela (Maman 100 jours)
- Pasteur Mukuna
- Audit Kabangu
- Mr. Mbuta Kamoko
- Mr. Christian
- Alice Ali

Since I believe in God, I cannot lie in the name of God or judge these people. However, all of these people, before and after Marie's death, were being mean, rude, and judging Ms. Marie. They insulted her, made negative comments about her, and talked about her behind her back. They provoked her on many occasions and disagreed with her. Also, they took advantage of her because she was too nice to them. However, after repeated insults, she became angry with them and argued with them. Ms. Marie was not as naïve as they thought. After divorcing her ex-husband, she was never romantically involved with other men or with other people's husbands or boyfriends. AMCC singers and pastors lied and told people that Marie had slept with other people's husbands and caused divorces. However, her enemies told lies about her, calling her negative and disrespectful names, like "bitch," "lesbian," and racial slurs. The AMCC singers and pastors did not like Marie, so they were rude, mean, and disrespectful towards her. These people wanted her to die, so they killed her with poison. I'm not trying to create a problem with the AMCC singers and pastors because I don't have personal issues with them. However, I'm very upset that they treated Marie badly and killed her. Before Marie died, she admitted that her enemies made her life miserable and judged her private life because she was single. These people judged and hated Marie, similar to the way in which people used to hate Jesus Christ. Like Marie, Jesus was innocent and yet people hated him and crucified him. Marie was a true daughter of God in the same way that Jesus was a true Son of God. Marie had a good musical career and a fiancé she was going to marry; however, she died as a single woman.

Ms. Marie Misamu suffered and died on this earth because other people didn't like her. Before she died, she admitted that she had an insecure life, which explains why God took her spirit to live with him. She is now in heaven together with Jesus Christ. We should thank God that we don't have problems like Marie did on earth and that she now lives in peace with God. However, her body is gone and her death is still very painful because we loved her so much. We will think of her forever. I loved Marie because, like Marie, I'm a true Christian who believes in Jesus Christ as my savior.

Marie Misamu had retired from her music with her other AMCC colleagues during her period of fasting. A few seconds later, she didn't feel very well. She drove herself to the hospital in Congo. Her colleagues and the pastors didn't take care of her while they were waiting for her to die. She died on that same day, January 16, 2016. AMCC musicians and pastors told the doctors that they wanted her to die, especially Mr. Patrice Ngoy Musoko, who pretended he was the leader of the AMCC. Marie didn't know that she was going to die. She didn't know that her colleagues and the pastors had conspired to kill her. When Marie had arrived at the hospital, she had told the doctors what treatment she needed. She had lost some blood from her body. They tried to add blood to her body, but the blood transfusion was not successful. However, they kept trying to add the blood to her body. This action is illegal because it could cause the patient infection, heart attack, and death. The doctors could have faced charges, prison time, or even the death penalty. In Europe, North America, Australia, New Zealand, and South Africa, improper blood transfusions are against the law. The doctors thought that Marie had diabetes, but her body showed high levels of toxins, indicating that her death resulted from poisoning rather than diabetes. The singers and pastors poisoned her several times by shaking her hand or through food and drink.

The same thing happened with the King of Pop, Michael Jackson in 2009. Jackson's doctors gave him the wrong medicine, which resulted in his death. The doctor knew that the medicine was wrong and that it would cause him more pain and that it would give him a heart attack. The doctor was charged for his criminal offense and put in prison for life. Since he was found guilty, he also lost his job. Although most doctors can be trusted, some doctors cannot be trusted because they are criminals. Several people have died because doctors have committed criminal actions. Doctors in the Congo are especially susceptible to crime because the Congo leader encourages the murder of innocent citizens. The healthcare industry is vulnerable to corruption and can be bribed into killing people, as in the case of Marie Misamu. In addition, the Congo government will murder people for protesting or send General Kanyama to kill citizens. People should know their rights. The doctors that contributed to Marie's murder should face life in prison or face the death penalty because of their illegal actions. The truth surrounding Marie's death will never be revealed because of medical secrets. The doctors may lie and claim that Marie's death was an accident; however, Marie's death was done on purpose. The Congolese government accepts bribes from AMCC musicians and pastors for their obedience to murder Marie. After Marie's death, her body was transferred to another hospital and she was later put in the morgue. The doctors in the second hospital were also complicit with the conspiracy, which explains why the truth was never discovered. The doctors completed a false application without asking her family permission. This way, the doctors can illegally take and use her organs for their own purposes. The doctors, singers, and pastors should be charged and arrested for their crime. However, Marie's death gave rise to different stories and false controversies. The Congolese journalist that covered the story took a picture of Marie's death body and posted it on the Internet. The journalist, who was supposedly Marie's friend, had no right to do that. It was illegal and inappropriate to take Marie's picture without asking permission from Marie's family. The journalist, named Carine Monkonzi, was charged and arrested. In addition, the police, military, and doctors charged people money to see Marie's dead body. The government's corruption prevents hospitals and police from treating citizens properly in the Congo. If a Congolese citizen lacks the funds to pay for treatment, doctors will kill them or let them die. The Chinese, Rwandan, and Indian doctors will murder Congolese patients.

Mrs. L'Or Mbongo is Marie's biggest enemy. She is a criminal and tarnishes the reputation of the gospel music industry. L'Or came from a family of criminals who murdered people with poison. Her mother died of poison because her mother was a criminal whose enemies killed her in revenge. Her mother had killed many innocent people in the Congo. L'Or's mother killed an innocent Catholic (poop) man who was a very good servant of God and spoke the truth. This is exactly the type of situation in which L'Or conspired in Marie's murder. L'Or and her mother brought criminal activity into gospel music by killing people with poison. Both women are hypocrites and taught their AMCC colleagues how to commit crimes and murder people, especially fellow Christian musicians. D'Or, Olive, and Olive's husband have perpetuated a significant amount of crime in the Congo. L'Or Mbongo is obedient to the Congo's corrupt leader and the leader's wife. All three were complicit in the murder of L'Or's supposed best friend. L'Or told her best friend that the leader's wife could braid her hair and gave her the address to the leader's house. When the best friend showed up at the leader's house, the leader asked L'Or's friend for her identity. When the friend explained the situation, the leader grabbed a gun and shot the woman. However, this is not the only incident of this kind. L'Or has killed many people with poison in order to receive money from the government. L'Or is also part of the country's corrupt politics. Although gospel concerts should be free, L'Or charged people $100 for attending the concerts. In gospel music, it is illegal to charge people for admission to concerts. L'Or is not a true servant of God because she charges money for her music and kills people. All AMCC musicians, leaders, pastors, and military were complicit in Marie's death. However, L'Or Mbongo is the most responsible because she had a significant amount of conflict with Marie. L'Or hated Marie and insulted her. Marie forgave to L'Or and the two women apologized to each other; however, L'Or never truly forgave Marie.

On occasion, L'Or sent Ms. Marie's adopted daughter to visit Marie at her house. Marie cooked dinner, and when she finished, she set the food on the table. After Marie and her daughter ate dinner, Marie left the room for a short period of time. While Marie was gone from the room, her daughter poisoned Marie's food plate and water. When Marie returned, she ate and drank without knowing that her food had been poisoned. Later that evening, Marie felt sick. Marie wasn't aware that she could call a poison control center and receive emergency treatment to remove the toxins from her body.

I don't understand how Marie's adopted daughter could have turned against her and accepted a bribe from L'Or. Ms.

Marie was a nice lady that raised her daughter properly, took care of her, and paid for her school. Marie gave her daughter a better life and job. Her daughter should have appreciated her; however, she accepted money from L'Or Mbongo to kill Marie. The daughter should have turned against L'Or Mbongo instead of murdering Marie. I don't understand how Marie's adopted daughter forgot about all of the good things that Marie did for her.

After the liberation of the Congo, Marie's daughter should be charged and arrested or even receive the death penalty. In addition, L'Or Mbongo should be charged, arrested, and receive the death penalty. These actions represent an illegal and criminal offense for both women. In many countries, the murder, poisoning and corruption rarely happen because the law restricts these actions in order to protect innocent people. However, third world countries, such as the Congo, do not have these laws, which leads to high levels of crime and corruption. Because such laws are absent, Marie died from poison that stayed in her body for a long time. Her body became intoxicated and couldn't function properly, leading to her death. This is not the death that God chose for her and she didn't deserve to die this way. At the age of 41, Marie was still a young and beautiful woman. She should have lived for longer on the earth. It is painful that she died so early and so young.

The AMCC singers should have come to visit her when she was sick. They only came after she died, which shows that they didn't care about her and even wanted her to die. On the other hand, her own family and her best friend visited her in the hospital. After her body went to the morgue, people came to visit her. Her funeral was at Stadium (Stade) De Martier in RDC. The military police were at the funeral in order to make sure that everyone was safe. However, General Kanyama and his employees were wrong because they weren't there for protection. They should protect people and treat people with respect. Instead, they charged people money, brutalized people, and arrested people. During Marie's funeral, three women were choked to death by the military police. Other people were injured and went to the hospital during the same time. Rather than killing people, the police should have checked the funeral attendees one by one. Also, the military police allowed some people to see Marie's body while denying other people this chance. Normally, a person's corpse has to remain unburied for two days. The funeral director should give people one week to see the body and share their sadness.

There is a significant amount of false prophecy, where some people use the gospel for fun and deception. However, this is not right. We can't use the gospel for our own selfish purposes. We need to take the gospel seriously and give people a chance and listen to them without judging or doubting them. Congolese people should understand before doubting and refusing, especially if they don't have evidence. There is no way to know if a prophecy is true or false. The gospel may provide Congolese people with their first and only chance to listen to the true gospel. It seems that these people completely forgot about the gospel and refused to listen to God. The Congolese appear to treat the gospel as a joke. Before they dismiss the gospel, they should find out if the prophecy is true or false. While some people believed the gospel, other people refused to take it seriously. Once the Congolese refuse to receive the prophecy without verifying it, they made other people angry. Nobody was arrested or charged for the prophecy. Nobody took pleasure in seeing Marie dead. Marie was not stupid and avoided trouble with other people.

Everyone in RDC and the whole world received news of Marie's death via the Internet. This is truly the message of God, and a true servant, Marie, shared the prophecy. A lady from Brazzaville shared and passed the message to Congolese people. Other people received the same message, which they then passed to other people. Mark and Mrs. Shaumba Ntumba received the true prophecy, which was the resurrection of Ms. Marie Misamu. God had a plan to bring her back to life. This was a true command that God gave to the Congolese. Normally, this should have happened without ignorance, doubt, excuses, jokes and sabotage. The Heavenly Father gave three chances and warnings. The Congolese should have obeyed God's command, because God's commands are important. If you want to be blessed for your whole life and want your country to improve, you should listen to God. The Congolese were sad and emotional over Marie's death. They should stop crying, come together and pray for Marie's resurrection in order to bring her back to life. Many of the Congolese population were truly excited that Marie would come back to life on January 29, 2016.

God told the Congolese that they don't need to bury Marie, to just wait until her body will come out of the morgue and go to the Stadium Martier in Kinshasa, RDC. As the servant of God, Mrs. Shaumba Ntumba will help to resurrect Marie Misamu and bring her back to life. However, the resurrection was in God's power rather than Mrs. Ntumba's power. On January 29, 2016, God ordered Mrs. Shaumba Ntumba to help with Marie's resurrection. The Congolese should obey God without doubting or questioning His word. People should follow God's commands and pray together as a group. Many Congolese, AMCC musicians, pastors, and military police disobeyed God and His command. God gave them a chance to obey Him; however, the Congolese authorities didn't want to allow other people to see Marie's resurrection. They thought that the resurrection was a joke and were rude, refusing to obey God and making inappropriate comments. Mrs. Shaumba Ntumba should have the chance to resurrect Marie and bring her back to life. Instead, the police and military forced her to leave the funeral. They disrespected and insulted her because she had told them about God's prophecy for Marie's resurrection. In addition, the police and military lied, saying that Mrs. Ntumba didn't tell them about the prophecy and didn't show up to the funeral. They stated that it was too late to fulfill the prophecy and resurrect Marie. However, they were wrong, because Shaumba had shown up to the funeral and they had forced her to leave. They had not given her the chance to resurrect Marie. Since they heard the message, they disobeyed God by kicking Mrs. Ntumba out of the funeral and lying about the situation. Shaumba was very insulted and disappointed by the police, the pastors, and the musicians that opposed Marie's resurrection. Marie's enemies were worried that her resurrection would mean that she would expose their secrets.

Patrice Ngoy Musoko and General Kanyama agreed that Patrice should arrive early to the cemetery of Necropole in Kinshasa, RDC. Patrice was at the cemetery before General Kanyama came with the body of Marie. As a result, Marie was buried too early, on January 29, 2016. General Kanyama was charged, arrested, and lost his job because he made all of the decisions for stopping Marie's resurrection. Specifically, General Kanyama forcefully stole Marie's body from the morgue and buried her body illegally without asking her family for permission. Marie's family should have complained and reported General Kanyama. Now, Marie's body is underground, which is painful and sad. Many people were complicit in Marie's death and in preventing her resurrection, including General Kanyama and Patrice Ngoy Musoko; however, L'Or Mbongo is the guiltiest person because she ordered Marie's murder, sending Marie's adopted daughter to kill Marie with poison. Both L'Or and Marie's adopted daughter should be charged and receive the death penalty, which is the law in the Congo. L'Or Mbongo has already been found guilty of her criminal offense. She is the real suspect; Marie's death was not Mrs. Shaumba Ntumba's fault.

In the Bible, the New Testament states that the miracle of the resurrection exists not only in the past but also in the present and future. In fact, Jesus Christ resurrected a lot of people before his death, such as Lazarus and Tabitha. Even after Christ's death, more people were resurrected. Regardless of whether a person has been buried underground or how long their body spends in a tomb, people can still be resurrected in the present day. Also, it doesn't matter if people took your organs out of your body; people that lost some of their organs can still be resurrected. People's physical bodies, in addition to their spirits, can be resurrected. If you have faith in Jesus Christ, you will experience your own resurrection after death. Many Congolese don't understand the true gospel; while some Congolese completely disregard the gospel, others doubt parts of it. Without faith and a belief in God, the Congolese will not experience their own resurrection. Lazarus was dead and spent a long time underground; however, Jesus still resurrected him and brought him back to life. The testimony of history, a Congolese man named Mrs. Mathieu was resurrected. This is not a joke; this is a serious matter of the gospel. We need to take the gospel seriously; we cannot play games with God. I don't understand why the Congolese continue to doubt the gospel.

In reality, a Congolese man named Mr. Mathieu, who was a real servant of God, was resurrected. We can never force God to resurrect someone because God chooses who he wants to bring back to life. We need to let God take his time and decide how to do his work. God loves us and will do the best for us. Mr. Mathieu was sick and died. He was buried underground and spent three years there, until his body rotted. A servant of God listened to God's command and order to enter Mr. Mathieu's tomb with his people. These people showed up at Mr. Mathieu's tomb and broke into his coffin. When they opened his coffin, they saw his body. They started to pray for fifteen minutes; however, after two seconds, Mr. Mathieu woke up and came back to life. His best friends and family already knew of his resurrection, while many other people were happy and excited. Everyone thanked God that Jesus Christ resurrected Mr. Mathieu. After his resurrection, people treated Mr. Mathieu well. Mathieu, along with his family and friends, gave testimonies, which are on YouTube and the Internet. These testimonies tell what happened to Mathieu and thanked God for His grace.

Two more women that were resurrected include Mrs. Domitila and Mrs. Animata. These women wrote histories about their resurrections, which occurred in the early 90s. These women are both Congolese. They had been sick and died, with their bodies going to the morgue and then put in coffins for one week. After a week, other servants of God that had been given orders by the Heavenly Father gave orders not to bury these women. At this time, President Mobutu, who was a good leader, obeyed God's orders without doubt and disrespect. One week after the burial, Jesus Christ resurrected Domitila and Animata on two different days. Today, both of these women are still alive. People were so happy and excited and many people gave testimonies to the resurrections. People that have faith will witness more of Jesus Christ's wonderful and amazing miracles. These resurrections provide proof of God's goodness and power.

After the death of Marie Misamu, Mrs. Shaumba Ntumba resurrected a little boy that had gotten sick and died. This boy is now alive and healthy. The little boy's mother was so happy and thanked God for his work. God can heal all types of diseases. Jesus Christ is the human manifestation of God. He never lies and always fulfills his promises. In the past as well as in the present, Jesus resurrects people who have faith in Him. Although the pastors and AMCC musicians used to preach, they have lost their faith. They lied to us for money and profit. They should have given Marie a nice funeral or taken care of her family, but they didn't do these things. They used theft and corruption to make money. They murdered Marie Misamu and prevented her resurrection for profit. In particular, Patrice, General Kanyama, and L'Or Mbongo were found guilty of Marie's death. These people killed Marie and blocked her resurrection; they shouldn't show up to her morgue or cemetery. In fact, they shouldn't visit Marie's family because they embarrassed Marie with their immoral and hypocritical actions. They embarrassed Marie's family and lied about her death. If Marie's real mother was a demon, as her conspirators claimed, why didn't her mother kill Marie when she was a baby? It makes no sense that a mother who wanted her child dead would wait until the child was 41 to kill her. In reality, false Christians murdered Marie and accused her mother so that they could get away with their crime. Marie's mother admitted herself to the hospital after the accusations and has since returned home. I hope that Marie's mother, Mrs. Sophie, is in peace. I understand that this situation is very sad and painful for her. Her family and her daughter will still experience pain and sadness for a long time. Marie's mother has high blood pressure due to her worries. Marie's mother may die of sadness, but we hope she stays alive. The accusations should be directed towards General Kanyama, pastors, and AMCC musicians because these parties contributed to Marie's death and stopped her resurrection. Many people have lost their faith in Christianity all because the conspirators prevented Marie's resurrection. Other people were arrested because they attacked journalists. People should not attack journalists and media members because these people are simply doing their job. Rather, they should attack the people that conspired in Marie's death and prevented her resurrection.

The AMCC musicians, pastors, and military police:

- Caused the real misery of Marie's death
- Caused violence and issued threats
- Caused death and committed crimes
- Committed torts and other violations

Although people may think that citizens caused Marie's death, it was the musicians, pastors, and military police. Other countries make mistakes but they never kill their own people or committed corruption by discriminating against innocent people. These countries will murder foreigners that break the law without discrimination. Some countries have a bad leader, so people will conspire against that leader and attempt to kill him. In this case, they can kill the leader without his awareness, bribe a gang with money, or turn an army against the leader. This is how you protect your country and liberate the country from a bad leader. After getting rid of the bad leader, the new leader can make rules against insulting people and discriminating against foreigners. They want to protect the citizens of the country and give people more chances than in other nations. If a bad foreigner can't follow the rules of the country, then he should be forced to leave; however, an innocent foreigner that follows the laws should not be deported. Countries should solve their own problems and not let other countries solve it for them. If countries can solve their own problems, they will gain respect. Third world countries like the Congo needs to create proper laws so that the Congolese become wise and respected by others.

Here are some questions that I have about the Congolese:

- Why are the Congolese not wise and why have they used a Rwandese leader?
- Why don't the Congolese want to know the truth and have faith in Jesus Christ?
- Why do the Congolese ignore the prophecy and live in cowardice?
- Why are the Congolese not nice to each other?
- Why do the Congolese hate, insult, and kill each other?
- Why don't the Congolese want to help each other and communicate with one another?
- Why do some Congolese prefer using discrimination against other peoples and races, especially those from Angola and Brazzaville, when these countries were joined in the past? This country was previously called the Royal Congo before

Europeans separated this country into Angola, the Congo, and RDC. Some Congolese have forgotten their history and continue to discriminate.

- Why have Congolese forgotten the Mobutu times, when there was no discrimination or tribalism?

There are some good people from Rwanda, Burundi, and Uganda; however, some of these people kill innocent Congolese with poison, weapons, knives, machetes and guns. These countries brought a criminal system into the Congo after Congolese politicians sold RDC. Many Congolese citizens lack a good education, which prevents them from having a good job and life. Some Congolese people prefer to kill their own people. The singers, politicians and pastors betray the Congo for money and power while many Congolese citizens and suffering and struggling. The Congolese need to wake up and do good deeds for their own country. They need to get the current leader out of power, which is what they have promised in the past. However, this time, they need to stop talking and start acting.

I thank God that the Congo will soon experience liberation. Congolese are sick and tired of having bad leadership. 8 million people have died in RDC, including the best singer, Marie Misamu. We will never forget her. We love her so much. She had many fans that loved her. Marie was a human being like the rest of us. I have loved Marie so much and I still love her. I consider her as a friend or a big sister although I never met her in person. I watched her DVDs, videos, and YouTube performances. I listened to her music on CDs and audio files. I wish that she could live for longer on this earth, but soon I will see her together with Jesus Christ in heaven. I hope that her soul rests in peace.

I also want to thank three of the best Congolese fighters, Conbantantte Boketshu Wa Yambo, Combantantte Esso and Ondonmbo. These three fighters are fighting for RDC and I respect them a lot. I want to wish them safety in Belgium and God bless! These three combatants, along with JF Ifonge, are true servants of God. God used Mr. JF Ifonge to save people and to save the children of God so that they can come back to Jesus Christ. JF Ifonge is taking people out of danger and away from Satan. Although some people believe JF Ifonge, other people deny that he speaks the truth. However, these people are wrong and should not oppose him.

After Marie's death, the police military chief, General Kanyama, lost his job and went to prison. When he got out of prison, he was attacked and almost killed by Congolese citizens because he had illegally buried Marie and prevented the resurrection. General Kanyama conspired with Patrice Ngoy Musoko, who is the first person that planned to stop Marie's resurrection and force Mrs. Shaumba Ntumba to leave the funeral. General Kanyama stole Marie's body and buried her illegally. Both men will never tell the truth about the incident. They made the situation worse by stopping Marie's resurrection and continuing to lie about the circumstances surrounding her death. As a result, they caused a serious protest and rivalry in Congo, which led to violence, vandalism, and crime. These men incited the Congolese population to issue threats and hatred. Even I was very upset and disappointed that these two men prevented Marie's resurrection. If someone in your family died and another person took illegal action to prevent their resurrection, how would you feel?

Patrice Ngoy Musoko endangered his own life because of his actions. A real servant of God doesn't need security guards to protect them because the Holy Ghost of Jesus protects people. AMCC's leader, Patrice Musoko, has no relationship with Jesus and the Holy Ghost. He doesn't have anyone to protect him, and he knows that the Congolese citizens will attack him and even kill him because he stopped the resurrection of Marie Misamu and buried her illegally. He is also corrupt and accepts money from the government for his actions. As a result, he needs security guards to protect him from people. Eventually, Patrice will run out of money and the security guards will stop protecting him. The Congolese citizens will still be angry and want to kill him. They also want to murder the police military chief, General Kanyama. Not long ago, Olive's entire family passed away. Some of the corrupt pastors, who receive money from the government, returned home from the funeral and died from an earthquake. This event shows that God was so angry with these people for what they did. God is almighty and nobody can play games with Him. God is still angry for what happened surrounding Marie's death and resurrection and will turn his anger towards the people that disobeyed him and caused her death.

I learned many things about death and life from the example of Marie Misamu. If someone treats you well, you should treat other people well also. Don't wait for someone to die and play the hypocrite. You need to treat people well during their time on earth. If you treat someone well during their lifetime and they treated you with respect while they are alive, when they die, you can mourn their death without being a hypocrite. This will show that you did love the deceased person. If people wait until a person is dead to show them love and respect, it will be too late and you will never see that person again. This situation will be painful for you and others. Later, you will regret your actions and be sorry.

The life of a person is never a joke. A person's lifetime is the most important part of their journey. While a human being is alive, we should treat that person well because once they die, it will be too late. We want to prevent regret by treating someone well during his/her lifetime. You should believe that people are telling the truth without insulting them or doubting them. People need to show real respect and love when a person is alive. We all aren't going to live forever on this earth, including myself, my coworkers, my supervisor, my manager, my family, my friends, my spouse, my partner, or anybody. People that cannot believe what I say without making jokes or insulting me, without treating me properly and without respecting me despite the fact that I never insulted anybody and judged or criticized anyone will regret it when I die. I want to ask these people not to come to my funeral because some people might regret their actions and be sorry. In particular, family members often experience regret and sorrowfulness because they didn't realize the truth of what people said. They don't realize that once I die, they can never see me again.

One example is a man named Tom from Trinidad. Tom was a very nice person and had the ability to fight for self-defence. Since he was a small child, Tom was not very strong and didn't know fighting techniques. However, as an adult, Tom got stronger and learned how to fight. He could defend himself as well as his mother and sister. He was never afraid of the police or any other citizen in Canada. Tom was not stupid, like his biological family and other people thought. He was criticized by other people and by his own family members, who didn't believe him. In 2012, Tom's mother was attacked and almost killed by his abusive stepfather. Although the police were on their way, they weren't close enough. Tom had to do something and separate the fight to save his mother's life. Tom didn't allow his stepfather to hit him. Tom was angry and would hit his stepfather back. Although Tom would fight back, he hadn't yet fought against his stepfather but vowed that he could do it the next time the stepfather abused his mother. This time, Tom jumped into the fight and saved his mother's life. However, his mother and sister still didn't believe that he would defend his mother without fear of the stepfather. Tom was never afraid of the stepfather. Tom didn't like to fight very often and only became involved in fights for his self-defence or the defense of his family. Since Tom only fought for defense, the police had no right to arrest him. Police are prohibited from discriminating against someone on the basis of their gender or skin color and they will lose their jobs if they do so.

On the day that Tom protected his mother from his stepfather, the stepfather called the police and lied. The police found that the stepfather was guilty and arrested him. Tom respected his mother and sister and would defend them from any attack. Tom's brother-in-law abused Tom's sister, Jasmina. Tom warned his brother-in-law, telling him that if he continued to mistreat Jasmina, he should leave the relationship. Otherwise, Tom told him that he would break his neck and put him in the hospital. Tom had threatened him several times because he was so angry about the way in which he treated Jasmina. However, many people, including his friends and his own mother and sister, continued to criticize Tom. Tom became angry about the way in which people treated him. He followed his mother's advice and started to train. His plan was to lose weight and then build more muscle. In addition, he wanted to join a fighting sport that enabled him to fight better and teach him techniques to defend himself. He believed that by learning self-defence, he could gain more respect from people in society. He knew that he could never fight against a woman; he could only fight with men. Also, he knew that you could never start a fight and that you should only fight for self-defence. You should avoid problems with the government, police, and society in order to keep a good reputation. Tom was an intelligent man, but his family and friends doubted him. They doubted him simply because he didn't like to fight. If something happened, Tom, rather than his family members, would receive the accusation. In Canada, you can't start a fight with someone; it is against the law. People in Canada respect the law, which is a good thing that I like about living in Canada.

God bless Canada and the Congo. I have a couple of Congolese friends in addition to friends from other parts of the world, such as Mexico. I'm half Haiti and half Congolese. I grew up mostly in Congo, but I live here in Canada. I'm going to tell you about the revelation that God gave me about Ms. Marie Misamu. We can't leave Marie's treacherous death the way it happened. We need real justice for Marie, which comes from God. We will wait for her resurrection. Here are the following things that you should know about me:

- I don't want revenge and I don't hate other people
- I am a servant of God and I don't live for my own fun or profit
- I don't support violence or celebrate someone's death
- I don't threaten, criticize, or offend other people
- I don't want any enemies and I'm not a hypocrite
- I'm here to speak the full truth, especially about Marie Misamu

Nobody is going to close my mouth. I would prefer to be in prison than to not speak my mind. Because of Jesus Christ, I am not afraid of anything, which shows that I am a true servant of God. I don't want successes or titles or fame. God gave me my abilities to save his children and take them out of danger.

I want you to listen to this very important message, especially Congolese people. This will be the first and last chance to hear my message. If you miss my message, God will become angry with you. Everything that I'm going to tell you, I want you to believe. I want Congolese people to obey God and follow his orders, commandments, and expectations. I don't want you to doubt my message or to criticize it. The entire world, especially the Congolese population, want justice for the death of Marie Misamu while we still wait for Marie's resurrection to come. We missed her resurrection the first time, which we regret. We shouldn't force God to do certain things because he loves us and we love Him. We shouldn't play games with God. We should give Him time and let Him perform His work. God will always keep His promises and He never lies. We will see His real glory as long as we are patient and repent ourselves and ask him for forgiveness without repeating our sins. In this case, he will still forgive us.

Mrs. Marie Misamu spent a long time underground. No matter how much her body rots underground, she will be resurrected later. She will come back in life and we will see her again. God promised us that we would see her physical body again on this earth. Since God made this promise, it will happen in reality. Nobody will stop her resurrection again because we really need her and we want her back in the real world. When this happens, our pain will be gone.

People shouldn't spend any money on her tomb as long as her name is on a big stone and her picture doesn't disappear. This makes it easier to find and recognize her tomb easily.

We want to bring Marie back to life and see her again because she was special for us. She was a gift that God gave us, as she was the best female singer of gospel music. She inspired many people, mostly young women, to have many chances and opportunities to become new singers of gospel music. Nobody, especially another female gospel musician, can inspire people in the way that Marie did. Marie is the only and best person to inspire other people in gospel music. Although I'm a Christian, Marie inspired me and changed my life so that I can become closer to Jesus Christ. Marie gave me the chance to see the real glory of Jesus Christ. Even Lazarus was rotten and spent a long time underground before Jesus resurrected him. In the same way, Jesus will resurrect Marie Misamu. We should obey Jesus Christ because he is the earthly manifestation of God. Jesus resurrected Tabita, who was a very beautiful young woman. Marie Misamu was also a very beautiful young woman. She was a true servant of God.

Mrs. Shaumba Ntumba, I want to pass you a message. I still respect you and trust you because you are also a servant of God. I want to encourage more people like you to follow God's instructions. People shouldn't take a long time and wait until Marie rots and turns to dust. If she remains underground for too long, it will be too late to resurrect her. We need to stop complaining and crying about her death because God has the ability to resurrect her. Since God is the only one who can resurrect Marie, we should put our faith in God. This is our second chance to resurrect Marie and bring her back to life.

Mrs. Shaumba Ntumba, don't be afraid or dread anything. God will be with you and the door is open for you to resurrect Marie. Nobody will stop you this time. When you visit Marie's tomb, take people who are true servants of God. Go back to Kinshasa, RDC. Go to Marie's cemetery and take your camera so that the public can see and believe her resurrection. People will break into her tomb for you and take her coffin from the underground. Then, people will open her coffin and check her body. Then, you guys will stay 5 or 10 meters away from her coffin. Then, Mrs. Shaumba Ntumba, you and your group will pray for 10 or 15 minutes. After that, God will do something. People will see that Ms. Marie Misamu will wake up and get out of the coffin. That young woman will become resurrected and come back to life. We will be so happy and thank God because Marie was very young when she died and it was not her time. We really want to see her alive again because we love her so much. She is like a mother and sister to us. Mrs. Shaumba Ntumba said that she is going to resurrect Marie. She needs to act on her promise because we are waiting for Marie to come back to life. If we don't experience Marie's resurrection, Shaumba, please don't talk to us anymore because we won't trust you. We still respect you and trust you now because we know that God gave you the job to resurrect Marie. We don't want to wait too long. We really want Marie back. This time, we want to go to Necropole Cemetery to resurrect her and bring her back to life. We don't want anybody else to be resurrected, only Marie.

After that, we want to see the real miracle of God in Congo and everywhere in the world. We still need servants of God. Next time, if someone dies while the true prophecy of God comes, do not disobey God. Do not bury people's bodies anymore or stop their resurrection. We want to see the real servants of God to come and resurrect people. We don't want other people to disrespect the real servants of God and kick them out of the funeral or cemetery. We need to give the servants of God the opportunity to bring people back to life. In addition, we want to see the real servants of God to come and heal people who have diseases. It is never too late to be healed by God. Although Marie is still underground and people think that it is too late, Marie will still get resurrected one day. Marie was a much better musician than her enemies, who will die soon and won't live past 2016. We miss Marie and we love her. The resurrection of Marie Misamu should come without doubts or excuses. Please, Congolese people, put your faith in God and ask for forgiveness. Repent without repeating your sins. God will still forgive your sins, I guarantee you, because you will see his glory during the resurrection of Marie Misamu. Even after Marie, other people will die and become resurrected. We need to teach people about real physical resurrection and spiritual resurrections.

I have another real message that God gave me. I want to share this message with the Congolese people as well as people in other countries. I am not lying about God's message. If I have been a sinner, I want to apologize to God and ask for his forgiveness of my sins. I love God and I know that God loves me. It is important to ask God's forgiveness because if people can forgive others, God can forgive them if they don't repeat the same mistakes. You should forgive people because forgiveness is very important. God wants us to forgive other people and to eliminate hatred, threats, and violence. Forgiveness brings peace and happiness. If we forgive, God will revenge our enemies. We don't need to seek revenge on our enemies because God will do it for us. We can't get justice for ourselves because the real justice comes from God.

God forgives more than people. He forgives all of our sins regardless of the wrongs that we committed. He still forgives our sins, even the ones that we didn't know we committed. Before He forgives you, you need to apologize to Him and repent without repeating your mistakes. Then, he will forgive you for real. We have grace because of Jesus Christ.

Sometimes, we commit sins on purpose; in this case, we know that these actions are bad regardless of our religious background. Some of these sins include using drugs, breaking rules, breaking laws, stealing, lying, murdering, preventing resurrections, disobeying God, insulting people, causing doubt, using alcohol, demonstrating hypocrisy, and taking the lord's name in vain. If you did something that you knew was wrong, you shouldn't do it. God, people, and the government won't forgive people that sin on purpose regardless of whether or not you apologize. Please don't play games with God. Even the Bible says that if someone kills a real servant of God, God will never forgive that person. God will kill that person and it will be the person's fault. He/she will deserve their death; it is the death penalty by God. It's not fair to take someone's life away because it makes God and other people very upset. This type of thing happened to Marie Misamu. These people killed Marie and stopped her resurrection without obeying God and without having faith. These people disrespected Shaumba Ntumba and kicked her out of the morgue and funeral after she spent time and money to travel from France to RDC. These people don't belong on this earth and they won't live past 2016. They really deserve the death penalty from God. In reality, they will die sooner rather than later. They put their lives in danger by committing immoral actions.

Mrs. L'Or Mbongo is the first person who will die because she is the first person who murdered Marie Misamu by sending Marie's adopted daughter to kill her with poison. L'Or was Marie's biggest enemy and everybody knew that because L'Or had a lot of rivalry and conflict with Marie despite the fact that Marie had never done anything wrong to L'Or. L'Or Mbongo killed Marie because of money; the government of RDC paid her to kill Marie. L'Or was trying to steal the success that God gave Marie. L'Or wasn't a successful musician because she is not a servant of God in the same way that Marie served God. Later, Olive and her husband, who are also bad people, will turn against L'Or Mbongo and kill her for her money. Specifically, Olive and her husband will give L'Or poison, which will cause her to become sick and die. L'Or will die because she put her life in danger; she will deserve her own death. Actually, the government has already poisoned L'Or's body, which will become intoxicated and make her sick. She is already sick now, but her illness will increase and she will die. L'Or Mbongo is the person most responsible for Marie's death. L'Or is the biggest criminal, murderer, and suspect in Congolese gospel music; she brought crime to gospel music. She should be fired from gospel music.

The pastors, General Kanyama, and Patrice Ngoy Musoko will die shortly after L'Or because they put their own lives in danger by stopping Marie's resurrection and disobeying God. They were disrespectful, critical, and doubt. These people will die from the angry Congolese citizens and gang members in the Congo. I have seen and heard many people threatening Patrice Ngoy Musoko. People have told him to leave AMCC and resign his leadership position; otherwise, he will die. Once L'Or dies, people will realize that this is very serious and I am not joking. I'm not threatening anyone; I am only conveying God's word. God is very angry with the false pastors, General Kanyama, Patrice Ngoy Musoko, and L'Or Mbongo. Since Marie's death and early burial, her murderers think that the problem is over. However, God's anger will never end until these people die. Once they have died, God will stop being angry. This show that people can't play games with God.

Mr. JF Ifonge was right about his prediction that L'Or Mbongo and Patrice will die soon. JF Ifonge is the best man in gospel music and always speaks the truth, which most people can't do. He is a real brother and servant of God. JF inspires me through his gospel music, which will help me to become closer to Jesus Christ. I want to go to heaven and see Jesus' glory. I want to thank JF Ifonge for saving my life and making me smarter. God bless you so much!

Mrs. Sophie, the mother of Ms. Marie Misamu, needs help and support without abandonment. She is not a witch and there is no proof that she committed witchcraft, so people should stop accusing her. People shouldn't concern themselves with the business of her family. She needs more respect from people.

Many Congolese people misunderstand Mrs. Shaumba Ntumba. They accuse her of claiming to have the power to resurrect people and use magic. However, Mrs Shaumba Ntumba has no power or magic and she cannot resurrect people on her own. She gets all of her power from God. Some people don't understand the nature of miracles, which ultimately come from God and Jesus. People should stop judging or criticizing Shaumba because true miracles or not humorous or imaginary. Only God or Jesus can resurrect people. God gave Shaumba the mission to resurrect and heal people. Although Shaumba has the ability to resurrect and heal many people, her power comes from God, rather than herself. Shaumba is a servant of God. Many other men and women are servants of God. Shaumba should not be disrespected because she is a woman; this is sexism. She didn't make up lies; the words that come from her mouth are the true words of God. People should have faith in God and believe His words. Congolese people need to repent and apologize to God and Shaumba, His true servant. They need to open their hearts to God's love because God loves them. The liberation and victory will come to the Congo because God has blessed this country with a true miracle. We can never stop people's resurrection because it will make God angry. Marie talked about her own death and resurrection in her music.

I want to send a message to Marie's real daughter, Ruth Misamu, and thank her. Ruth, I know that your mother's death is very painful for you. Many people still feel sad that your mother passed away. I realize that you and your family experience more pain and sadness than the rest of us because Marie was your family member. We know about the goodness of your mother, but you know more about her than we do. You have more experience with your mother because she raised you. Right now, we are happy that you are still alive. We thank God that we can see you and talk to you. God will always be with you and make you stronger. I know you still think about your mother, Marie Misamu. I know that it is still difficult and painful to think of her death. We loved your mother so much and we love you right now. Right now, you have a successful career with gospel music. In the future, you will become the best gospel singer, just like your mother.

We are so proud that you can benefit from your mother's music and influence. You are very much like your mother, which is a blessing from God. We wish good things for you for the rest of your life. Don't let people fool you about things that don't make sense. Please obey your mother and do what she told you. Follow God and Jesus and obey them in the way that your mother did. Your mother was a real servant of God. We know that you are wise and beautiful, especially in comparison to all of the Congolese women of your generation. Your mother, Marie Misamu, was the most beautiful Congolese woman of all time. Don't let people insult you or say negative things about you and lie about you, like they did with your mother. In particular, Aaliya Star needs to stop taking negatively about you and lying on the Internet. I know that her behaviour makes you angry, and you have the right to complain about it or report it. Make sure that you finish your school, get your diploma, and get a good job. You can build your own business or follow in your mother's footsteps. I hope that you find a good husband to marry, one who will treat you with respect and make you happy. I hope that you will have children. We are here to help you with anything that you need from us; however, we can't make guarantees. We want to take away your sadness and pain. You are like a second chance for us after Marie's death. We really need you and we love you so much while you are alive. We are so happy and proud of you. You are everything for us, just like your mother was everything for us. We still love your mother, who was a very beautiful woman. She was like our own aunt or mother. We hoped that Marie Misamu could still live for longer on this earth without dying early, because Marie was still young when she left this earth. We wish you could still have your mother with you. We still have faith in

God and are waiting for God's miracle. This time, people need to repent and obey God without doubting Him. We are still waiting for the resurrection of your mother, so that she can come back to life and receive good treatment from people. We want her to live for a long time into the future, so she can give her testimony about what happened to her. We will always feel the pain of her death.

We are here to protect you from potential enemies, including the church pastors, AMCC singers, Patrice Ngoy Musoko, and L'Or Mbongo. They want to use you for their own profit and success before taking advantage of you. Don't let this happen to you, like it did to your mother. Don't spend time with these people; keep your distance and stay away from them. These people are bad people and hypocrites; they were never your mother's friends. In fact, they were enemies of your mother and killed her. Remember that these people are murder suspects for poisoning your mother. They also conspired with the government to kill Alain Mobto with poison because they are corrupt. They poisoned him 7 times in 2013 and stopped your mother's resurrection. They should ask for forgiveness. Those people are dangerous and cause real pain or stress. Patrice and L'Or are the guiltiest parties in your mother's death. You cannot hang out with those people anymore. You should only spend time with your own family members, your mother's friends, and your friends. God bless and be safe.

Patrice never supported the AMCC; rather, our brother, Mombaya, who died in 2007, was a true AMCC member. Mombaya was also killed by Olangi and Patrice; Patrice wanted power and status in the AMCC in order to make more money. Patrice Ngoy Musoko stole money from Marie Misamu's funeral. I remember when Aime Makengo, another gospel musician, became sick. No pastors or AMCC musicians visited him or took care of him because Aime wasn't a member of the AMCC. Patrice, the AMCC musicians, and the pastors waited for his death. They will never come to visit or help anyone when that person becomes sick. Patrice is very disrespectful and commits illegal actions by burying people illegally without asking the family's permission. Although Patrice and his colleagues never visit people, they will show up at their funeral in order to bury them illegally. Patrice and a few of his colleagues showed up at Aime's funeral despite the fact that they didn't visit him in the hospital. Many people were upset, rightly accusing Patrice of hypocrisy. Patrice is not a true servant of God.

The real servants of God are fighters like Boketshu Wa Yambo, Esso, Ondonombo, Celezino and JF Ifonge. I want to thank these people for serving as true inspirations to the Congolese people. I also want to thank them for informing people of the truth and fighting against corruption in the Congo. Many Congolese people are now wise about Congolese rights and want to save the children of God from corrupt Congolese gospel. Many of our Congolese brothers and sisters are no longer fooled by their emotions. Good Congolese people will repent and come back to Jesus Christ. If all Congolese unite under the goal of taking Kabila out of power, he will leave the country at the risk of being killed. We don't want Kabila in power anymore, so he, along with his people, should leave the country. I have a vision that God gave to me in the same way that God has affected other visionaries. I am here to help people and save the children of God from false Congolese gospel.

In North America, Europe, Australia, New Zealand, and South Africa, the Congolese world music and gospel was officially banned on a permanent basis. Congolese musicians were not allowed to come to these countries and perform concerts because most Congolese musicians engaged in corruption by accepting money from the Congolese government. These musicians didn't care about the Congolese citizens, many of whom had to struggle and suffer. While the population struggled, the government and musicians hoarded the money without sharing. The RDC government brought corruption and killed innocent citizens in the RDC.

I'm asking you to help Combatantte Esso, Combatantte Ondonmbo, and JF Ifonge to follow my advice. I have a good idea of how to remove people from the false Congolese gospel. In Congo as well as the rest of the world, including Europe, USA, Canada, Australia, New Zealand, and South Africa, I want to help Congolese people by telling them the truth. If you want to improve and progress in your life without malediction, you need to know the truth. All of the church pastors and AMCC singers are false prophets of God. Please throw the videos, audios, DVDs, and CDs of these people in the garbage and delete their music from the Internet and YouTube:

- Patrice Ngoy Musoko
- Jose Nzita
- Aime Nkano
- Mbuta Kamoko
- Matou Samuel
- Pasteur Mutumbo
- Pasteur Sony Kafuta
- Mike Kalambay
- Moses (Moise) Mbuyi
- Christian Mbongo

- Pasteur Kakienza
- Pasteur Kiziamina
- L'Or Mbongo
- Esther Ekawa
- Esther Malela
- Pasteur Mukuna
- Audeth Kabango
- Mrs. Olangi
- Thomas Lokofe
- Alice Ali

All of the people listed above are false because they care only about money and accept money fro the government for corruption. They don't care about the Congolese people, who struggle and suffer. They fool people by teaching them the false gospel and kill people, including their own colleagues. As a result of their corruption, you shouldn't listen to their music or their preaching anymore. Their files on the Internet and YouTube should be deleted and shut down. However, they will continue to produce music and sell their music to stores and the Internet. So people will keep buying their CDs and DVDs, but we will cancel their products and make new rules prohibiting people from buying their music. We want real discipline and order in our nation. People that disobey our fighters and us will face real trouble. We don't want a problem with those people, so we don't buy their music anymore. These false prophets will be prohibited to enter any studios to record music because they were wrong and committed crimes against many people. We are very upset about this corruption and we want the true gospel rather than the false one. In addition, the false pastors will be prohibited from preaching in any country of the world, including

Europe, North America, Australia, New Zealand, and South Africa. The Congolese people don't want these false preachers back in their own country because they were the enemies of Marie Misamu and served as accomplices to Kanyama, Patrice Ngoy Musoko and L'Or Mbongo in her death.

Unlike the false pastors, Pasteur Walesa is a true servant of God and can continue to preach while the rest of the pasteurs are prohibited from the Congo. All AMCC musicians and pasteurs will never be allowed to sell products or merchandise. Soon, the real servants of God and the true victors will come to the Congo. The following deceased musicians are real servants of God and people can still buy their music and merchandise:

- Brother Mombaya
- Brother Alain Moloto
- Brother DeBaba
- Brother Bimi Ombale
- Brother Guaylen
- Brother Clockson
- Brother Aime Makengo
- Sister Marte
- Sister Marie Misamu

Although these people are no longer alive, people can still listen to their music and pay them homage. Other musicians, who are true servants of God, are still alive, so people can still buy their CDs and DVDs:

- Brother Carlito Lasa
- Brother Denise Ngonde
- Sister Annie Mobejo

- Sister Blanche Tidulu
- Sister Mama Costa Deboraha

Everything that I have said is the truth. Hopefully, you will understand and believe me without insulting me or creating controversy. I want to share my sadness about Marie Misamu because I still love her so much. I still think about her a lot and cry over her passing. I won't ever forget her because she was the best star in Congolese society. Marie's mother, Sophie, lost a few children before Marie died. There are problems within their family, and I hope that she can fix it and solve the problem. We cannot interfere with the family's business because it is not our problem and we don't want to separate or destroy the family. By interfering in the family business, we are showing disrespect to not only the living family members but also to Marie. Since we love Marie so much, we must respect her family. People accuse her mother of murdering her, but nobody in her biological family has mentioned this issue. Before Marie died, she never said anything negative about her mother. This means that the accusations against her mother are lies. There is no proof that her mother is a witch. I want to ask you to keep following God's commandments without making excuses or doubting Him. If people continue to disrespect God, the Congolese population will become more upset and want revenge. People should not make threats, cause violence, or commit crimes. What I speak is not my imagination, jokes, or lies. Pasteur Bobo, I respect you a lot, but please stop doubting the gospel. Mrs. Sophie cannot be abandoned because she is an elderly woman. She deserves more respect from other people, who should provide her with help and support. I encourage everyone to talk to the real servants of God. I prefer that people take Sophie to

Pasteur Walesa, because he is a true servant of God. Pasteur Walesa has more experience in the gospel and can harness the true power of God. That's why Mrs. Sophie Batekila needs deliverance from Pasteur Walesa, who can pray for her and give her testimony. Sophie didn't commit any wrong action and truly wants her daughter back. People should take Sophie and Pasteur Walesa to the Necropole Cemetery, where Marie's tomb lies. They should call Shaumba Ntumba and hope that she can show up to the cemetery. Even if Shaumba doesn't show up, people can break into Marie's tomb, bring her coffin from underground, and open her coffin. Then, Pasteur Walesa can pray for 10 minutes. After this time, I can guarantee you that Marie Misamu will become resurrected and come back to life. Once Marie has received treatment, she can give her testimony. Marie's resurrection will represent the real glory of God. The population of Congo as well as the rest of the world wants Marie to return to this earth because she was still a young woman. This will allow Marie's mother to live in peace again. This time, nobody will stop Marie's resurrection. God never lies; he promises us that the people who prevented Marie's resurrection will die and that they won't be able to stop her resurrection again.

I just want Marie to come back to life and I want to see her again.

Don't judge me.

Don't ask me dumb questions.

I care much about Marie Misamu and I cry a lot for her when I am emotional and sad.

Don't tell me that I talk too much about Marie and no other things. I'm not the only one who is affected by Marie's death. Lots of other people, especially her fans, are also affected.

I'm not worried too much because I will continue my own life and build my future. The pain will last forever because I miss Marie although I've never met her. I still love Marie so much. She was a good person and the best music star that I have ever seen in my life. I really love her so much and think about her a lot.

I share my sadness with people that I know in person. I share my sadness about famous people that I liked and have seen before. However, I share my sadness mostly with my own family members, such as my aunt, grandmother on my mother's side, who have been dead for a long time. It was more painful for me. I share my sadness with my best friends. People need to stop judging us because Marie's death is very painful. I share and cry with only people that I know.

Let me ask some questions about Congolese people who are ethical Christians:

- Why Congolese are people judging others that are single or don't have spouses, especially attractive women without husbands?
- Why do Congolese people have negative thoughts about people that are single? If a single man or woman visits somebody, they are not trying to steal their spouse.
- Why do some other nations, especially Congolese like to disrespect single people, especially women, and treat women like animals?
- If you are a real Christian and you know somebody that is single or has a problem, you should help them or pray for them so that they can have a better life and find someone to marry rather than

judging them. People can't judge another person's private life because they don't have any proof

If you want people to treat you properly without insulting you, you should treat other people with respect. Marie Misamu was not the only single woman in the Congolese community. Many other Congolese were also single, including some other female gospel singers. However, nobody ever criticized these women. People only insulted Marie Misamu because she was a real daughter of God.

I want to repeat that we also love Mrs. Sophie, the mother of Marie Misamu, and we need her while she is still alive. Mrs. Sophie needs more help and support. She needs people to pray for her so that she can get deliverance and live in peace again. We want Mrs. Shaumba Ntumba to come back in Kinshasa to resurrect Marie Misamu because we still love Marie. We really like Marie and we can't live without her. She is the best icon that we ever had and we don't want to miss her forever. We don't want to hear excuses about Marie's missed resurrection; otherwise, we will become angry. We ask two things:

1. The deliverance of Mrs. Sophie while we still respect her
2. To receive the resurrection of Ms. Marie Misamu, so that she can come back to life and we can see her again.

Ms. Marie is like our sister and mother of the Congolese nation, a beautiful young woman. For us, it is very difficult to stop thinking about her. Even myself, I'm still emotional. I cry every night when I'm sad.

L'Or Mbongo worked for Olive as a secretary in the government. L'Or's life is in danger because Olive and her husband, Kabila, are dangerous murders. Soon, Olive and her husband will turn against L'Or and kill her. She will die in 2016. However, I'm not threatening L'Or; I'm only predicting what will happen because she has put her life in danger by conspiring with the government and killing Marie. Similarly, Patrice Ngoy Musoko's life is in danger because he is working for the RDC government for Olive and her husband. Patrice won't live beyond 2016 because Olive and her husband will turn against him and kill him. Both Patrice and L'Or deserve their own deaths. Pasteur Kakienza, Kanyama and Sonny Kafuta will die soon because they opposed God's prophecy by disrespecting Shaumba Ntumba and refusing to let her enter the morgue and funeral. As a result, they prevented Marie Misamu's resurrection. I was so upset about the fact that Marie's resurrection was blocked that I said all AMCC singers and their records should be prohibited, especially L'Or and Patrice. In addition, they should be prevented from coming to Ruth's future marriage. My brothers, Boketshu, Esso, Odonmbo and JF Ifonge need to take action to shut down all of the pastors and musicians so they can never work again. Please contact Congolese journalists, especially Mrs. Shaumba Ntumba. We love Ms. Marie so much and we can't live without her. That's why we need Mrs. Shaumba to have another chance for resurrecting Marie. Shaumba needs to return to RDC and go to Necropole Cemetery. We were Marie's fans, and we will all be excited when she comes back to life again. Since God promises us that Marie will come back, nobody can stop Mrs. Shaumba Ntumba from resurrecting Marie; otherwise, God will stop them and kill them. This is the job that God gave to Shaumba. Please don't play games with God and joke about His words. Mrs. Shaumba Ntumba is here to help us and we need to thank God for that. We still need her to resurrect our sister Marie, so that her physical form can return to earth. We can't miss our sister Marie forever. We hope that soon in the future that Marie can remarry and build her life again. Many people, especially Congolese people, should belief in Marie's real resurrection, which exists not only in spirit but also in body. Ask the true Christians, who will tell you about resurrection. Many people want Marie to return in her bodily form. We can't wait to see her for real because we love Marie so much. We want to relieve Ruth's pain and allow her to see her mother again. We want to make her happy and thank God. Please don't spend any money on building Marie's tomb because the resurrection will come soon. We don't know when it will come; only God knows for sure. I hope that you people understand the real gospel.

Resurrection for Ms Marie Misamu

Hello, everybody. I'm a friend of my friend. and I'm half RDC and from Brazzaville, Congo. Everything that my friend Jessie said in his chapter, "Homage for Ms. Marie Misamu," is the truth. Everybody in the Congolese community and every other place in the world knows this. I don't want to offend anyone or cause controversy. I don't want to promote violence, threats, or criticism. I'm not here to judge anyone and I don't oppose Congolese people; in fact, I have a few Congolese friends myself. I want the entire world, and the RDC, to know the truth about what I'm going to say about Marie Misamu. This situation bothers me and hurts me significantly, because, like other Congolese people, I loved Marie.

I don't understand how the Congolese people made fun of Marie, who died four months ago, because the Bible said that if a person died and will never return, that person is gone forever. We should respect death and respect people who have passed away. We can't make fun of people who have died because if we die, we don't want other people to make fun of us and look at our picture like the Congolese people did to Marie Misamu. The Congolese people wanted to publish pictures of Marie's body in the morgue after she passed away, which is disrespectful. It is not cool at all. Many people were angry with the Congolese people. How can Ms. Marie Misamu come out of her tomb to make a concert, talk and sing from midnight to 6 a.m.? It doesn't make any sense because Marie was already dead. It can't happen and it will never happen. This belief comes from the imagination of the Congolese people. We aren't fooled to believe what other people think or say. Marie was a real servant of God.

The Congolese people need to stop making fun of Marie as well as causing controversy and spectacles. In addition, they need to stop making lies about Marie singing at night. It is not nice anymore. It is painful and offends her fans like us. The leader of the AMCC, named Patrice Ngoy Musoko, and his group, the Church Clock in Kinshasa, RDC, were corrupted by the government. In addition, pastors such Kakienza and Sony Kafuta, also experienced government corruption. The government paid the AMCC and pastors to embarrass Marie after her death. They allowed people to make fun of her and create a spectacle out of her death. These actions bothered us and hurt us, as we loved Marie. In particular, Marie's daughter, Ruth Misamu, is not happy about this situation. The AMCC, Patrice, L'Or Mbongo, Sony Kafuta, and Kakienza did not like Marie while she was alive. These people were hypocrites and were her enemies. Shame on those people. They are false servants of God.

Prior to and following Marie's death, there was controversy and embarrassment regarding the publication of her pictures. Patrice bribed the doctors to send Carine Monkonzi to take Marie's picture while she was in the morgue and publish the picture in the media. Patrice Ngoy Musoko bribed doctors in a Chinese hospital in RDC long before Marie's death. When she showed up at the hospital, the doctor provided improper treatment, which resulted in Marie's death. This is how Marie died, but nobody will tell the truth. Marie's death was illegal, and here in Canada, this behavior is against the law; someone will get arrested for providing improper treatment. Marie was transferred to another hospital, and other doctors illegally removed her organs. What were they going to do with her organs? Maybe sell them to get money? I don't know. Her organs were taken out of her stomach, all because Patrice Ngoy Musoko asked the doctors to perform these actions without asking the permission of Marie or her family. In addition to Patrice Ngoy Musoko, L'Or Mbongo is the guiltiest person. She was the most responsible for Marie's death because she hated Marie. L'Or sent someone to kill Marie with poison. L'Or disliked Marie while she was alive. After Marie was dead, L'Or showed up at her funeral and bribed someone $100 to bury Marie illegally. The people who killed Marie and stopped her resurrection have disobeyed God. They stole her body from the morgue and buried her illegally. Bad people, such as L'Or Mbongo, Patrice Ngoy Musoko, Sony Kafuta, and Kakienza all profit while other people suffer and die in the Congo. Eventually, these people will die, especially L'Or Mbongo, as her life is already in danger, because Kabila and OLive Lembe will kill her. L'Or is a corrupt, money-loving person, who is also a hypocrite. However, I'm not threatening her; I'm simply stating that her involvement in corrupt activities will eventually hurt her. My two brothers, who are servants of God, Tambwe Teach and JF Ifonge, said that L'Or Mbongo will die soon. Once L'Or and the other people responsible for Marie's death die, God's anger will be over. The Heavenly Father is so upset with them and lacks forgiveness for them because of what they did. They knew that their actions were illegal in the gospel, especially L'Or Mbongo. She will die first because she kept embarrassing God. She refused to stop embarrassing Jesus Christ all because she wanted to murder people for profit. You shouldn't perform illegal actions for money, because God said that money was free in the gospel. L'Or is not a real servant of God; she will deserve her own death. That lady is a criminal. Her spirit has already died, and her physical body will die soon. Soon, Olive will turn against her and kill her. L'Or will never stop her illegal and immoral actions because she loves money so much.

L'Or is Olive's secretary, and she has been corrupted by the Congolese government and the bad Rwandan leader, who is in power. JF Ifonge is right about the fact that God gave him a vision. Patrice Ngoy Musoko, L'Or Mbongo, Sony Kafuta, Kakienza, and Kanyama don't belong on this earth anymore; eventually, they will die and never return. L'or will die first because she is more corrupt than any of the other people. All of these people experienced corruption from the Rwandese leader, who bribes other people to commit crimes and murder innocent Congolese citizens. Although I don't oppose General Kanyama, I think that he is the biggest military leader that I have ever seen in my life. Kanyama supports Kabila because Kanyama profits from killing innocent Congolese people. Also, General Kanyama stole the body of Marie Misamu in order to stop her resurrection and bury her body illegally. Kanyama forced Mrs. Shaumba to leave Marie's funeral and threatened her. In addition, Kanyama raped many beautiful young women in the RDC. The AMCC, including Patrice and L'Or, bribed people to put pictures of Marie's dead body on Facebook and other social media. Patrice and L'Or were also involved in Marie's murder. Before Marie died, L'Or made a false accusation against Marie. Specifically, L'Or claimed that Marie was a wizard that killed her own oldest brother, which is not true. After Marie died, L'Or made a false accusation that Marie's own mother was a witch and had killed Marie. There is no proof for these accusations; the AMCC and government are the ones that murdered Marie. In particular, the doctor gave Marie improper treatment that resulted in her death. The doctor should be charged and go to prison because his actions were illegal.

What I'm about to tell you is a real warning that God gave me through a vision. This is not a joke. This is not my imagination. This is not a lie. I don't like to force people into believing falsehoods and I don't like to pretend to be God. I have to share an important message with the Congolese people regarding their true liberation through God. God's victory will come soon, and this will happen in reality. I need to do the job that God gave me; otherwise, He won't be happy with me. All Congolese need to repent for their actions or they will die. God is very upset with the Congolese people for their immoral actions.

This is the message that God gave me. We do not live in the Old Testament anymore. Before Jesus Christ came to this earth, there was no liberation or resurrection for us. Now, if we have total liberation or resurrection, it is because of Jesus Christ who came to this earth to pay for our sins. Jesus Christ did not live for himself; He lived for us. People shouldn't add or delete anything in the Bible because that will make God angry and will put a curse on you. We are all Christians; we believe in God and Jesus Christ. Jesus is our savior as well as the Son of God. We know that God, Jesus, Satan, and witches exist. We know that the Bible never lies, because it was written by God and Jesus, who always tell the truth. God and Jesus love us, and we love them. We are not permitted to worship other people as we worship God and Jesus. Also, we are prohibited from mixing up the Old Testament and the

New Testament. We know the Bible, so people can't fool us by telling us lies about the Bible.

If you are a true Christian, you shouldn't believe in false miracles. You should believe in real miracles and resurrections. If you don't believe in true miracles, then you will be cursed for the rest of your life. The curse will pass through your generation as well as the next generation; this is stated in the Bible. We know that nobody will live forever and all of us will die at some point. We need to be patient and let God perform his work; then, we will see His glory. God always stays the same without changing. We can't play games with God; we will all die regardless of what we do. Although God knows the reason why we have to die, He will not tell us; we just have to trust Him and have faith.

The resurrection occurs when a person's spirit and body come back from the dead. There are people in the 21st century that were dead and then experienced resurrection; in fact, some of these people are currently alive. Resurrection is the best miracle; it has happened a lot in the RDC with true testimonies. These miracles have occurred without lies, theft, identity theft, imagination, bribery, or profit; they occur only by the grace of God. People that have experienced resurrection are not making it up in order to obtain money and fame. True Christians that have faith in God and repent their sins will receive the glory and miracle of God. People that were resurrected were raised from the dead and still live today. They have real proof, evidence, references, and witnesses. Congolese people need to stop causing doubt and threatening people. Many Congolese people claim that they are Christian and yet they don't believe in miracles and resurrections. People that stop believing in God's true miracles will become cursed. They need to put their faith back into

God and stop trying to prevent God's attempts to resurrect people. Even if you are a government, police, or military member, you can't stop God's actions. People that disobey God will cause their own curse and death.

Although many people in the Congo have experienced resurrection, people in other countries have also been resurrected. Specifically, people in South America, Canada, USA, and Europe have experienced these miracles. Many people believe that resurrections happened only in the past, such as in the case of Jesus raising Lazarus from the dead after he had spent several days underground. Jesus resurrected many people in the past, before and after Jesus himself experienced resurrection. In the future, more people will be resurrected, especially people who believed in God and Jesus, such as Marie Misamu. People have the right to seek the resurrection of innocent people, such as Marie Misamu. Marie was one of the best singers in the Congolese gospel music industry. She was a true star and almost the queen of gospel music in the RDC. We don't want to live without Marie.

Most people will still die and never return to the earth. Resurrection provides eternal life for your body and spirit. My knowledge of the gospel comes from God. I am telling the truth without lying or being a hypocrite. People will receive the miracle of God only if they have faith. People that lack faith in God and Jesus will not receive the miracle unless they repent their sins. If a Christian person dies and someone stops God from resurrecting that person, God can still resurrect that person at a later time, even if they have been underground for a long time. People need to ignore the lies of others and listen only to God. People don't need to wait for Jesus to return to the earth in order to experience their resurrection. Marie Misamu will experience her resurrection even though Jesus hasn't come back yet. Marie has been underground since January 29, 2016. Although people prevented her resurrection, she will still experience resurrection because of the glory of Christ. Kanyama thinks that he has more power than Jesus Christ by blocking Marie's resurrection. Although I have nothing personal against Kanyama, I think that he mistreats people and abuses his power; many people are upset with him.

Christians understand that Jesus Christ is the Son of God and also a part of God. We know that Jesus can heal and resurrect people. We also understand how the Old and New Testament work and what God means in these books. Because of our knowledge in the Christian religion, people cannot fool us about aspects related to religion and miracles. We only obey God and Jesus Christ; we don't allow Congolese people to fool us into thinking differently than God's word. Why do people lie about the words of God and Jesus Christ?

God will resurrect people regardless of whether they have lost their organs, been buried, or were dug out of their graves. God can perform any kind of miracle regardless of how long a person has been buried. People can lie underground for 3 or 4 days or 3 and 4 years. Even if they have an odor, God will resurrect them. It is never too late for a dead person to come back to life and enjoy a full life like other people. I have seen and heard of many dead people being brought back to life. They have given a testimony about what happened to them and the miracle that God gave to them. Only God or Jesus Christ can heal or resurrect people. God and Jesus can perform other miracles, such as healing people that are sick, handicapped, mutilated, deaf, blind, or in a coma. This is the truth. These miracles make people's lives better. These miracles happened in the past and they still happen today. Even Lazarus was a dead person that had been buried underground for a long time before Jesus Christ resurrected him. Lazarus had been dead for 3 to 4 days before Christ resurrected him. Why don't the Congolese understand this resurrection, and the gospel, in the same way that they did in Mobutu's time?

I don't understand why the Congolese refuse to believe in the gospel. In the Bible story about Lazarus, John 11.38-44, many people called Jesus Christ a magician. Although Jesus was not a magician, he had his own power and could use this power because he was the Son of God. However, he didn't use his own power while doing a miracle. Jesus performed many miracles, but most of them occurred because of Heavenly Father's power. If we receive great miracles today, they come from Jesus Christ and nobody else. Jesus gave us permission to perform similar miracles to the ones he did; although we can perform miracles, we are not better than Jesus. When we perform miracles, they are always because of God's power and not from our own power. We don't have the power on our own to perform miracles. Congolese people keep refusing to believe in God, which is why they have been cursed for the rest of their lives. They should only blame themselves because they did not put their faith in God and Jesus.

In Peter 9.39-40, Jesus gave us permission to have the power to perform miracles. Peter explains that this power belongs to God rather than our own power. When Jesus performed miracles, he didn't do them for his own selfish needs, like fame or money. Jesus cared for humanity and paid the price to liberate us and cleanse us of our sins. Jesus showed his love for us by sacrificing himself for us. If you are a real

Christian, then you should put your faith in God and believe in resurrection, which includes refraining from preventing the resurrection of others. It is illegal and a criminal offense to stop someone's resurrection. People that prevent God or his true servants from resurrecting others disrespect God. Actions such as removing a dead person's organs or burying a person not only offend people but also anger God. These are criminal offenses that intend to reap profit at the expense of ignoring God. They can result in the death penalty or a life sentence in jail. People that take these actions will not receive God's heavenly kingdom. God doesn't forgive these actions, especially false people that use Jesus Christ's name for insulting other people.

Jesus Christ gave us permission to make great miracles. The first person he blessed with this ability was Peter. This power includes the following abilities:

- Heal all kinds of diseases, including AIDS, HIV and cancer
- Resurrect dead people and bring them back to life
- Hunt all kinds of demons
- Help people with many types of problems
- Ensure that people can have a better life, job, and families

However, there are some restrictions to this God-given power:

- Gospel acts should be performed for free and you cannot use miracles to reap profit and fame
- Make sure that you know God and Jesus Christ and receive Jesus before going to heaven. Make sure

that other people know and receive Jesus Christ so that they can go to heaven. Heaven is more important than earth; earth is merely a transitory state before the final destination of heaven. People live eternal lives in heaven.

- If you are a sinner, you need to apologize to God and ask his forgiveness. God will forgive you for the sins that you committed by accident. God will forgive you if you repent and promise not to repeat your sins. Once you know that a certain sin is wrong, you need to stay out of trouble with God. God doesn't forgive sins that you commit on purpose because you knew that you were wrong. Please don't play games with God.

- Do not oppose God or stand against his word

- Do not disrespect or prevent the servant of God from performing his/her work

- Nobody can stop another person from resurrecting somebody. Once you have attempted to resurrect a person and somebody tries to stop you, you need to go back and attempt to finish the work that God gave you. You shouldn't give up trying to resurrect a person because someone stopped you the first time. If you give up, God won't be happy with you. If God sent you to do something, you should do it without giving up, especially if you have promised people that you will resurrect someone. If you fail to resurrect a person once you have promised to do so, people will think that you are a false servant of God.

- If God assigns you to do something, you need to perform the action without allowing other people

317

to stop you or talk you out of it. Even police, soldiers, security guards, and the government cannot stop your mission because God is more powerful than any of those people. People that try to stop you from completing God's task will anger God and become cursed.
- People cannot add passages or delete passages from the Bible or they will be cursed for the rest of their lives.

Not all Congolese are bad people; however, many Congolese are not good people. RDC needs a liberation and victory. The Rwandese people have committed immoral actions towards innocent Congolese people by murdering with guns or poison as well as raping Congolese women. While many Rwandese people are guilty, others are also guilty, including Burundians and Ugandans. With Congolese, their biggest faults involve the fact that intelligent Congolese sold their own country to foreigners, most Rwandese, to rule RDC. In my entire life, I have never seen a country become ruled by people from a foreign nation. RDC is the only country in the world to be ruled by another country. This is a curse for Congolese. In Mobutu's time, it was never like that. During this time, Mobutu ruled a just country. Although Congolese made mistakes, they did not make huge errors, like allowing a Rwandan man to rule the country without justice. The Congolese cannot accuse other people or blame them for their own mistakes. They should blame only themselves by allowing an enemy of the Congolese to rule in their own country. Other African countries, such as Nigeria, Ghana, Morocco, Tunisia, Egypt, and Angola, as well as other countries such as Canada, the United States, Jamaica, Trinidad,

Tobago, Haiti, and Latin America and European countries have made their own mistakes. However, they have a strong sense of discipline and rules that prevent them from hating and killing each other. They will never fall for corruption or kill their own people. Even Rwandese citizens aren't like that, at least with their own people. The Congolese people of the RDC are the only nation in the entire world that allows corruption and foreign rule as well as manipulation from other nations. Today's RDC is like a jungle without rules and justice; the RDC has weak and unenforced laws. The Congolese refuse to stop hating and murdering their own people. They go too far and do whatever they want, which includes abusing their own power. Specifically, Congolese can shoot their own people or kill their own people with poison at any time. Rwandese can manipulate or bribe Congolese into killing their own people both inside and outside of the RDC. If someone dies, they will take someone's organs away illegally and sell them for profit, as in the case of Marie Misamu and Papa Wemba, who passed away at the end of April. In addition, the Congolese will bury people illegally. Both of these offenses are illegal criminal actions.

In the past, the Congolese respected the dead people. Citizens and fans of famous musicians and other celebrities mourned their beloved by burying them appropriately at a funeral. There were no issues, such as people being kicked out of a funeral, arrested, assaulted, or even murdered by soldiers or police. Rather, the police and military provided appropriate security that kept order and minimized disruptions, preventing anyone from causing problems. The police would never take away people's graves, steal organs, or bury people illegally, like General Kanyama did in the case of Marie Misamu and Papa Wemba. Kanyama lost his job; however, he was hired for a second time and repeated his crimes in the case of Papa Wemba. This doesn't make any sense, because the government knew that Kanyama was not going to change. After the incident with Papa Wemba, General Kanyama was arrested for a second time. I hope that he has lost his job forever and never returns to the police force or military for his illegal actions. He is the biggest criminal police officer in RDC because he used to kill his own people. The government has corrupted him, especially Kabila, for whom he works. Kanyama has been bribed by Kabila in the same way that Patrice Ngoy Musoko and L'Or Mbongo were corrupted. They are all secretaries of Olive Lembe and Kabila. Olive, Kabila, and L'Or Mbongo also conspired in the murder of Marie Misamu, who was an innocent woman.

I want to thank Mrs. Amazone, the wife of Papa Wemba. I respect her a lot and I also respect Papa Wemba, who was an international musician of music and Congolese music like Marie Misamu. I was upset that Lambert Mende bribed a young Ivorian man for money and sent him to kill Papa Wemba. Papa Wemba had been singing on the podium without paying attention to the events around him. The young man changed the microphone quickly, put poison in the microphone, and brought it back to the stage. Papa Wemba grabbed the microphone without knowing that it was poisoned. Then, Papa Wemba began to sing, and within two seconds, the poison affected him through his nose, mouth, and stomach. He quickly fell on the floor and died immediately of a heart attack. After his death, people embarrassed Papa Wemba and his family by posting pictures of his dead body on the Internet, even when his body was in the morgue. This was the same thing that happened to Marie Misamu. It is very disrespectful.

Mrs. Amazone was right to report what had happened to her husband. There was enough proof and evidence to support his murder. The Ivorian and Congolese governments are prohibited from stopping people's rights to report murders to international courts. Lambert should be charged, arrested, and receive the death penalty because he is the most responsible for Papa Wemba's death. Also, the Ivorian guy that poisoned Papa should be charged, arrested, and have the death penalty because he is the person that switched and poisoned the microphones, which was what killed Papa Wemba on April 24, 2016, in Abidjan, Ivory Coast. Papa Wemba was buried in Kinshasa, RDC. The police should perform an autopsy on his body to investigate the cause of death and allow his family to receive justice. However, the Congolese people refuse to conduct such an investigation, which constitutes an offense and a criminal action. They should also conduct a similar investigation for Marie Misamu's death; it is not too late. Marie's family could report the situation to an international court, especially the way in which she was killed. The family could say how the doctor gave Marie the wrong treatment, which resulted in her death. The doctor should be charged, lose his job, get arrested, and even receive the death penalty. Ms. Marie Misamu needs real justice from her death, which was an illegal action and a criminal offense. However, the doctor will never tell the truth. Olive Lembe and Kabila also conspired in Marie's murder, but L'Or Mbongo is the biggest perpetrator because she had hatred and conflict with Marie. Patrice and Kanyama also had a role in Marie's death. As a true servant of God, I guarantee that Marie will soon experience resurrection. We just need to pray and put our faith in God without thinking negative thoughts. Kanyama, Patrice, Sony Kafuta, and Kakienza will die soon, in the year

2016. L'Or Mbongo will die first and it is going to happen. These people won't live much longer because they committed crimes. I don't understand why Congolese people play games with God and disobey Him simply for the sake of profit. The people that killed Marie, took her organs, buried her illegally, and prevented her resurrection all disobeyed God. They will die shortly to pay for their sins; in fact, God has already sent a virus to kill them. Kabila and Olive should leave RDC without returning for another term; however, they refuse to leave their positions of power. I guarantee that Kabila, Olive, and Kanyama will get assassinated by Congolese rebels. Shortly afterwards, RDC will experience liberation. The Congolese will need to repent for their sins in order to avoid death. Many people will die in RDC because God is very upset with the Congolese people and their actions. I don't understand why Congolese people still consider the gospel as a joke.

God provided me with a message of warning that I want to share with you. God is upset and will send a virus to RDC. We need to take this warning seriously rather than treating it as a joke. Since God gave Jessie and me this command, you need to obey us, and God, who issued the command. We aren't looking for money, glory, power, or fame. We aren't lying to you or providing you with a false gospel, because God would punish us and we don't want that. You may think that we are playing a game, being hypocrites, or making up secrets. This is not what we intend. I want to emphasize the importance of obeying God's messages and recommend that you don't disobey or ignore any more of His messages. Everything that I'm going to tell you will happen. The true prophecy about Marie Misamu is real. Marie Misamu was supposed to experience resurrection; however, this did not happen because Congolese people ignored God's message, doubted Him and disobeyed His commands. The Congolese people refuse to obey God despite the fact that they identify themselves as Christians. If they are truly Christians, they should believe in resurrection. However, they have lost their faith for the sake of profit. After the Congolese people prevented Marie's resurrection, even more Congolese lost their faith in God. The blocking of Marie's resurrection caused threats, violence, and protests. During this time, other innocent Congolese were attacked, including a journalist. Rather than killing innocent people, the protesters should target the real culprits, such as Patrice Ngoy Musoko, General Kanyama, Kakienza, Sony Kafuta, and L'Or Mbongo. These people are the true threats. In addition, the Congolese people refused to pray together as a group, which would enable Marie's resurrection.

Initially, two prophets, one named Marie from Congo Brazzaville, and another one, Petronie Mukandi, predicted Marie's resurrection. However, General Kanyama and Patrice Ngoy Musoko stole her corpse from the morgue. Later, Kabila and Patrice bribed the prophets to distract the Congolese citizens. These two false prophets lied to us and gave up on Marie's resurrection. These two prophets are hypocrites and false servants of God who played games with us. We thank God and respect Him regardless of whether he wants to take Marie forever or resurrect her. We don't play with God's plan or try to change his intentions. Also, we don't want Congolese prophets to give us excuses for Marie's missed resurrection, such as the fact that Marie's organs were stolen and she was buried. These people claim that since Marie has spent too much time underground, it is too late for her resurrection. People that make these statements lack faith in God. People that keep preventing her resurrection will die soon because they insult people, lie, and create false beliefs. Many

Congolese people, even Christians, don't believe in resurrection. They make negative statements about Marie, but we don't want to hear these things anymore. We want people to stop blocking Marie's resurrection and stop ignoring God's true messages. The Congolese disobey and disrespect God and His true servants. In addition, the Congolese exhibited sexism against Mrs. Ntumba Shuamba simply because she is a woman. People don't know whether or not Marie will actually return to this earth. They have lost their faith in God. The curse that God put on the Congolese for their lack of faith and immoral actions will last the rest of their life. The Congolese need to repent or they will die. Just because Marie is dead and buried does not mean that God has forgotten and forgiven people for their actions. God is very angry with the Congolese and has already unleashed a virus in RDC because their murdered Marie, prevented her resurrection, disobeyed God, and blocked God's message. The Congolese committed all of these actions for the sake of profit. The Christian Congolese are worse than non-Christian Congolese because they pretend to be Christians but are actually hypocrites. People keep supporting bad government in RDC.

It doesn't matter what the Congolese people think or say about Marie's resurrection. God doesn't care about people's opinions because God is all-powerful. Although Marie lost her organs, was buried illegally, and lay underground for more than 6 months, God can still resurrect her and put new organs in her body. God will not necessarily resurrect her soon, but he will eventually bring her back to life. She will return to this earth and live for longer so that she may complete her mission. She was only a young woman of age 41 whose mission wasn't yet complete.

This is a serious warning from God, and Jesus will assist in carrying it out. We can't force God to do anything; we have to let him do his work and be patient. If God promises us something, we have to be patient because it might take a long time. However, I guarantee you that Marie Misamu will be resurrected and return to this earth. When she returns, she will give her testimony and we will thank God. The prophets Marie and Petronie Mukandi need to stop lying to people and telling them that Marie is gone forever. Marie is gone now, but she will soon return to this earth. We are still patiently waiting for Marie's resurrection, and we will never give up until she has been resurrected. We don't want to miss the opportunity for her resurrection, like we did before. This time, there will be no more doubt, delay, discrimination, lying, or disobedience. No one will kick out the servants of God or use violence and threats against them. No one will block Marie's resurrection. If any of these things happen again, those people will die on the same day or night. The virus is already in RDC, so the Congolese need to repent and apologize to God and Ntumba Shaumba, giving her another chance to resurrect Marie. This time, Marie's resurrection will happen and the people who try to prevent it will die. This is no joke. The Congolese that refuse to repent will die that night. God's anger still remains.

We want to see a new miracle in RDC because we love Jesus Christ, and he loves us back. The next time someone dies, the true prophesy from God will come, and a true servant of God will resurrect that person without having their mission prevented. People need to receive the message of God and obey Him without causing disturbances or blocking people's resurrection. After Marie's resurrection, we want other people to also experience resurrection so that they can come back to life and experience healing from diseases, especially cancer, HIV/AIDS, and Ebola. We want people to have a good life, job, and marriage. We want people to put their faith in God and repent for their sins. Although we want miracles and resurrections in RDC, we can only resurrect people that God chooses. In the Bible, Peter resurrected Tabitha after she had died, and she came back to life. Pastor Israel and Walesa can support us and invite us to the resurrection of Marie Misamu. These pastors are true servants of God because they have resurrected people before. Congolese people, please listen to Jessie and me as well as to Papa Charles Iwo. We must obey God and fulfill the obligations that He imposes upon us. This is the most important message in all of the world's media. I repeat again, whoever tries to disturb Marie's resurrection will die the same night. We live in an age similar to Noah, who received God's commandments and tried to transmit them to the people; however, people didn't listen to Noah. People took his message as a joke, which incited God's rage, causing him to drown people. This is the same thing that will happen to the Congolese people and RDC. We are the servants of God and everything that we tell you is the truth. Our eyes are like those of the eagle, who see what God shows us. The Congolese people don't want to interfere with Marie's resurrection. God is very angry because the Congolese insult Jesus Christ. The Congolese need to ignore the two false prophets, Marie and Petronie Mukandi. Rather, they should listen to Mr. Boketshu, Mr. Esso, and Mr. JF Ifonge, who are the true servants of God. Mr. Tambwe Teach and Pastor Francis, two Congolese men that live in Paris and Brussel, disobeyed the government and the servants of God. I don't understand why the Congolese people disobey God but they don't disobey the government.

Disobedience of God results in a curse and death. I repeat again, Marie Misamu will eventually be resurrected and will soon return to the earth. Many people are waiting for her resurrection, so it will happen for real. Right now, she is in a peaceful place with Jesus Christ. Since Marie left us, many people have passed away from a broken heart because they loved her so much.

Mrs. Shaumba Ntumba, I want you to know that we still respect you and acknowledge you as the servant of God. We hope that you don't give up on Marie's resurrection. It was not your fault that people stopped you from resurrecting Marie and you were right to complain to the media and the Internet. Although some people closed the door on you, another door will soon open. A young male child was dead in the morgue, but Shaumba, you resurrected him. Now, you can return to resurrect Marie. We don't want to force you to complete this job or put pressure on you. However, you shouldn't publicly complain and make promises that you can't keep or give up on the mission that God assigned you. People will think that you lied and they will be disappointed. Don't put your life at risk and let people threaten you because of this incident. Some other people went to prison and were cursed for the rest of their lives because of this situation. For example, people that promise to pay the government a penalty but take too long to pay can be arrested and go to prison. This is exactly what you can face if you disobey God. Please do the job that God gave you. You can prove that you are the real servant of God by performing your duty. Do not complain or give excuses through the media. We want to see real action in order to prove your status. Don't listen to other people or give up on your job or resurrecting Marie. We are very serious about this situation and we don't want you to cause a protest. When are you going to resurrect her? We have been waiting so long for you to resurrect her in Necropole; we don't want to hear any more excuses or we will become very upset with you. This time, if people try to stop your resurrection, such as government, police, military, or cemetery employees, they will die instantly. Since Jesus Christ wants Marie's resurrection, nobody can stop it. Nobody can stop you from resurrecting Marie. You need to act on this duty because you publicly stated that you are the force of God and that you will resurrect Marie at the Necropole. Why did you give up? People are starting to lose their patience. Although Marie was buried, it is not too late to resurrect her. If you don't do anything about this situation, it could cause a curse, and we don't want that. We are encouraging you to return to the Necropole and resurrect Marie. We still need your help and we trust you. I guarantee you that you will succeed, because it is your responsibility. Keep praying to God and you will receive his answer. Why did you take so long to resurrect Marie? This time, take people that you can trust back to Kinshasa. Go straight to the Necropole Cemetery. Find Marie's tomb and have people dig out her coffin. Open the coffin to see if her body is still there. Move away from the coffin and pray together for 10-15 minutes. Then, Marie Misamu will be resurrected and come back to life. Prepare the media so that the public can see that you are the real servant of God and approve of you. Many people need and want Marie alive again. If you fail to resurrect her again, you will be in big trouble because it was your responsibility and you took too long. I guarantee that Marie Misamu will be resurrected and come back to life and God will give her new organs in her stomach. God promises us that he will resurrect her and give us grace. I believe in Jesus' name; this time will receive her resurrection and miracle. Once Marie has been resurrected, we will all have faith in God and repent for our sins. We still trust God. This time, Mrs. Ntumba Shaumba, please succeed in your mission to resurrect Marie. We still respect you and know that you are a real servant of God. We know that you still have the power that God have you. Please do the job that God gave you and I guarantee you that God will bless you more. Many true Christians received the same message and prophecy of Marie's resurrection. Although Marie didn't get resurrected yet, she will still be resurrected soon. Don't listen to other people in the RDC. Just listen to us and obey God. Thanks, Mrs. Ntumba Shaumba, please contact us if you have a question and we will email you back. God bless.

Congolese people said that the mother of Marie Misamu is going to experience deliverance and peace. However, she still has not received these things. We need to see deliverance for Mrs. Misamu's mother because God expects it to happen; otherwise, God will become angry and Congolese people will die. Mrs. Shaumba Ntumba, I have another question for you. You said that you are going to the Necropole Cemetery to resurrect Marie Misamu because her family and fans loved her so much and need her back. When are you going to resurrect Marie? God gave you this responsibility and you should act on it without delaying or making excuses. By resurrecting Marie, you will show that you are the real servant of God. You don't have to give up. We don't want to rush you or put pressure on you. Just keep following your gospel and perform you job without taking too long. God bless you more.

God showed me that Patrice Ngoy Musoko, L'Or Mbongo, Kanyama, Sony Kafuta and Kakienza will die sooner rather than later because they have refused to repent for their actions. Those people are false servants of God because they stopped Marie's resurrection and buried her illegally without obeying God's message. These people were silly for ignoring God's message of Marie's resurrection. In addition, they disrespected Marie's death and embarrassed her family. These people are immoral hypocrites that commit illegal crimes according to the gospel. Mrs. Shaumba, this is not your fault; they should have given you a chance to resurrect Marie without kicking you out of her funeral. Patrice, L'Or, Kanyama, Sony Kafuta, and Kakienza rejected their faith for the sake of profit. Patrice stole money for Marie's funeral and used the money for his own profit; Mrs. Ntumba Shaumba, you are correct about Patrice. Patrice, the leader of the AMCC, is a liar and a criminal who sold Marie's organs for profit. Remember that L'Or Mbongo will die sooner rather than later because she is the most responsible for Marie's death. L'Or cares only about money and profit. Those five people, and the rest of the AMCC musicians, didn't even visit Marie's grave after she was buried. They are prohibited from visiting her tomb. However, you can still come into her tomb and resurrect her; it is not too late. Like you, I am also a servant of God in the name of Jesus Christ.

If those five people and the AMCC musicians visit Marie's tomb they will die that same night because they killed her and were her enemies. God gave us the ability of an eagle to see far into the distance before something happened. God showed me everything that happened before and the things that will happen in the future. God never lies. Although people won't believe what we tell them, these things are still going to happen. Marie's resurrection will eventually occur, and people will tell me that I was right because everything that we tell you is true. Jesus always remains the same; he never changes. Marie will still be resurrected in the way that Jesus was resurrected from his tomb. Marie will not stay forever in her tomb. Now, she is dead, but she will not be dead forever. Right now, she is taking a long break in heaven with Jesus Christ, but she will still complete her mission on this earth and have a long life like everyone else.

We tell you about the prophecy of Marie's resurrection because God gave us the duty to pass the message to you. Please keep the following things in mind:

- We don't want to become heroes
- We don't want to make money
- We don't want to fool people for entertainment
- We are not imagining things
- We are not trying to cause controversy
- We aren't trying to force God into doing anything

We don't want the Congolese people to have ill feelings towards us because they don't have faith. Many people in the RDC claim to be Christians but they don't have faith in God and Jesus. Mrs. Ntumba Shaumba told the truth. Jesus never lies. Congolese Christians used to believe that Jesus resurrected people. However, they have lost their faith by disobeying God and Jesus. They blocked other people's resurrections for the sake of profit, as in the case of Marie Misamu. Congolese Christians no longer believe in resurrection; rather, they engage in hypocrisy, lying, and insulting other people. Regardless of whether they're Christians or non-Christians, Congolese are all the same; they all oppose people's resurrections. Congolese will never tell the truth. If God hadn't predicted Marie's resurrection, then we wouldn't worry about it. God promised us that he would resurrect

Marie. Even if it doesn't happen quickly, God will still resurrect her sooner or later and we will see her again. We just need to keep the faith in God and be patient. I guarantee you that it will happen for real. We will receive His miracle and see His glory. We don't want glory for ourselves; we only want to see God's glory.

Don't think that the five people who killed Marie, stole her organs, and buried her illegally can block the message of God and her resurrection. These people tried to sell her organs and bury her illegally for profit. However, the problem is not over and it will never be over. Those five people committed a criminal offense; they should be charged and go to prison or have the death penalty. It bothers me that a young, beautiful woman died early. I loved her so much and she still needs justice for her death. In fact, both Marie and Papa Wemba suffered unfair deaths for which they still need justice.

God has shown that Kabila and Olive Lembe will suffer their deaths at the hands of other authorities or Congolese citizens. Kabila and Olive want to keep their power and continue ruling for a third term. However, the Congolese citizens no longer want them in power. They should leave RDC and never come back. Because Kabila refuses to give up his position of power, he is putting his life in danger and will soon get killed. The same thing applies to Patrice Ngoy Musoko. However, we do not hate him or wish to see him dead. His life is in serious danger because Congolese citizens have been threatening Patrice that he should leave AMCC. The previous leader of AMCC, Mr. Charles Mombaya, died in 2007, and Patrice took over as the leader. However, Patrice is a bad leader and refuses to leave AMCC. So, RDC citizens will likely rebel against him and possibly shoot him.

The gospel will continue to exist in RDC after the liberation of Congo; however, AMCC will no longer exist. All of the musicians, their records, and their videos will be banned and never come back.

Congolese people are hypocrites because they always talk badly about people, even good people. When a person dies, Congolese people talk nicely about them once they have passed. I don't understand why they couldn't talk nicely about someone while they were still alive.

The great singer Victoria Ellison is sick and has been in the hospital in RDC for a while. The Congolese have ignored a man named Malembe Chante, refusing to send him money and help him. The same thing applies to a man named Kokodioko. I respect Kofie Olimide, Werrason, and J.P Mpiana, but they can help these two people. I don't understand why they don't do anything, especially since Malembe and Kokodioko will eventually die; they have been sick for a long time and are not receiving proper treatment. Why do the Congolese people wait for Malembe Chante and Kokodioko to die and act hypocritical about their deaths? Kokodioko still has a mental illness; I don't know what's going on (finally I thank God that Malembe Chante and Kokodioko are better now). The Rwandese people need to stop separating us from our own people; they should leave our country alone and go back to theirs. The Rwandese have killed our citizens and raped our mothers and sisters with weapons and poison. In addition, they have murdered many great musicians in RDC, including Madilu System, Pepe Ndombe, Babia Chorco Ndoga, Alain Moloto, Mombaya, Sister Marte, Father Tabuley, Mr. Guylain, Ms. Marie Misamu, and Papa Wemba. We lost all of these people, who were killed with poison by the Rwandese people; this is very painful. Fans will cry for the musicians that they have lost. It doesn't matter whether or not a fan has met a musician; the fan can cry for any musician that dies. Even musicians cry for a fellow musician that they have lost. People shouldn't judge others or listen to what people say. Personally, I don't care what people say.

These people are the real servants of God. They will tell you the truth and tell you that everything we say is the truth.

- Pasteur Francis Lola
- Tambwe Teach
- Pasteur Walesa
- Pasteur Israel
- Brother Charles LWO
- Papa Moliere
- Brother Elizier Ntambwe
- Papy Mboma
- E.X. Catcheur (a Congolese wrestler from America that lives in Brussels, Belgium)
- Mrs. Ntumba Shaumba
- J.F. Ifonge
- Boketshu
- Combattante Esso
- Brother Celezino

Unlike the people listed above, there are two false servants of God: Prophetese Marie and Petronie Mukandi. Initially, these propheteses said good things about Marie Misamu; however, they lied and were corrupted by the government. Patrice Ngoy Musoko bribed them with money to post propaganda on the Internet, opposing Marie's resurrection. I was so offended by what they posted, and I'm sure that other people were hurt as well. We can't live without Marie Misamu; we just want her back and we love her so much. Our pain will never go away since she passed away. Our hearts are still broken.

Hi Everybody! I'm a Swedish-Canadian guy but I grew up in a Congolese community in Montreal. My two best Congolese friends. The three of us are Christians; we both believe in Jesus Christ as our savior. I'm going to give a testimony about the experience I had. In Italy, there was a beautiful young woman named Sabrina. Although there are many beautiful Italian women, Sabrina was the most beautiful Italian woman that I have ever seen. In fact, I almost fell in love with her; however, she had her own spouse and two beautiful adult daughters. Sabrina was very respectful, friendly, and outgoing with people. She was a true Christian. In 2012, Sabrina was sick for a while and she died at the end of January at age 40. Her biological family, including her daughters and her best friends, were so sad and cried. Sabrina's body was in the morgue for two weeks before the doctor's took her organs from her stomach illegally without asking permission. This incident occurred in the city of Torino, Italy. After two weeks, her family and friends came to her funeral, which lasted for three days. God sent a message to Pastor Berto, telling him to resurrect Sabrina. The pastor came from Rome to Torino and planned to resurrect Sabrina. However, the false servants of God and police officers opposed Sabrina's resurrection by preventing Pastor Berto from resurrecting her. They threatened him and blocked him all for profit. The whole city, including Sabrina's family and friends, were upset with the police officers because they had blocked her resurrection and buried her illegally. The false servants of God had obeyed the police officers, so Sabrina was buried in 3 days. Two months later, in June 2012, there was a protest against the false servants of God and the police officers, especially the police chief of Torino. The entire city was upset because people loved Sabrina so much. The police officers and the false servants put their lives in danger because they had kicked Pastor Berto out of the church. They shouldn't have kicked the pastor out of church and blocked Sabrina's resurrection, stolen her body, and buried her illegally. These are the reasons that people were upset with the police officers, which resulted in violence, threats, and fighting. Some of the false servants of God and police officers were killed by Italian citizens. They government experienced significant difficulty in controlling them because the citizens were so powerful. In September, the police officers and the false servants of God faced life in prison because they had tried to block Sabrina's resurrection. Justice came after Sabrina's death. Pastor Berto went to another town to resurrect two teenage boys whose bodies were in the morgue. This was an amazing miracle from God. However, Sabrina spent three years underground and developed an odor. God promised people that he would resurrect Sabrina, so Pastor Berto returned from Rome and took his people to Sabrina's cemetery. His people broke into her tomb, and opened her coffin to check her body. Her body was all right, so Pastor Berto and his people stepped back from the tomb. They prayed for 10 to 15 minutes. After 15 minutes and 2 seconds, Sabrina came out of her coffin. She was resurrected in 2015 and God gave her new organs in her stomach. When she returned, she gave her testimony about what had happened. Her story was true, and she didn't make up lies or imagine anything; it was a real miracle. Many people thanked God and put their faith back in God after seeing her resurrection. We still thank God that Sabrina is alive.

We need to put our faith in God and repent for our sins. I guarantee that even if God doesn't act quickly, he will still perform his miracles as promised. We are all the children of God; we need to exercise patience and let him perform his job. We don't know God's exact plans; even if God decides to take our sister Marie Misamu forever, we will still thank him. However, since God told us that he would resurrect Marie, God will keep his promise, even if Marie is underground for a long time. Eventually, the resurrection will happen for real. I guarantee the Congolese people that like Sabrina, Marie will get resurrected.

Jesus was never a selfish person; his resurrection was for our benefit. Even some people don't believe that Jesus was resurrected; however, it happened for real and is a true story. I know that Marie Misamu was the best singer in the entire gospel music industry. She inspired many people, even myself, to become closer to Jesus Christ. She is the best performer that I have ever seen in my life. She was a true servant of God. Although she is dead, she is not gone forever. Don't listen to the Congolese people that say that Marie will stay in her tomb forever; they don't know anything about gospel music.

There are many beautiful women in the world, but Spanish and Latino women are the most beautiful women that I have ever seen. I have seen attractive Congolese women in the Congolese community, but Marie Misamu is the most beautiful Congolese woman that I have ever seen. Marie has nice long hair and makes effective use of makeup and clothing to suit her face and body. Her daughter, Ruth, is also beautiful like her. However, Marie is the most beautiful Congolese woman ever. If she were still alive, I would wish that I could date and marry her as well as have kids with her. I wish that

God could give me a kind, beautiful wife like Marie or a Latina/Spanish woman. I apologize to Congolese people and hope that they don't take my opinion about Marie's beauty seriously. This part is just my opinion about Marie. I still feel bad that Marie is not alive anymore. She will still come back and give her testimony. I hope that God can give her a new husband, so that she can continue to have a long life like everyone else. When she was alive, I loved her so much and I still love her very much.

If the Congolese people can't improve their country, they will never experience progress. They need to help Marie become resurrected before too long. People have been resisting and seeking God's plan to return her to the earth; however, they shouldn't forget her, because it is going to happen. The type of cemetery doesn't matter; a person's tomb can be in hard or soft soil in order to experience resurrection. Even if a person isn't a Christian, they can still be resurrected. Regardless of whether a person has been underground for 1, 2, or 4 years, God can still resurrect them. However, if a person has been underground for a very long time, such as 6, 8, or 15 years, it is too late to experience resurrection. At this point, you will be dust and ashes. Sabrina is still alive; although she lost her organs, God provided her with new organs. No matter what soldiers, police, government, or false servants of God think, they cannot hide the truth. They can hate us, charge us, arrest us, or even murder us if we speak the truth, but the truth will still emerge. Remember that we don't hate or oppose anyone; we are children of God and we want liberation for the people of the Congo. This is the mission and responsibility that God gave us. God bless.

Hi, this is me again. God showed me that Congolese people shouldn't take any action concerning Marie Misamu's grave. Her grave doesn't doesn't need a tombstone because her resurrection will come soon. The Congolese need to have faith in God rather than continually trying to prevent her resurrection. This situation is the fault of the AMCC musicians. Even if they spent money on Marie's tombstone, the stone will still rot. God will send his servant to break the tombstone and resurrect Marie. This time, the government, police, soldiers, AMCC, and other Congolese citizens can't prevent her resurrection. Otherwise, they will die on that night; God will murder them. If Congolese people continue to disobey God, he will murder them. God is still upset, and he has unleashed a virus in the Congo. Patrice Ngoy Musoko, Sony Kafuta, Kanyama, and Kakienza will all die soon, especially L'Or Mbongo, because they conspired with Kabila and Olive Lembe to kill Marie Misamu.

Let me address Mrs. Ntumba Shaumba again. I still respect her. However, Ntumba, you said that you would travel to Necropole to resurrect Marie. She has been in her tomb for nearly eight months now. Why haven't you brought her back yet? You should try to resurrect her again. Why are you neglecting the job that God gave you? This situation will cause a protest throughout the whole world and the RDC because many people are expecting her resurrection. Don't let people get to the point where they protest. If we find out that you were lying to us, you will be in very big trouble. Some people know where you live and have your address. People will come and vandalize your house. Do not let this happen. Although we are disappointed, we still trust you. Some people have been accused and threatened after the death of Marie Misamu, while others were killed. Since people blocked her resurrection and kicked you out of the funeral, it was not your fault. If people continue to cause problems and prevent her resurrection, they will die. This is all Patrice's fault because he set everything up. L'Or Mbongo is the guiltiest party because she, along with Olive and Kabila, killed Marie. L'Or Mbongo will die first because she is the most responsible for Marie's death. She is the biggest criminal ever in gospel music. I can't live properly anymore without Marie alive because I loved her so much and her death is painful for me. My heart is broken and I will never forget her.

Freedom Speech

I like to talk about freedom. Freedom is not about religion and politics like people think. In reality, people want challenge and change in order to make the world a better place. We want to find a solution, which is where the freedom speech comes in.

Many people live in democratic countries like Canada, USA, Australia, New Zealand, South Africa, and European nations. In these countries, nobody will stop you, arrest you, or kill you. It doesn't matter if you're a permanent resident, citizen, or landed immigrant. Nobody will charge you or deport you to any country nor will they make you lose your permanent residency or citizenship. In free countries, people can share their own opinions in public and criticize the government. People can disagree with each other or publish a book with your own thoughts. People can do anything in a democratic country, as long as they don't use violence, threats, and curse words or discuss sensitive topics like crime and terrorism. We shouldn't offend our fellow citizens or the government because you can't disrespect people in public. People can't use sexism, discrimination, racism or any other form of prejudice. You will be charged for those offenses. When publishing a book, you can use your real name, but you don't have to. It doesn't matter if people use their real names, fake names, or nick names. Many famous people use aliases when publishing a book. You can use any name that you want as long as the government can trace your identity so that you pay your taxes. You shouldn't have trouble with the government because the government doesn't control what people say or publish. People can publish books on their own and still make money. They don't need to depend on the government to publish a book and have success. People can either publish independently or publish with a company, but in either case, they aren't controlled by the government.

I feel sad that people died in Brussels, Belgium and the Ivory Coast from terrorist attacks in 2016. These attacks resembled those in Paris, France in November 2015, where many innocent people died. We need to fight ISIS because they cannot continue to attack innocent people. This is not right; the government should do something about it. Why do bad governments in Europe, North America, South Africa, New Zealand, and Australia discriminate against black people without giving them permanent residency or citizenship? Why do the government allow refugees that are Arabs, Asians, Mulattos, and Latinos into the country? Later, the Arabs will turn against the governments of these countries and commit crimes. Black people never commit terrorist acts but still experience discrimination because of their skin color. This is not fair. I'm not asking people to discriminate against Arabs, Asians, Mulattos, and Latinos or to deport them to another country. Please don't discriminate against any of these people and do not deport them, but do not deport black people. The government and police shouldn't promote threats and violence against black people. I still respect the government and police and I don't have any problem with them.

I disagree with the policies of Donald Trump, but it doesn't mean that I'm against him. Let me tell the truth. He thinks that he is a legitimate presidential candidate and that people will vote for him. I don't think that many people will vote for Donald Trump, and he will never become president of the United States because he would bring more corruption to the world. He will cause a real war, worse than that of George W. Bush. I still respect Donald Trump and George W. Bush; however, Donald Trump can't show discrimination, racism, and hatred towards newcomers, refugees, and immigrants. He can't dislike black people, Arabs, Asians, and Latinos. He can't deport foreigners, such as Mexicans, who have spent a long time in the US. Donald Trump will never be allowed to make bad laws in the US. If he tries to make unconstitutional laws, other people will kill him because he put his life in danger. I'm not making threats; I'm telling the truth.

Message for RDC (Congo)

This is a message and command that God gave me and I have an obligation to obey his command. I cannot keep any more secrets; otherwise, God will be upset with the Congolese, because God's word is serious and not a joke. I'm not talking about politics; however, I don't intend to threaten, enact violence, or insult anyone. I do not want to cause disturbances with the police, military, or government of any country.

In a short period of time, RDC will become liberated and have the full freedoms of the democratic country that it once was. I don't understand why the Congolese people allowed Kabila to stay in power for one more year; it doesn't make any sense. The Congolese people want to achieve freedom and escape pain and slavery from the Rwandese people, who are ruling RDC. This is a real curse for the Congolese people, which I have never witnessed in my life. Kabila can't stay in power for another year because he should leave the country. However, Kabila will remain in RDC until December 19, 2016. This is not fair.

Kabila should give up his power in RDC and leave the country right now. Since Kabila refuses to leave RDC, someone should kill him. Why can't the Congolese people kill Kabila and why do they increase his ego despite the fact that he's already very arrogant? He has been in power for a long time, since 2001, and he will stay at least until the end of 2016.

Why do Kabila and Mende not respect the constitution in RDC? Kabila and Mende, along with their people, are murderers and criminals. They are the only ones that caused massacres in RDC, especially in the East Congo, such as Bukavu, for killing many innocent people and sending soldiers from Rwanda, Burundi, and Uganda to kill Congolese citizens and rape beautiful Congolese women. Kabila and Mende still continue to commit crimes in RDC. The Congolese need to make their own decisions, which will allow them to liberate their country and establish their own rules. This is how the Congolese will gain more respect from other nations. If the Congolese killed Kabila and Mende, and they allow all of the citizens to partake in sharing the power, then the country will have true freedom. Nobody can take away your right to fight for your own country. The Congolese people need to know their own rights and stand up for them. However, the Congolese people need to get wise like some other nations. I guarantee that the RDC will become liberated soon, in this current year of 2016. We don't want to wait any longer. We want to experience the liberation of the Congo since we have been waiting a long time.

Olive Lembe doesn't know that her own husband has used her to gain power; however, her husband, Kabila, has another wife, who is Rwandese. They have been married for a long time and have two children. Olive doesn't know that Kabila used her wealth to gain power in RDC and that he is cheating on Olive with another wife. Why doesn't Olive realize that because she is a rich woman living in the Congo, she can do anything that she wants? I guarantee that Kabila will soon leave Olive and kill her. Olive will die soon because Kabila's other wife will put poison into her body without Olive's awareness. Although Olive has a lot of money, the money didn't come from her own pocket; she married a husband that has a lot of money, which he obtained from committing crime and theft. It doesn't matter whether or not Olive gets treatment for her poison, the poison will never leaver her body and allow her to heal. The poison has been in her body for a long time and she has been sick from the toxins for a while. Olive Lembe will still die soon. She is an immoral person who has been corrupted by her husband. She is a criminal and murderer, especially from killing people with poison. She committed crimes because she came from a poor family; however, she is still the biggest demon on the Congo. Everyone in the Congolese community and every other police in the world will know this. I don't need to prove Olive's evil nature, as there is already proof. Before marrying Kabila, Olive had two other husbands at different times and had a child with her first husband. She divorced and killed her two ex-husbands for their money. She is not a real Christian because real Christians don't commit crimes. Olive is also partly responsible for the death of Marie Misamu, who died from being murdered with poison. Olive colluded with L'Or Mbongo in order to kill Marie. Together, Olive and L'Or are guilty for killing Marie Misamu.

Kabila will soon dump Olive Lembe and return to his Rwandan wife. Kabila will still get killed and die because he refused to leave power despite the fact that Congolese citizens no longer want him in power. Why are the people in power, such as Kabila, Olive Lembe, and Mende, so arrogant? All three of them will soon die.

The European and the Americans cannot continue to make decisions for RDC simply because RDC is the richest country in the world in terms of its resources. They need to leave them along. Why keep harassing the Africans?

Kanyama, the police chief, has finally been sanctioned for the actions that he has taken. In addition, Kabila, Mende, and the other people in power need to receive sanctions. All three men have performed immoral actions in Kinshasa, RDC. Although Kanyama did a few good things, he performed more immoral actions than positive ones. Kanyama understands that the leader, Kabila, is not a part of the RDC and that Kabila is an immoral person who kills his people. Celestin Kanyama has a strong military force in RDC; he could turn against Kabila and kill him. Why did Kanyama refuse to kill Kabila? Because Kanyama allowed Kabila to corrupt him for money. Kanyama preferred to abuse his power, turn against his people, and kill his own people like Saddam Hussein did in Iraq. Kanyama is exactly like Hussein, so there is no forgiveness for him and his actions. He knows that harming his own people is wrong, but he continues to do it anyways. He abused his power and murdered his own people. Even at the funerals for the great RDC musicians, such as King Kester Emeneya, Ms. Marie Misamu, and Papa Wemba, Celestin created a lot of disorder and disrespected the citizens. He insulted the musicians' fans, beat them, kicked them, and tried to choke them to death. Furthermore, Kanyama blocked the resurrection of Marie Misamu for stealing her body and burying her illegally. Similarly, he also stole the body of Papa Wemba and buried him illegally. Kanyama lost or got suspended from his job countless times, indicating that he should lose his job forever. In addition, Kanyama was arrested and put in prison several times. Finally, the Americans arrested him and placed sanctions on him. Kanyama deserves everything that happens to him because he was not wise or good. Since Kabila and Mende betrayed him to the Americans, he will likely die soon.

Ms. Marie Misamu will still experience resurrection regardless of how long she has spent in her tomb. She has been underground for 7 months now, and even if she is underground for one year, it will still happen. She has been dead and buried since January 2016. The AMCC musicians and pastors didn't take care to keep her tomb clean or even visit her tomb. Even up until now, they still haven't done anything. However, we don't need them to do anything to her tomb, and we don't want the government to do anything to her tomb because they didn't like her when she was alive. They murdered her and interfered with her funeral by falsely accusing her mother of being a demon. The government only helped her mother on one occasion; the rest of the time, they provided no help or support. In particular, Patrice Ngoy Musoko visited Sophie Misamu for one day only. Patrice and L'Or conspired in the death of Marie Misamu. They accused her innocent mother of being a demon in order to try to escape their own crimes. In addition to Patrice and L'Or, Pasteur Sony Kafuta and Kakienza are also demons for their role in Marie's death. These four people created disorder in Marie's family, dividing Marie's mother from her siblings and Marie's daughter, Ruth Misamu. Due to the false accusations against her, Sophie has been prohibited from receiving help, support, or money from her sons or daughter. Congolese citizens have been fooled into thinking that Marie's mother is a demon and that she murdered Marie. Mrs. Sophie's money can't be taken by her children or by Olive Lembe. She can't be treated badly because she didn't commit any crime. Mrs. Sophie should have money to live and receive good treatment. Since she has been sick for a while, she needs more help, service, and support in Congolese society. She should be treated with respect. Mrs. Sophie is not dead; she is still alive and we don't want her to die. Patrice Musoko wants to wait until Mrs. Sophie dies and bury her quickly and illegally in the same manner in which she buried Marie Misamu. Ms. Marie will still be resurrected one day.

If Mrs. Sophie is killed, Patrice Ngoy Musoko, L'Or Mbongo, Sony Kafuta, and Kakienza will receive more accusations and people will murder them, causing them to die on the same day. Mrs. Sophie can't die like that just because her daughter was a gospel musician. Marie was her only daughter. Patrice Ngoy Musoko often makes money when people die. Among the four people responsible for Marie's death, L'Or Mbongo is the guiltiest party because she sent Marie's adopted daughter to kill her with poison. That woman is a real murderer.

Mrs. Sophie can't die. Thank God she is alive. Why can't Marie's family solve their problems with their mother or go to a real servant of God to try to solve their problems? They should also talk with Ruth to apologize and help to solve the family issues. Marie's siblings shouldn't treat their mother like that. Mrs. Shaumba Ntumba has been waiting for so long, and we don't want her to wait any longer. She needs to return to the Necropole Cemetary to resurrect Marie because she promised that she is going to bring her back. If we find out that Mrs. Shaumba Ntumba lied to us about resurrecting Marie, then we will be upset with her and turn against her. She needs to take action because this time, we want her to return to Necropole Cemetary to resurrect Marie and bring her back to life. Then, God and the Congolese citizens will be happy with her. Since God gave her the job of resurrecting Marie, she needs to complete this mission. We still respect her and we are not angry with her yet. Patrice, L'Or, Kafuta, and Kakienza will die shortly because of their criminal action against Marie Misamu.

On June 27, 2016, people from all over the world heard the news that Mrs. Sophie isn't doing well. After four months of being underground, Marie's tomb has gotten dirty despite the fact that it should be kept clean. Now, seven months after her death, Marie's tomb is still dirty. We don't need people to take care of her tomb because she will be resurrected. During her lifetime, people didn't like or respect her, so nobody has bothered to clean her tomb. The AMCC and pastors stole money and cheated, especially Patrice Ngoy Musoko and L'Or Mbongo. These two people are real demons and fool people in the name of Jesus.

Some people falsely claim that Ms. Marie Misamu is in hell and others have posted her picture on the Internet. People keep saying false lies about her. She was a servant of God in this world, so she is now in heaven, not in hell. If people continue to manipulate her memorial, other people will die. God said, "Don't touch my servant, judge, or play with my servant." People shouldn't disobey God. That makes other people angry, and God gets more upset about that. The Congolese people should respect the death of other people, because we are all going to die and nobody can live forever on this earth.

Someone should ask the Congolese people, "When you die, would you like people to make fun of your death or stop your resurrection? How would you feel if someone stopped your resurrection?" I'm not saying that all Congolese people lack intelligence; actually, many of them are quite intelligent. Many of today's Congolese people don't respect other people's deaths and resurrection. This is not just my own opinion; it is a serious matter that came from God's word. Congolese people should believe in the true miracles of God without doubting the gospel. People that doubt the gospel will experience curses and even death, because God becomes angry when people disobey Him. In particular, if Ms. Marie Misamu can't be resurrected anymore, L'Or Mbongo, Patrice Ngoy Musoko, Sony Kafuta, and Albert Kakienza will die because were the ones that murdered her, blocked God's message, and prevented Marie's resurrection. The mother of Marie Misamu has been abandoned. However, Sophie shouldn't be abandoned for a long time. God has told us that Marie Misamu will be resurrected; although it hasn't happened yet, it will happen eventually, regardless of how long Marie spent underground. Marie Misamu won't stay underground forever or for a long time, like 10 years. Marie will be resurrected and come back to life because God never lies to us. Shame on these people.

Homage for A Friend

I want to thank A friend and his whole family because he was my best friend. He passed away on June 30, 2016. It was very painful for me, because he was a good person and he was never a troublemaker who insulted other people; he always respected everyone.

Rest his soul in peace. It was still painful for us and for his family because we can't live without him. Let me explain what happened to him.

A friend, who was Afro-Cuban Canadian, wasn't treated very well by his mother, older sister, younger sister, or two younger brothers. If his mother or two sisters asked him to help them with any job, he would always perform the job without complaining or refusing. He had no difficulty with comprehending either English or Spanish, his native language. If they explained the work to him properly and showed him what to do, he wouldn't cause any issues. However, they got angry at him and said that he didn't listen. Come on! He was treated badly by his own family members, who never appreciated him in the house, leading to problems and arguments. That's why he left the house.

Some temp agencies treat their employees in the same way. He worked for temp agencies, and while some of them liked him, some company employers and employees as well as even people from the street didn't treat him with respect. Every time he accidentally made mistakes, people took issue with him. He didn't like the attention and tried to avoid causing problems. In particular, a man from New Brunswick and an older woman from Alberta never showed him how to perform his job with a proper explanation, so these people treated him badly and insulted him. The employers and employees lied and said that he didn't listen to people and had a problem with the English language. However, people can't get angry with someone else or blame that person if they don't know how to explain the job properly to the other person. Come on! If you want to be treated with respect by other people, you should treat others with respect. People should know this Golden Rule. Why hurt someone?

An older Native man was very rude to him at the temp agency. Both men worked at the same agency and were sent to work on the garbage truck picking up garbage. The older Native man worked on one side of the street while he worked on the other side. They were both busy because there was a lot of garbage to pick up and throw in the truck. Initially, both men were helping each other, but he was too busy on his side of the street to jump to the other side. Although the older Native man asked a friend for help, he had too much garbage on his side. Rather than being understanding, the older Native man got angry, argued with him, and blamed him despite the fact that he was very busy. The older Native man was so rude to him by insulting and disrespecting him; he acted as if he were his supervisor. By the end of the day, he was angry. Many people had taken advantage of him because he was too nice to people. However, he was not stupid like people though. He was treated very badly.

On Wednesday June 22, 2016, a friend came from the Bay LRT Station. After getting off of the train, he went upstairs and went straight to the temp agency to see if they had any work for him. Before he got to the office, a young beautiful black lady, who was sitting down, started yelling at him and disrespecting him. Although she didn't even know him, she acted rudely to him asking him, "Why are you looking at me? Don't look at me like that! Just go away, walk away." However, he hadn't been looking at her; he had done nothing wrong to her. He ignored her without paying attention or answering, and just walked away in order to avoid any problems.

Later, a friend became sick and died from cardiac failure because he had too much stress in his life, especially concerning problems with people, such as his mother, older sister, and younger sister. In particular, his younger sister insulted him the most. Now, his family regrets that he died. He died at age 32, which is too young and too early to die. People in his biological family didn't know his importance when he was alive.

The two chapters, "Message for RDC" and "Homage for A Friend," are both written by me, I am an Mulatto, half-Congolese, half Belgian. I can speak Swaheli, French, and English. I want to tell people that the world that we live in today is very bad. I don't want to insult anyone; I only want to tell the truth. Christian was not truly the husband of L'Or Mbongo because his heart was twisted by L'Or, the biggest criminal and demon musician in RDC. L'Or could find her own husband to marry, but she didn't do that. Instead, she stole the husband of another gospel singer, Fideline. L'Or's actions were very immoral because Christian belonged to Fideline, who eventually married another man. L'Or also murdered Marie Misamu because of her jealousy and hatred towards Marie, who was a much better gospel musician than L'Or. In fact, Marie Misamu was the best gospel singer in

RDC. L'Or Mbongo won't live long enough to grow old; she will leave this earth soon because God has not forgiven her for what she did to Marie. L'Or knew that her actions were wrong but she killed Marie anyways. I'm not judging L'Or; however, the death of Marie was very painful for many people, including myself. Many of us loved Marie very much and she left the earth too early. We want to state the sentiments that come from our hearts. We will keep thinking about Marie forever, and we are still waiting for God to make a second attempt at resurrecting her. We want Marie brought back to this earth because we love her very much. We can't miss Marie forever and we can't live without her.

Why Are Congolese People Silly?

In our chapters, "Homage for Ms. Marie Misamu, "Resurrection for Ms. Marie Misamu" and "Message for RDC Congo," we told the truth about everything that is going to happen, so we didn't tell any lies. We aren't going to tell you the same things again because we already told you everything. The true prophesy and message of God came on January 29, 2016, when Ms. Marie Misamu was dead. The Congolese people disobeyed God, and they didn't provide Mrs. Shaumba Ntumba with a chance to resurrect Ms. Marie Misamu. The Congolese people were wrong, and blocked Marie Misamu's resurrection, especially Celestin Kanyama, Patrice Ngoy Musoko, Albert Kakienza, Sony Kafuta and L'or Mbongo. All of these people participated in causing her death because when she was alive, they didn't like her, so it is their all fault. Mrs. Shaumba Ntumba said that she was going to the Cemetery Necropole to use the power of God to resurrect Ms. Marie Misamu. Unfortunately, Shaumba didn't succeed in her mission and gave up, which was not good because she promised people that she was going to resurrect Marie. She should keep her promise and resurrect Ms. Marie Misamu. When she is going to do that? We still want her to resurrect Ms. Marie Misamu. I still trust Shaumba and we still have faith in God; however, this time we want a real miracle, which will come from God. Specifically, we are still seeking Ms. Marie Misamu's resurrection from God. Ms. Marie has spent a while in her tomb, 9 months now, but her grave is probably dirty and rotten, so it doesn't make any sense. If we find out that Mrs Shaumba Ntumba has lied to us, then we will become upset; I guarantee that some people who know where Shaumba lives will vandalize her place and the whole world, especially RDC, will create a real protest. These evens are going to happen for real in RDC as well as other Congolese nations, So, Mrs. Shaumba, don't let this happen, especially if it is too late to resurrect Ms. Marie. Otherwise, L'or Mbongo, Patrice Ngoy Musoko, Celestine Kanyama, Albert Kakienza, and Sony Kafuta will die this time, because they are the only ones who murdered her, disobeyed God and His message, kicked Mrs Shaumba Ntumba out of the funeral and blocked the resurrection of Ms. Marie Misamu. I want to know the truth. Why can Ms. Marie Misamu no longer be resurrected anymore? We still know in our minds that God promised us that Ms. Marie would be resurrected; even if it didn't happen quickly, it will happen later. It doesn't matter if people build her gravestone or not.

Although people want to build Marie's gravestone, the gravestone on her tomb will not last long on Maric's tomb because people will break it. Even if the Congolese continue to block her resurrection, Ms. Marie Misamu will still experience her resurrection regardless of the circumstances. There's no point in spending money to build her gravestone; we don't need it because her resurrection is still coming soon although we don't know when. Why are the Congolese people so silly? Why don't they give another second chance for resurrecting Marie Misamu? Please give our people, and Mrs Shaumba, a second chance to resurrect Ms. Marie Misamu. She cannot spend forever in her tomb. The Congolese people cannot block other people's resurrections without having faith in God and continuing take the gospel as a joke, causing doubt. It is in the Bible that doubting the gospel will cause curses and deaths. Why put your own life in danger and play with God? For this incident, you won't get to experience God in heaven. The money came from everywhere; people spent money on Ms. Marie's funeral while she was buried Illegally. Why were Patrice Ngoy Musoko, L'or Mbongo, Kakienza, Sony Kafuta, Celestin Kanyama and AMCC the only people to quickly bury Ms Marie Misamu without thinking and why they didn't build her own gravestone on her tomb shortly after? Even her friends, some of her family members, and the musicians didn't build her a gravestone.

When she died, no one visited her tomb, including her mother. This shows that when Ms Marie was alive, nodoby liked her at all. These people are hypocrites: Patrice Ngoy Musoko, L'or Mbongo, Kakienza, Sony Kafuta, Celestin Kanyama and AMCC. These individuals used her funeral for their profit and they stole all of her money. They will never tell the truth; they will keep lying and refuse to give money back to her mother and her family members. We said that we don't need her friends, the musicians in her group, and even some of her family members or some other Congolese journalist in RDC and Shaka Congo (we respect him).We don't need them to spend money and build her gravestone because they didn't think about building a gravestone before. Why do they hurry now to make her gravestone for January 16, 2017? It's because they don't want her resurrection to come. These people try to play games with God and they just want to profit by pretending that the money comes from their own pocket. We don't want her to stay in the tomb because we loved her so much while she was alive. When she was alive, many Congolese people didn't like her, including Patrice Ngoy Musoko, L'or Mbongo, Kakienza, Sony Kafuta, Celestin Kanyama and AMCC. So, these people are hypocrites because they didn't visit her mother or her family. We aren't stupid and the Congolese people can't fool us. The Congolese people in other parts of the world don't send money because they try to use the money for theft. It makes us upset. Why are the Congolese people still silly? Those people have been corrupted by the government, including Patrice Ngoy Musoko, L'or Mbongo, Kakienza, Sony Kafuta, Celestin Kanyama, and AMCC. These people keep supporting Kabila, seeking money from the RDC government, and murdering innocent people. Celestin Kanyama's sanction cannot disapprove because he still supports Kabila for his profit and he still kills many innocent Congolese Citizens, refusing to stop committing crime. People are getting upset with Kanyama.

How come the mother of Ms. Marie Misamu passed away on July 27, 2016? She has been abandoned by her children, the AMCC, and Patrice Ngoy Musoko. She worried about the death of Ms. Marie Misumu, which has caused her to experience high blood pressure. This time, we want a miracle, so both Sophie and Ms. Marie Misamu should experience resurrection. Sophie shouldn't die; I feel so sad and upset. Sophie's death is the fault of Celestine Kanyama, Patrice Ngoy Musoko, L'or Mbongo, Kakienza and Sony Kafuta's. We told people that if Sophie died, this time, they would face greater accusations, which would result in more serious revenge. This time, people that know their address will vandalize their house and possessions or even murder Celestine Kanyama, Patrice Ngoy Musoko, L'or Mbongo, Kakienza, and Kafuta.

These people really deserve their own death and it is entirely their fault. It is going to happen. We are not threatening violence against them; we are just speaking the truth. God has shown us before what will happen to them. They are false servants of God. There are many Congolese journalists throughout the world in Europe, North America, Australia, New Zealand, South Africa, and RDC, who broadcast on all Congolese channels and sites, including Casarhema, Etio Du Ciel, Congo France, Avis Du Public, Tokomi Wapi, Eliezer Ntambwe, Edtuard, La Voie Celeste, and Alvine Beya. We ask these journalists to do us a favor; we want them to contact and interview Celestin Kanyama, Patrice Ngoy Musuko, Kakienza, and Sony Kafuta. The journalists should ask why these criminals made the decision to kick Mrs Shaumba Ntumba out of the cemetery and block Marie Misamu's resurrection without obeying God's message and without having faith in God. Why did L'or Mbongo murder Ms. Marie Misamu by sending her adopted daughter to murder her with poison? Why did Mrs Shaumba Ntumba not return to the cemetery to resurrect Marie anymore and when she is going to do that? We have been waiting for Marie's resurrection for a long time. We don't want to wait anymore; we want to see a real miracle of resurrecting Marie and Sophie. We spoke about the things that bother us and hurt us; these words came from our hearts and we are upset about the whole incident. Anyone who wants to contact us and ask question with respect, we will answer all people, including the Congolese citizens and Congolese journalists. Here is our email **jakodepo10@gmail.com**

We want the journalist who lives in DC to do us a favor and ask some questions. Specifically, the journalist should ask why Patrice Ngoy Musoko and the AMCC musicians switched Marie Misamu's body from one hospital to another hospital. They should also ask the doctors why they illegally took Marie's organs from her stomach and why Patrice Ngoy Musoko bribed the doctors to take Marie's organs out of her stomach.

We had a female friend pass away two months ago from Marie Misamu's death and the fact that her resurrection was blocked. This friend was a fan of Marie Misamu's. We all want true justice for her death and we still want to see her resurrected. Her mother passed away all because of this entire incident.

The journalist should ask Patrice Ngoy Musoko why he took all of the money from her funeral and never gave it to her family, lying about it afterwards? Why? It is all his faulty and he is in big trouble. Also, General Kanyama, L'Or Mbongo, Albert Kakienza, and Sony Kafuta are all in big trouble because of this whole situation, especially for Marie's death and her mother's death. These people were responsible for tearing Marie's family apart. Congolese people are silly because they don't like to hear the truth. They only like to threaten and murder people that want to tell or hear the truth.

Before other people build her gravestone, we want to know if Marie can still be resurrected. Her tomb has been abandoned for 8 or 9 months now. We don't want anyone to build her gravestone yet or spend any money because we want Marie's resurrection. The Congolese people should put their faith back in God, and we will all see his glory. Ms. Marie Misamu will be resurrected and maybe even her own mother will come back to life. We guarantee that both Marie and her mother will be resurrected by the glory of God and provide a testimony. This time, we don't want to hear any excuses or doubts about the gospel; otherwise, God is going to cause curses and deaths. God's revenge is going to be manifested and many people will die because of Marie Misamu's death. Please stop making jokes about the gospel. This time, we want to see the glory of God; we want to receive the resurrection of Ms. Marie Misamu, a real miracle from Jesus Christ. Please give us one more chance. This time, we are asking you to allow Mrs. Shaumba Ntumba to come back to Kinshasa and enter the Necropole Cemetery to resurrect Marie Misamu and her mother Sophie. Please don't cause doubts or problems like before. Congolese people should give people a chance in the same way that people in other nations do. Why are Congolese Christians acting in this way? That's why we are getting upset. We will eradicate the false Congolese gospel from everywhere in the world. We are not joking or playing games anymore. We don't care if Congolese people hate us, charge us, arrest us, or put us in jail. We don't care and we are not afraid of them. In fact, we are not afraid of anything because we believe in Christ and we will receive the Heavenly Father's kingdom. Don't play with God; otherwise, it will put a curse on you and cause your death. Congolese people have strong hatred for people that know the truth. In particular, Congolese Christians are hypocrites and some of them are even worse than Congolese atheists. False Christians are the only people who embarrass and insult Jesus Christ as well as other Christians. Miracles not only involve healing people with diseases but also involve resurrecting people who have been dead. These are real miracles of God. Our sister, Marie Misamu, should receive the miracle of resurrection because she was a real servant of God. Resurrection involves not only your spirit but also your physical body. People who are resurrected will not live forever on this earth; resurrection provides them with the chance to live a full life like other people in the world. Eventually, Marie will be resurrected regardless of attempts to stop the miracle. Congolese people need to open their hearts. Why are they so silly?

The children of God will still be liberated in God's glory. The Gospel Musicians, pastors, politicians, police officers, and soldiers that supported Kabila will die when Kabila loses his power. All of these people will be killed by the Congolese Combatants of Europe when they return to the RDC and the RDC will be liberated. All bad Congolese citizens will also die from the good Congolese citizens. However, the bad Congolese will deserve their own deaths, especially Kanyama. This is going to happen for real. This is their last year living on this earth. This situation resembles that of Benito Mussolini, who was killed by the Italian citizens because he was a bad person and supported Adolf Hitler. Mussolini was a dictator and betrayed his own nation by supporting Hitler and killing innocent Italian citizens. God has already shown us what will happen to bad Congolese leaders who betrayed their own nation. We are not against anyone; our job is to speak the truth. Nobody can force us to stop speaking the truth and we will never stop speaking the truth until Marie Misamu becomes resurrected and the children of God are liberated in the name of Jesus. Congolese people should have faith on God and it is obligation and it is in Bible. I don't understand it's because why Congolese people don't have faith at all on God while Congolese people cannot hold against God while it is not right at all against God. We know that Congolese people hate the truth because they won't pay attention. It doesn't make any sense.

Why do Congolese people act stupider than citizens of other African countries? Why are Congolese people so silly, especially because they don't want Marie resurrected? Why can Congolese people not get along with one another like people in other countries? Jesus Christ will come back soon. Please, Congolese people, please repent. We understand the revelation of the Bible, but they don't. Congolese are only fooling people in the name of Christ. I will post all of my chapters, "Homage for Ms. Marie Misamu," "Resurrection for Ms. Marie Misamu," "Message for RDC," "Homage for A Friend," on social media, like Facebook, YouTube, and other Internet sites so Congolese people and the whole world will see. And we wanted a good challenge in Congolese Gospel and over place in the Whole World. Thanks

God bless you guys so much.

These proof that these people are still corrupted by the of government in RDC (Congo) and (Pastors at Kabila, C Kanyama receives supports pastors).

Government, Police and Military are Members of the KKK

In the 1960s, the Klu Klux Klan (KKK) used to kill black people as well as burn their houses and hang them because the KKK didn't like black people. Today, the KKK has become disbanded due to human rights. This organization is shameful; they can no longer dress in white clothing and cover their faces. However, many white people in the United States have changed their strategies regarding the killing of black people and eliminating blacks from the United States and the rest of the world. This type of racism resembles the way in which the German people would oppress blacks in Germany, Europe, and the entire world, because the Germans are still racist and continue to murder black people like the Americans do. The government, police, and military have enough power that nobody can tell them what to do or not what to do because they are too powerful; they can abuse their power and kill people in any way that they wish. However, this behavior is still against the law.

There some people that are still members of the KKK, but they can't publicly declare their status because their membership is embarrassing. For this reason, there are many people in the United States and Canada who dislike black people. These people will often apply for government, police or military jobs. For this reason, there are many bad governments, such as Republicans and Conservatives in North America, especially in Canada and the United States. Many members of the government, soldiers, and especially the police are members of KKK because they don't like black people; they are still racist and continue to kill many black people in North America. However, these people are under-cover KKK, including North American federal governments. Their undercover KKK membership is illegal. The same thing happens in Europe, especially in Germany, UK, and Netherlands.

Many citizens of Europe, including the federal govern-ment and especially the police, are members of Nazis who still discriminate against black people and commit racism. These Europeans also continue to kill many black people, who die every year. The same pattern occurs in Eastern Europe, South Eastern Europe, and Russia, as these people still discrimi-nate against blacks and kill black people. This behavior is still wrong and it's against the law. Many people have become angry with the government. Mostly, policemen and police-women are guilty of black people's deaths. Policemen and policewomen won't receive entry into heaven because they will die; nobody is going to live forever on this earth.

I don't understand why someone would want to take someone's life away if nobody has taken his/her life. So, at the end of the day, God will judge the police and ask why the police have murdered innocent people. The police are never allowed to murder people because it's against the law. However, police continue to murder people; they don't seem to care that murder is wrong. Many police conspire with the government and loose their jobs because of their actions. Murder is never right; the police need to stop killing innocent people. Murderers like police will not go to heaven;

that's what the Bible states. Personally, I'm not critical of police brutality; it is the public who criticize the police and the public will never stop criticizing police officers because they will continue to commit illegal actions like murder. Police crime and police brutality makes me angry; however, I'm not against the police.

What I am about to say is the truth. Racism in North America, Europe, Australia, and New Zealand, especially in the United States, occurs against blacks rather than other races, such as Asians, Arabs, Mulattos, Jews, Caucasians, Latinos, Indians, and Aboriginals. Blacks are unique in that they experience racism and murder throughout the entire world. These occurrences make me angry; I feel extremely insulted and experience pain in my heart. I can't believe that racial profiling and discrimination against black people continues to exist. People from North America, Europe, Australia and New Zealand, and South African want to eliminate black people from the entire world by murdering them, shooting them, poisoning them, and infecting them with diseases, such as Ebola, AIDS/HIV, or cancer. Jesus will not let this happen; he will still protect us without being afraid. This behavior is similar to how Hitler taught the Germans to eliminate certain races from the earth. However, the complete genocide of black people will never happen.

I'm not against any government, such as Conservatives or Republicans. I just speak the truth and their behavior makes me upset. For example a young boy named Muhammad was arrested in the United States. He was not a terrorist simply because of a picture that he drew; he drew a watch and not a bomb. Nor did he have a bomb. Some white American elementary or junior high student called the police on him without verifying the truth. The police shouldn't arrest an innocent boy like that. The white policeman should have verified the truth before being brutal and arresting him. That police officer lost his job because he demonstrated brutality with an innocent child and the male schoolteacher was accused and got suspended for one month. The next time an incident like this happens, the teacher will lose his job. The Americans need to stop discriminating against and insulting Muslim people. The police officer and teacher discriminated against Muhammad only because he had a Muslim name. Just because someone is a Muslim doesn't mean he is a terrorist; he is an innocent child. I am not defending a Muslim people in particular; I'm not a Muslim, but I have friends who are Muslim. Muslims are people like everybody else. The Americans, Canadians, and British need to stop discriminating against Muslim people. Most Muslims are not terrorists because terrorism has nothing to do with that religion; we should respect Islam people because they are all human beings like us.

Two Louisiana policemen in the United States were charged and lost their jobs for murdering a man and his innocent six-year old son. That man was an alcoholic or drug dealer; he and his son had no weapon. The two policemen could have smashed the window, grabbed the man, threw him on the floor, and arrested him. In this case, the police would have been doing their jobs; however, the police shouldn't have shot and killed that guy and his son. The police claimed that they killed the man because his car collided with the police cruiser; however, this incident doesn't warrant police officers shooting them and killing them. Once the two policemen came out of their car, they started to shoot the man and even kept shooting the six-year old boy. The boy received multiple gunshot wounds to his head and died. Basically, the two

Louisiana policemen killed that innocent six-year old boy. Later, the two policemen were charged and lost their jobs; shortly after, they received the death penalty in the United States.

In South Carolina, a police officer at Spring Valley High School was charged and lost his job for racial profiling. I don't understand why the black high school teacher couldn't solve a problem with his own black student instead of calling the police. It was not right what the teacher did; he was suspended. The black teenager should not interrupt the class and make noise. Also, she shouldn't refuse to obey a teacher in the middle of his lessons. Once the high school teacher called the police, the police arrived at the school. The policeman was requested to remove the student from the classroom; however, he brutalized and assaulted her by pushing her and throwing her on the desk and handcuffing her. In addition, the police arrested other innocent black students. The policeman's behavior was not acceptable, as he hurt a black female student. Policeman should not treat women in this way. After the incident, many black students skipped school or couldn't concentrate on their studies and homework, which would help them to receive good marks for passing their courses and obtaining their diploma. This, in turn, would allow them to have better jobs and lives. However, black students couldn't have those chances if they failed and were kicked out of school, all because a policeman was racist and abused his power. The policeman beat and assaulted black students. He almost murdered a black teenage boy and assaulted a black teenage girl. All of the students in the school had cameras on their cellphones and filmed the officer assaulting the students. This provided proof that the policeman was guilty. The officer was charged and lost his job; now, he's in prison. He will experience real prison life. The actions that he performed were illegal; after the female student girl refused and resisted, the police showed direct brutality against her. However, it doesn't matter if someone refuses or resists against police authority; the police cannot brutalize someone simply because that person has refused or resisted. It is still illegal for the police to brutalize someone; the police can still lose their jobs for this action. Many police officers have lost their morals, which is not the way that they should operate. I have tried not to insult the police officers despite the fact that many police officers aren't doing their job correctly, which leads people to become angry with them. The police officer at Spring Valley High School in South Carolina was a very immoral person; eventually, he lost his job because he deserved to lose his job and spend life in prison.

Countries such as Canada, the UK, Australia, and New Zealand cannot discriminate against people and deport immigrants from the country because it is against the law. When people spend a long time in their countries, they should have permanent residency or citizenship without experiencing discrimination. If immigrants promise to become a permanent resident or citizen without lying or changing their mind, the Immigration Department or government cannot cancel their permanent residency or citizenship and keep questioning immigrants. These actions are discrimination and against the law. It doesn't matter whether someone is a regular citizen who works for immigration or government, is a governor, is a minster, or is the Prime Minister; nobody can question or report you based on your status in Canada. This is immoral and illegal, as it constitutes discrimination. Nobody can stop you or has a right to report or complain about you. People have a right to complain and report illegal immigrants as long that person has all paperwork as proof with them during court. The immigration officials, governors, or government employees will get in big trouble and lose their jobs for refusing to give someone the proper status, such as Permanent Resident or Citizen. The government should give proper statuses to people without questioning them or complicating the process, as this is discrimination. The Prime Minister or his minsters cannot refuse to help people who have problems because it is part of their jobs; otherwise, without their help, people will have problems. Otherwise, the government officials will lose the next terms and nobody will vote for them anymore. That's the policy for helping people.

Race Wars & Police Brutality

One young Congolese woman was victimized by the police in Brussels, Belgium. Before she came to Belgium, she went to the Belgian Embassy in the RDC. The Ambassador told her that she could come to Belgium without any problems. This young Congolese woman and her parents had been immigrants and lived in Belgium for about 25 years. Her whole biological family, including her parents and her young siblings, are all permanent residents or citizens of Belgium. She could have also achieved resident or citizen status if her parents influenced her to come to Europe. When she came to Belgium, she had been living with her parents for 7 months. She was not a criminal nor had she broken the law. She hadn't done anything wrong. However, the government treated her badly, disrespected her, and committed discrimination and racism against her only because she was black; this is not right and shouldn't happen to her. She was charged by the police and brutally arrested by 5 policemen. After, she was deported from Belgium to Congo, and her parents were upset. Her parents were in the Belgium airport to bring her straight to an airplane for her deportation. The young lady had asked to use the washroom, but the police refused and continued to treat her badly, as if she was a thief or criminal. At the end of the day, she felt angry because she hadn't done anything wrong and was innocent. She screamed for help while the 5 policemen, along with 5 other officers, abused her. They used force against her and embarrassed her in public at the Brussels Airport. Many people were upset at the 10 policemen, and other people swore at the police when they forced her into an airplane.

However, the cops removed her from the plane and brought her back to the airport. Then, they brought her to a police military helicopter by a secret route. When people became angry with the police, the officers started to accuse her of resisting arrest. They argued: "we tried to gently put you in a plane, but you started to embarrass us in public, making other people angry at us for no reason. We are so angry with you that we could shoot you and kill you right away." The police told her this lie and abused her by violently forcing her onto the airplane. This incident wasn't her fault; the police and government were responsible for this situation. However, the policemen around the police military helicopter continued to mistreat her, attacking, beating, and kicking her in the stomach. The 10 male police officers men threatened her again with violence and used racial slurs against her, calling her a "black monkey" and claiming that black people don't belong in Belgium and other in European countries. Although the police officers almost killed her, she survived the Belgium police attack, went to the hospital, and was brought to the refugee centre, where she was not allowed to go outside because her life was in danger from abusive police treatment. Everything that the policemen did to her was against the law and was filmed on camera. Her parents were upset with the government and the police; they reported the incident to the court and found a good lawyer to help them and defend her. The police and government separated her from her family, who isn't allowed to visit her or even contact her anymore; in addition, the government and police threatened her family members. Later the lawyer was upset with the police and government because their actions are wrong and illegal. The lawyer claimed that the government and police can't deport the young lady from Belgium to Congo and they can't use discrimination and racism against her because of her skin color. In addition, the court ruled that the police can't arrest her, threaten her, put her in the refugee centre, or separate her from her own family. Finally, all 10 policemen were charged for their illegal actions against her. All 10 police officers lost their jobs and have spent their whole life in prison because the incident had been filmed, catching the policemen on camera. The government had to pay her damages for mistreating her. She had the opportunity to stay in Belgium, and after two months, she became a permanent resident and citizen of Belgium. Fortunately, her parents had spent a long time in Belgium, so wasn't considered an illegal person in Belgium.

One man, who had Congolese, British and Indian heritage, had lived in the UK since he was a small child. He had grown up in the UK and had British citizenship. Although he has Congolese ancestry, he didn't know anything about Congo or know anyone in Congo, and he had a British accent and British mannerisms. He had never done anything wrong or committed a crime, and he had no criminal record. The government knew that he was very nice and respectful person. He always worked hard and automatically paid his taxes to the government. He had been a soldier in the British army and visited different countries, but he had never commited a crime in any country. Although I don't know the exact problem, I do know that the government could have solved the problem instead of deporting him. Part of the problem resulted from a journalist. While some journalists are ethical, many journalists are liars, and hypocrites that accuse other people of illegal actions. Once, this British man was interviewed by a female journalist a few times. After the interview, the journalist and some of her travelled outside of the UK to find his biological family and interview them. The journalists wanted to and check his background without asking the man's permission and without his awareness. When they got his information, the female journalist and her coworkers should have told the truth about him, but they didn't do this. Rather, they twisted his story, made false statements against him, and secretly filmed his private life without his knowledge or permission. As a result, he got in trouble with the government, which lead to brutalization and arrest from the police. Then, he was deported from the UK to Congo because the government believed the media's false report about him. Although I don't know the exact story that the journalists told about him, the government should not have deported him because of the reporter's false information.

In this case, the government's actions were truly illegally because the Congolese-British man was a British citizen who had had lived his whole life in the UK. The government shouldn't have taken his British citizenship away and deported him from the UK, which forced him to part from his British wife and his two sons, 2 and 4 years old. The journalist claimed that this man had committed murder while in the British army; however, the female journalist female was a liar and wanted to destroy his life. When the police arrested him, they used brutality. Since he was innocent, he felt upset about the brutalization that the two police used against him. The officers pushed him on the floor because he refused to comply with their deportation orders. Two policemen grabbed their guns and shot him 40 times. He died in the London airport, and his British wife was very upset. The female journalist, her coworkers, the government, and the two police officers were responsible for the innocent man's death. All of these people were charged and lost their jobs. Now, the two police officers are in prison serving life sentences. The journalist and her coworkers were arrested and lost their jobs. The public protested against the government, the journalists, and especially the police for their brutality. The man's British wife, who loved her husband very much, passed away from a heart attack because she was so sad that her husband had died three years ago. As a result of her death, her two children are left with no one to care for them. The government and police didn't care about the man, his wife, or their children. After the wife's death, another protest arose in London, accusing the government and journalist along with her colleagues. However, the protesters mainly targeted the two police officers with accusations, threats, and violence. While the citizens and other immigrants in the UK were angry, some other people killed the police with gas and fire. In one incident, 4 policemen sitting in their car had died. This incident created a rivalry between the police, government, citizens and immigrants. In Sweden, police officers were charged for criminal offenses and lost their jobs for murdering and threatening innocent citizens and immigrants.

Journalists can perform illegal actions against you after they have interviewed you; you never know what they will do with the information. Once journalists interview you and get to know you, they want to interview you again, and some of them may try to force you to tell them confidential information about your life. Once malicious reporters get your information, they may illegally film you and take your pictures without your knowledge or permission. It doesn't matter if you have refused to conduct subsequent interviews; they will interview your family members, your friends, former acquaintances, or your lawyer without asking your permission. Your family members, friends, and acquaintances may provide false or inaccurate information about you while you were telling the truth. Once you share the information about your private life with journalists, they have a permanent record of your information. They will check your background; they will film you and take your pictures so that they have access to your private life. The journalists that interview your family and friends without your knowledge and without asking your permission are committing illegal acts, especially the ones that get your information and your address.

The journalists should share the truth about you to the media; however, most of them twist your story to make false statements or provide false information about you. Although the government knows that journalists lie, they won't consult the source; they will immediately believe the journalists without believing you. Through the deceit of journalists, people get in trouble with the government despite the fact that they have done nothing wrong. These misunderstandings could cause people to get deported out of their country, arrested by the police, or killed by the police. After their deportation, people can become ill with heart disease and die. The police or government can separate people from their family members, spouses, children and best friends. They will forbid people to contact their friends and family and keep controlling people in other ways. All of these consequences are not right and against the law, so the journalists and police will get caught, especially if someone has proof or evidence. The police, government, and journalists can also get in trouble and lose their jobs because these actions are really against the law. As a result, many citizens get upset and threaten the police with violence. Journalists are never to be trusted because of all these consequences. If you are doing some undertaking or you have published something, you should mention it to your friends, family members, or people you know and can trust, so that they can refuse journalists from any companies, like national or international channels, CBS, CCB, BBC, CNET, to interview with them. You yourself should also refuse any interview offers; although it is your choice, I advise you against speaking with journalists.

Here are some rules to remember when speaking with journalists:

1. Don't let any journalist interview you
2. Don't share any information about your private life with any journalist
3. Journalists are not allowed to force anyone to interview with them
4. Journalists can't have your information and your address.

These rules of advice will help you to avoid problems with the government and police, such as deportation from any country, arrest by the police, and even death. For these reasons, we can't trust the journalists. I don't want to generalize journalists or criticize them; I tell the truth about what people have experienced with them. Many journalists have destroyed people's lives and caused people's death. In these cases the journalists, rather than the citizens, are responsible for these incidents; however, the police are even worse. You can report journalists if they have taken illegal actions against you, and if you have proof of their guilt, they can be charged and lose their jobs. Most journalists don't do their jobs properly. Sometimes, they exaggerate information and tell lies about people to make profit, which makes people angry with them. Journalists put their own lives at risk if they don't know that their behavior is illegal, because when people become angry, they may attack the journalists. If any journalist films you with cameras or interviews you without asking your permission, you shouldn't get offended unless it is a serious offense. In particular, you shouldn't swear, attack them, or even yell at them. Otherwise, you will make the situation worse and create more trouble for yourself. If you make journalists angry, they may report you to the police or the courts. Since you don't want this situation, you could report them to court. Some journalists are hypocritical and exploit people without their awareness. For example, malicious journalists filmed a British princess naked and published the video in the media. Rightly, the Princess was angry. How could the journalists film her naked in her private residence without her awareness? Eventually, the journalist lost his job because of this incident. His actions were illegal because journalists shouldn't go to her house without asking her permission. For this reason, public journalists aren't to be trusted any more because you never know what they are going to do with your information. That's why you should be smart with them and be careful with what you say during an interview; in fact, I suggest that you don't ever interview with them. The female journalist that lied about the British and Congolese man entering the UK illegally claimed that she made a mistake. However, she didn't make a small mistake because her lie could cause him to face deportation, while a minor mistake wouldn't cause a major issue like this. This problem should have been fixed instead of deporting him from the

UK because he followed all of the rules and laws. This is why people become angry with the government and police.

A man named Roberto came to the United States from El Salvador; he had an American wife and 4 sons. Roberto was a very good husband who took responsibility for his wife and children, and he was a hard worker that owned his own construction business and always paid his taxes. The government and police knew that Roberto was a good and honest person who had no criminal record. However, the government and police mistreated Roberto by exercising discrimination and racism against him because he was of Latino origin. That was not right. They shouldn't charge him, arrest him, separate him from his wife and children or take his American citizenship away and deport him back to El Salvador. The way in which the police and government treated him was wrong and against the law. Roberto's wife, sons, family members, friends, and his employees were upset with the government and police. Roberto lost everything, including his own business, which was really upsetting. Robert had lived in the US for a long time, about 25 years. Since he came to the US when he was 14 years old, the government shouldn't deport him and take his US passport away.

Another man from El Salvador, Andrea Mendes, lived in Chicago, USA for 5 years. He had become a permanent resident of the US and he had never committed any crime or broke the law, so he didn't have a criminal record. He left his wife and daughter in El Salvador, so after five years and two months, he tried to bring his wife and daughter to the United States, but he didn't have enough money. His wife talked to him on the phone so that Andrea could arrange for his wife to send his daughter to live with him. The wife went to the American Embassy, who approved of the move.

Andrea was so happy when his daughter came to the United States. She lived with him for 3 years in the United States. Three years after his daughter moved to the US, he tried to arrange for his wife to come to Chicago. When he asked the government, government agreed that his wife could move to the US. However, the government started to harass him and discriminate against him because he is a Latino man; this is wrong of the government. The government should have given him the proper application to fill in for moving his wife. He could read, write, and speak English fairly well but not as fluently as most citizens in United States. He had found out that the government had been lying to him about allowing his wife to come to the US. Now, he was facing to deportation from the United States to El Salvador. In two months, he would have to leave his daughter. The government and police threatened him several times and separated him from his daughter, forbidding him to have contact with his daughter anymore. They also nullified the permission they had given his wife to come to the US, so that his wife is no longer allowed to come to the US. This situation was so frustrating for him, especially since he received no justice for the discrimination against him. He had even spent lots of money on lawyers that refused to help him in this situation. Andrea's friends and daughter were so upset with the government and police. Many Latino communities protested the incident. They believed that the government shouldn't deport him from the US, stop his wife from coming to the US, and leave his daughter in the US without the opportunity to contact her parents. Nobody was going to take care of his daughter or pay for her schooling. The government can't separate people's families, spouses, and friends, especially people that have known each other for a long time. Why couldn't the government allow both Andrea and his daughter to become American citizens and why couldn't they allow his wife to come to the US and become an American citizen over the next three years? Deportation and discrimination is truly against the law. In Andrea's case, the government didn't provide him with a real reason. They claimed that he broke the law for fighting with someone; however, Andrea was defending his daughter when an American citizen attacked her. Andrea had apologized to the government, and they had forgiven him in the case that he didn't get in another fight. They shouldn't make excuses to continue complicating the situation. His deportation caused a six-month protest in Chicago. The government and police need to stop deporting and oppressing people because these actions violate the law and put the government and police at risk of a public protest. Finally, the court ruled that Andrea and his daughter could become US citizens and he could bring his wife to the country.

Monica is a 26 year-old Mexican-American who lived in Miami, Florida for 12 years. As an American citizen, she had never committed a crime or broke the law in the United States. She had a very good education and surfed as a hobby. She had completed her high school and college diplomas. Monica had a good job in Miami and always paid her taxes. Since her father died from a car accident and her mother died from breast cancer, Monica was adopted by Americans when she was 15. She used to speak and understand Spanish; however, she no longer remembers the language. She has a vague memory of Mexico and has forgotten her Latino cultural heritage. Monica's gestures, accent, and culture resemble those of Americans. However, she identifies herself as an American; she loves the US because she grew up in the States and was raised by American stepparents. She was respectful and obedient to her stepparents, and they treated her with respect. Later, the Miami government discriminated against her because she has Latino heritage. However, they shouldn't classify her as a Mexican or Latino because she is not part of that category anymore. The American government can't deny her rights or take her citizenship away and deport her from the US to Mexico. These actions are discrimination, racism, and against the law. The police had threatened her several times. Finally, the policemen and policewomen lost their jobs because of that behavior, which put her life in danger. Finally, her stepparents, stepsiblings, and friends defended her against deportation. She can never leave the US because she doesn't know Spanish and she doesn't know anyone in Mexico. Now, she can stay in the United States and keep her American citizenship because she has lived in the USA for a long time.

Daniella was an 18 year-old Colombian-American who was born in New York. Her accent, culture, and gestures all resembled those of Americans because she is an American citizen that grew up in the states although her parents came from Colombia. Danielle and whole family lived for a long time in the United States. However, the American government took away her citizenship and deported her from the United States to Columbia. These actions caused a major protest in the Latino community, which involved fights with the police. Daniella doesn't know anybody in Columbia or any Columbian culture, so she can't survive in that country. Her whole life is in the United States rather than in her parents' country. The United States can't remove her citizenship and deport her; these actions constituted discrimination and racism against Daniella only because she is a Latina; this is wrong. She was a very kind and innocent person who had never committed a crime or broke the law. She had never done anything wrong, so she can't be treated badly like that by the government.

In Toronto, there was a protest against the Immigration board because of the way in which the government treated an Indian lady, who had lived in Canada for 35 years. She had never done anything wrong, committed a crime or broken the law. I don't understand why the immigration board couldn't solve the problem and fix it with her. According to the government, she hadn't filled in some document. This doesn't seem like it was a big problem, so the government could have warned her nicely so that she can correct her small mistake and avoid repeating it again. The government shouldn't deport her from Canada to India and take cancel her Canadian citizenship; these actions were against the law because she only made a minor mistake. This small problem shouldn't cause her to get deported and lose her citizenship. After her deportation, she wasn't allowed her to have any more contact with her husband, children, grandchildren, and family. After she arrived in India, she died of a heart attack because she missed her family and she loved Canada. After her death, there was more protest against the government, immigration, and police. Other Canadian citizens were upset and protested with violence and threats, while her family was extremely angry. Some police were attacked and killed by other citizens, while other citizens burned police cars and buildings. There was lots of violent fighting between the police and citizens, which created a terrible situation. The Indian lady's family and the citizens accused the police, government and immigration board.

Police Criticism

Members of the public criticize the police and the way in which they perform their jobs, especially the unnecessary police brutality. I'm not criticizing the police; I'm only sharing the opinions of people that are upset with policemen and policewomen officers. Here are some examples:

In Rohnert Park, CA, a policeman was caught on camera and lost his job because of illegal police brutality. When the older policeman came out of his car, he pulled a gun on an innocent man and threatened him with violence because that man was filming on his cell phone. The civilian told the officer: "put your gun away from me, please; I haven't done anything wrong to you." In response, the policeman refused to listen to him and continued to point his gun at him with threats of violence. However, the civilian's friend saw the incident and secretly filmed it. The friend was right to film the police to make sure that they are doing their job properly. The civilian and his friend were complaining that the older officer was wrong, and they showed the videos, which had proof and evidence. That's why the police officer in Rohnert Park was caught on camera and lost his job. He was performing illegal actions, which, as a police officer, he shouldn't do.

A Boston officer was caught on camera and lost his job because he threatened a cameraman and pulled a gun on him, waving it in his face.

An Austintown, OH police officer was caught on camera and later lost his job because he illegally arrested a man who was filming in public. However, the man had gotten permission to film in public, so the policeman shouldn't have stopped him. This incident doesn't make any sense.

A Philadelphia cop and co-workers were charged and lost their job because they arrested a black man, punched him, and pointing a gun on him, while other officers handcuffed him. The public was upset with the officers for their illegal actions. They were caught on camera and lost their jobs. That black man was innocent and hadn't done anything wrong nor had a weapon.

An innocent 14 year-old black boy was sitting down. Although he hadn't done anything wrong, a policeman started harassing that black teenager by slapping him, pulling him, and brutalizing him. That teenage boy became upset and swore at the officer. However, this situation was not the boy's fault; it was the policeman's fault because he didn't respect the boy. The cop called eight of his coworkers, and when they arrived, all nine officers assaulted the boy, throwing him on the floor and putting him in handcuffs. It was wrong of nine cops to gang up against a single boy, especially since he was black. The nine cops were caught on camera; as a result, they were charged and lost their jobs for harassing, assaulting, arresting, and insulting the boy because of discrimination and racial profiling.

In New York, one shabby black woman, who hadn't done anything wrong, had a problem in a clothing store. I don't the exact problem, but the store employees treated her poorly and discriminated against her. Then, they called the police. When the police showed up at the store, a young male police officer started to brutalize her. He provoked her into fighting by slapping her in the face and forcefully assaulting her. The other five police officers threw her on the floor and kicked her before arresting her. The officers started choking her; when she couldn't breathe anymore, she died from a heart attack. The six policemen were caught on camera, charged, and lost their jobs for brutalizing, assaulting and murdering her. Now, the police officers face a life sentence in prison for racial profiling because she was black. In addition, the clothing store employees were accused and lost their jobs.

In another incident that occurred in New York, two policemen were caught on camera, charged, and lost their jobs for racism and brutality. These two male officers showed up at the metro to arrest a black woman who had done nothing wrong. She asked the two police officers: "Why do you guys detain me and why I should get off of the metro?" The police didn't want to give her a specific answer because they knew that they were wrong. The police grabbed her aggressively, pulled her out of her chair, forced her out of the metro, threw her on the floor, and put handcuffs on her. Then, the two policemen beat her with sticks until she was almost dead. However, she was taken to hospital and managed to survive the incident. Later, the two male police officers were arrested and charged. They will now spend the rest of their lives in prison because of their illegal actions and racial profiling.

In Chicago, two policemen and one policewoman are now in prison because they illegally assaulted an innocent black woman on a plane. The employees of Spirit Airlines had harassed her and discriminated against her. After they called the police, the officers came onto the plane and forcibly removed and brutalized her, claiming that she was disruptive. They assaulted her, breaking her arm only because she was a black person. Later, the employees were accused and lost their jobs. The public was very angry with Spirit Airlines as well as the police.

In another incident in eastern USA, policemen were accused and are now in prison because they pulled an innocent woman out of her car. They used brutality to throw her on the ground. One officer grabbed a knife, stabbed her, shot her in the head, killing her. These two policemen lost their jobs and face the death penalty.

In Turkey, two policemen were charged for killing an innocent woman in Istanbul. Now, they are in prison for life because they shot her twice.

In New York, 10 police officers are in prison for life because of their racial profiling against an innocent black woman. She had called 911 for some problem. When the officers arrived, they should have asked about the problem. However, one policewoman started to accuse her and yell at her. Then, the officer grabbed a stick to hit her, while a policeman ran over to her, threw her to the floor, and kicked her 5 times in the head. In total, 10 police officers attacked an innocent woman. After they kicked her several times, she was bleeding badly. She was rushed to the hospital, where they discovered that she had suffered brain damage, and she later died. The 10 police officers were charged, arrested, and lost their jobs for their racial profiling and murdering an innocent black woman, who was the mother of two young children.

One former police officer in civvies was charged and lost his job for throwing a black woman on the floor and continuously assaulting her although an older woman had attacked the black woman first. The older lady was also charged and lost her job.

In an airport, a policeman was charged and lost his job for illegal actions and racial profiling. He had beat a black woman and shot her 12 times, killing her.

In Texas, a policeman was charged and lost his job for racial profiling against a pregnant black woman. He had slapped her and sexually assaulted her. Similarly, in Chicago, a white officer lost his job and was charged for punching a pregnant black woman.

The Mexican President was very angry with American police that use racial profiling against innocent Mexican immigrants in the United States, especially for deporting them and killing them. These actions are against the law, and police shouldn't act like that. One innocent Mexican man, a Latino, was had no weapon or no drugs and he hadn't done anything wrong. However, the police stopped him and shot him twice for no reason. The officer that killed him was charged, lost his job, and faces the death penalty in Texas.

A man in Fort Saskatchewan, AB was charged and faces life imprisonment for shooting his ex-girlfriend, a mother of 5 children.

Swedish police officers were charged and lost their jobs for mistreating innocent people, yelling at people, assaulting people with sticks, killing people with guns, and fighting with civilians. These officers are often racist against foreigners, mostly black people in Sweden.

One British officer lost his job for assaulting an Iranian woman and breaking her ribs during a political protest. Normally, people shouldn't show their anger with the police; however, people have a right to be angry with the police, as long as they don't yell at them, swear at them, and touch them. The police don't have the right to attack you and arrest you for no reason. These actions are illegal, so the police can be charged and lose their jobs.

In September 2015, policemen were caught on camera for mistreating, deporting, and murdering refugees in Hungary. These refugees were newcomers to Hungary, so they may have accidentally made a mistake. However, the police attacked them and brutalized them. In particular, the police attacked and beat young children, and they attacked and sexually assaulted women. The Hungarian policemen used more violence against people. They killed people without burying them; they cremated or drowned the bodies. In addition, they put people in prison to die without allowing their friends or family to contact them. These actions are morally wrong and against the law. Later, Hungarian police officers were charged and lost their jobs. Although the Hungarian leader was removed from power because he made bad laws and angered the citizens, the police were more responsible for discrimination, racial profiling and murdering immigrants and refugees in Hungary and deporting them. In addition, Hungarians shouldn't built higher gates or fences between the Hungarian and Serbian borders to prevent people from other countries from entering Hungary. One female journalist in Hungary was charged and lost her job because she performed illegal actions, such as tripping and kicking people that were refugees in Hungary. When the refugees tried to escape police brutality, the journalist tried to stop them. The brutal police lost their jobs for bothering innocent refugees and immigrants.

Six California policemen were charged for the illegal action of stopping an innocent man, detaining him, beating him, assaulting him, and stealing $5000 of money from him. The police thought that the innocent man was a drug dealer but he wasn't one. He worked as an employee at a temp agency, where he worked to pay his rent, bills, and taxes as well as save money. This man was the husband of one wife and the father of 7 children. However, the police assaulted him only because he was black. The six police faced a sentence of life in prison.

In Edmonton, AB, Canada, a Canadian man that worked at a temp agency, TLC, was stopped by the police when he came from work. This man was coming from work after midnight, because he worked from 3 p.m. to 12 a.m. At 1:30 a.m., the police in Edmonton detained and stopped him for nothing while he was innocent. The police assaulted him and threw him on his back at West Edmonton Mall despite the fact that he had no drugs or weapons. One officer stole $300 of his money $300; the officer took $100 for himself, and $100 for each of his two coworkers. They laughed at him, made fun of him, and spit in his face. A police helicopter had the camera on and a machine gun ready. As a result, this innocent Canadian man got killed and shot by a machine gun from a police helicopter. The other policemen in the mall shot him twice more. All officers involved in the situation were charged and face life in prison. Why were these policemen acting illegally and telling lies about the man fighting with cops? The surveillance camera showed everything; the Edmonton police were wrong because that guy was innocent. This incident happened in 2008.

In another case, The RCMP were caught on camera for arresting an innocent man and taking him to prison. When they put him in prison, two policemen started to attack and assault him. They smashed his head on the floor, causing bleeding and damage. He was taken to hospital and became handicapped, leading to his death two months later. The two policemen lost their jobs and went to prison. Another RCMP officer was charged and lost his job in Alberta for illegally arresting an innocent man in a public library and murdering him by choking him to death.

Toronto officers illegally arrested two innocent men. A police officer in the metro station assaulted innocent men, punching them seven times until their faces were injured and bleeding. Later, the Toronto cops lost their jobs.

One undercover RCMP cop displayed racism against an innocent man from India. The officer stopped the man, yelled at him, threatened him, and swore at him. The officer was caught and lost his job. Similarly, other undercover EPS police lost their jobs for racial profiling and fighting with an innocent black man in West Edmonton Mall.

The Jasper, Texas citizens were angry with two officers because the government didn't charge the two officers and make them lose their jobs. A black woman had an unpaid, overdue traffic ticket and attempted to pay it. She gathered her money to pay the tickets, but the policemen arrested her. After they arrested her and took her to prison, the lady asked if she could phone her family and explain the situation so that they know where she was. Although she took only 5 minutes, the police hung up the phone on her. Although she didn't argue with the police, two officers grabbed her hair and slammed her down on the floor. They beat her until she sustained many injuries; she was almost killed by the two white racist policemen. The surveillance camera saw everything, including two police officers pulling her, hair, stripping her naked, and sexually assaulting her. They almost raped her and killed her. Six months ago, two policemen, Ricky Grisson and Ryan Cunningham, were charged and lost their jobs. Now they will spend their whole lives in prison. If that lady had died, they would have faced to death penalty.

On August 6, 2015, one RCMP police officer in Prince George, BC, Canada was caught on a smartphone camera and lost his job. I don't know the exact problem, but the officer had thought that a guy broke into a store because the window was broken. However, the man didn't steal anything from store; he just slept near the door of store. When the police showed up, he ran away from the police although he

392

was innocent. He shouldn't have run away from the police; it didn't make sense. Once he started running, the police followed him, caught him, pushed him on the floor, and put handcuffs on him. The police officers began sitting on his body so that the guy couldn't breathe anymore. Once another cop arrived, the innocent man was already dead. That's why this policeman was accused and lost his job; he totally murdered an innocent man.

In Hungary, a female journalist was charged and lost her job for stripping an innocent refugee man on the floor because he had run away from police. That lady was caught on camera and lost her job because she shouldn't kick someone on the floor.

Some men in India attacked a woman, poured acid on her face, and killed her. They should be charged and have a life sentence in prison because her actions were racist and a criminal offense. The Somali community, as well as other communities, was angry with the Indian men.

Many people complain about North American police and UK police, especially those in the United States. For example, if you are looking for a place that you can't find, and you need to find the place for something important, like a job interview, school, or banking, cops should help you find it. If you ask an officer about that place, they should explain it to you or show you a place without creating complications or harassing you. However, some police officers kill people, especially single women with children or sexually assault women. Furthermore, police can also ask questions, such as "Where are you going? What are you doing? What time do you have to be there? What time are you coming back?" Then, they can tell people: "If you don't show up or come back, I'm going to charge and arrest you" The police can't treat people like that and ask people questions that are not their business. Also, police can't for people's ID, especially innocent people who aren't criminals that have robbed a bank or store. Why do North American and British police have suspicions about innocent people and refuse to help them? For this reason, people no longer ask the cops for directions or trust them. They prefer asking someone else who can respectfully help them. The North American police and British cops abuse and still abuse their power because they think they can do whatever they want and murder you anytime; however, that's against the law. In the United States, police are worse and more brutal than police in Canada and UK. United States officers refuse to listen to President Barack Obama only because he's black, which is racism. The United States refuses to stop racism, discrimination, crime, and guns. In particular, the police won't stop abusing their power. If they see a black person in the street, the police will stop black people and kill them, so that they can exterminate all black in the entire US and then the rest of the world; that's what Germany wanted to do to the Jewish people. It's wrong and illegal that the police still kill black people in the US. The police and white citizens like to vote for bad leaders, like the American Republicans. If the police continue their illegal actions of murdering black people in US, they will ruin President Barack Obama's reputation by provoking him to say something, which may lead them to murder him. Then, there will be a war in the US; the police will have provoked the war by continuing to kill black people and engage in racial profiling. President Barack Obama is a good person and he's not going to die. If every policeman and policewomen murder innocent people, they should be charged, lose their jobs, and receive a life sentence in prison or the death penalty for their illegal actions. A good government should be strict with police brutality. The United States should stop guns, crimes, racism, discrimination, and police brutality because those issues can cause a serious war. I'm not trying to provoke a war in the United States or any other country. If something happens, please don't blame me or label me, because I have nothing against any country, especially the United States. Barack Obama and new Italian Latino pope are 100% right, but nobody obeys them, especially Republicans. I'm not talking about politics and I'm not against American Republicans, but I speak the truth.

One police officer was charged and sentenced to life in prison because he shot a black man named Samuel Dubose, an innocent person that had done nothing wrong and had no weapon. The young police officer stopped Samuel for no reason and asked him for his ID. Samuel Dubose showed one piece of ID but had left the other one at home. Then, the police started brutalizing him and opened his car. Samuel defended himself, so the police officer grabbed a gun, pointed the gun at Dubose, and shot him in the head, causing Dubose to die in his car. Later, that cop was charged, arrested, and lost his job.   In Ohio, a police officer was charged, lost his job, and received the death penalty for killing an innocent young 16 year-old black boy. Although the boy had no gun, the policeman stopped him. The boy obeyed the officer's request to get out of his car. Then, the police officer grabbed a gun and shot the boy once in his stomach. The boy died within 5 minutes. The 34 year-old policeman lost his job and received the death penalty.

The Edmonton police should be charged because they assaulted an innocent man named Peter. They charged and arrested Peter without any evidence that he did anything wrong. The police put Peter in prison in some part of an old building that had no camera. Later, some people witnessed two police officers assault Peter and injured part of his body. Peter was in the hospital for a while. Later, the two policemen were charged and lost their jobs because of their criminal offense.

The United States is so complicated with racism. Why can a black person never become a president if that person is good and knows how to rule the country? Why do people use violence and threaten black people that intend to run for president? Skin color shouldn't matter; if you were born in the United States, you are still an American citizen. So anybody can become president of the United States as long they can run the country successfully. The presidency shouldn't be restricted to white people. Discrimination and racism cannot continue to exist in the United States.

In California, 10 police officers, eight white officers and two Asian officers, were charged and lost their jobs for racial profiling and assaulting an innocent black man in a wheelchair. With one plastic leg, this man had no power to attack police officers. However, the police officers mistreated him, pushing him on the floor, assaulting him, and illegally handcuffing him. All 10 officers harassed one innocent black man; this was wrong and racist. One white lady tried to tell the officers to stop; she said, "Stop! Enough! Leave him alone! He's innocent. I was there and I saw he had done nothing wrong." One white cop took offense to her statement, and without listening to her, the white cop swore at the white young lady. "Shut up bitch! Who you think you are! Do you think that handicap in a wheelchair can't attack a cop? Mind your own business or I'm gonna arrest you, bitch!" This white cop was also charged and lost his job for saying negative things and threatening that white young female.

In Pennsylvania, USA, a 45 year-old policeman rang the doorbell of a Mulatto woman's home. When the Mulatto woman heard the ring with her daughter, both women asked, "who's this?" The officer answered, "I'm a police officer; open the door please." The Mulatto woman replied, "I'm coming; give me a second, I have to throw clothes on." However, the Mulatto woman opened the door shortly after. The lady respectfully asked the officer the problem, but the police didn't want to tell her specific details because he had planned to harm her. The police officer entered her home illegally without respecting her and asking her permission to enter her home. That lady told him nicely that his actions were inappropriate and embarrassed her in front of her six-year old daughter. The officer replied by disrespecting her and her daughter with threats of violence. He told her, "you don't have the right to tell me anything. If you make one more comment, I will arrest you. I can do whatever I want and enter anyone's house. So women don't have the right to tell male officers what to do." The lady nicely asked the officer to respect her, but the officer raised his voice and yelled at her. Without the officer's knowledge, the lady had a private surveillance camera at her house. The officer forcefully brutalized her and sexually assaulted her. The officer couldn't make an excuse for his behavior. He stripped her naked and embarrassed her in front of her daughter and also in public. He put her handcuffs on her hands. That Mulatto woman was innocent without doing anything wrong. She had been respectful to the officer. However, the officer had disrespected her, illegally arrested her, illegally touched her belongings, and destroyed her belongings by throwing them through the house without cleaning up. He shouldn't have performed these actions because they were illegal. When she came out in public, people laughed at her, made fun of her, and embarrassed her because the police had arrested her naked. Two weeks later, she came out of prison and made a complaint that the 45 year-old policeman was wrong for illegally entering her house, destroying her belongings, harassing her, sexually assaulting her, stripping her naked, embarrassing her in front of her daughter and the public, and arresting her illegally. She had a video with proof of the officer's actions. One week later, the policeman was charged, lost his job, and went to prison. The policeman shouldn't have performed these actions because they were against the law.

One Jamaican man in the United States was very big and muscular; he was stronger than most people, including police officers. This man hadn't committed any crimes or done drugs; He was a very good person and respected all laws. This man had played sports and was trained to defend himself. However, he never started fights with people; he would only fight to defend himself. If the police wanted to arrest him, they would have difficulty tasering him to calm him down or even trying to shoot him. Neither the police nor the citizens could kill him, because that guy was too strong and powerful. That Jamaican man was the strongest and most muscular in his community, so nobody, even another muscular man, would give him trouble because he was very muscular and powerful. He became a part of the government and a police chief; he was a good ruler and a good person.

One man, an American and British citizen, had left the UK a long time ago, and his British passport had been expired for 5 years. This man was planning to go back to London, UK to see his biological family that he missed. Although there was a British embassy in Chicago, he went to a European British embassy to renew his British Passport because he had dual citizenship. Your passport can have expired for 5 or 10 years and you should be able to renew it at any time, as long you were never a criminal. The UK ambassador said they at they could renew his British passport anytime without complications. However, they asked him a bunch of questions: "Where are your travel documents? How long have you been outside of the UK? What did you do for work? How did you make money and survive? Where did you work or study? What are you doing here in this country?" The British Embassy or any other European Embassy, such as the Netherlands, shouldn't ask people these questions, because it shows discrimination and racism. Embassies should let you renew your expired passport anytime and allow you to pick up your passport without problems or complications. If someone with a lot of money or a high status complains or reports an embassy employee, then they will lose their job because it is against the law to refuse to allow someone to renew his/her expired passport. The government can't stop you from renewing your passport and it is also against the law to arrest someone trying to renew a passport. That Jamaican man was right to renew his passport, and the ambassador can't interrogate him with discrimination by asking him questions about his private life, which is none of their business as long as he was never a criminal. This was the first time that he tried to renew his British passport because he lived in the UK for a long time and grew up in the UK. He became angry because the British embassy shouldn't question him and refuse to let him to renew his British Passport because he had left the UK for 10 years. It doesn't make any sense. Once he became angry, the Ambassador called the police in Chicago. In 5 minutes, the police showed up. They should have asked him about the problem because he knew his own rights. However, the 5 policemen started to brutalize him illegally and try to arrest him. He became angrier, and five more policemen showed up. All ten policemen started to fight with him, but this man was too powerful. He fought with ten police officers in self-defense; first, they tried to taser him, but it didn't work. Then, they grabbed a gun to shoot him on his chest or head, but it didn't work because he was too fast, strong, muscular, and powerful. Five cops were injured and went to the hospital, while the other 5 cops attracted the anger of their own community, because the Jamaican man was innocent and it wasn't his fault. Five policemen were charged and lost their jobs because that guy had no weapon, and they shouldn't have pulled their guns out and tried to shoot him because it was against the law. All 10 cops were charged and lost their jobs for brutalizing and assaulting him while he had defended himself against the policemen. He didn't mean to fight with them because he showed respect to the policemen, but they hadn't shown respect to him. The incident was the fault of the police and the British Ambassador rather than the man. They had discriminated against him all because he was black. Later, 6 female employees and 4 male employees lost their jobs because their actions were against the law. This is a true story that actually happened in the US, and a popular movie has been made out of this incident. Some people believe this story while other people won't believe it. This story happened around 2009 or 2010. 10 male police officers learned their lesson and lost their jobs, showing that they can't mess with innocent people, especially those who are very muscular.

In Maryland, US, the Montgomery County Police Officers saved the life of a nine month-old baby girl but brutalized the mother. I don't know the exact problem; the mother may have had a drug addiction or been driving above the speed limit. She hadn't done anything wrong when the police stopped her. However, the officer, James Herman, grabbed her aggressively and broke her arm rather than helping her solve the problem. She had been nice and respectful to him, so he should have treated her the same way. James Herman should respect women because he has a mother, sisters, aunties, and female cousins from both of his parents' sides. Policemen should know how to respect women in general. James Herman received a warning and suspension for two weeks; if the problem occurs again, James Herman will lose his job. It is against the law to disrespect or assault women.

In Canada, four male police officers, which were trained very well and knew fighting techniques for defending themselves and defending others, shot and killed a 16 year-old white boy who didn't have a gun, bomb, machete, or other major weapon. However, the boy had a small knife and was playing with it. He could have been a drug dealer, but I don't think that he was a drug dealer. I don't know the exact problem, similar to the situation with innocent Sammy Yatim, who was killed in Toronto by police officer James Forcillo. Likewise, this teenage boy was innocent, as he hadn't attacked anybody or didn't do anything wrong apart from having a small knife. The boy was 10 meters away from four policemen. When the police officers asked him five times to drop the knife, the boy should obey them, but he didn't listen to them. The police officer should have used a taser to restrain the boy and calm him down without killing him. Although the boy should have obeyed the police, the 4 officers shouldn't have killed him. When I heard the news from someone, I, along with other people, was so angry at the four white police officers because they killed an innocent teenager; the four men shot him six times and killed him. Regardless of the problem, police officers are not allowed to shoot and kill people in Canada and the United States because it is absolutely against the law and they will lose their jobs and spend their whole life in prison; that's the law and the law can't be changed for the citizens or police officers to murder people. The government knows the identity of criminal citizens, especially criminal police officers, who are worse than citizens. Criminal police officers won't stop committing crimes and murder, which isn't fair because people get angry. The laws for criminal police officers and criminal citizens can never be changed. Criminals should learn real lessons by spending the rest of whole their lives in prison, which will be nobody's fault but their own. Soon, the four Canadian police officers will be charged and lose their jobs; they should spend their whole lives in prison because they killed an innocent man for no reason. Why they couldn't they taser him to take his knife away and arrest him? Some police officers are good, but many police officers are bad people. I don't want to generalize police officers; I want only to speak the truth. The job of a police officer is to protect people rather than shooting and killing people. These 4 policemen wee wrong for murdering an innocent guy.

In the UK, one male police officer was charged and lost his job. He's now in prison now and he's going to spend his whole in prison. He displayed racism against an innocent black guy, shooting him 12 times for nothing. The policeman shot him and killed him only because he was a black. I am so angry about that situation.

The Government Cannot Stop Immigration From One Country to Another Country.

The government cannot make laws to stop immigrants, newcomers, and refugees from coming into a country. The government, security, and police cannot stop people all of the time to ask them questions, such as "Where are you going?" What are you doing in this country? How long are you going to stay in this country? When are you going to return to your own country?" Furthermore, they cannot threaten to charge you or remove you from the country, because it constitutes discrimination. Government, police, and security cannot ask people those questions because it is not their business. People can show their passports to security officers, and the appropriate airport authorities can check to make sure that passengers aren't breaking laws, such as terrorism and crime. However, people that respect the rules and laws should be free to go. Authorities need to ensure public safety by making sure that nobody has any weapon, bomb, or other dangerous item, because nobody wants a problem. However, they don't need to ask people about other citizenships because it is not their business, especially if someone isn't a criminal or terrorist while respecting laws and rules. You only need to show security officers your current passport. They don't need to know if people have dual citizenship; people should keep their dual or multiple citizenships as long as they don't break the law and respect the rules. The government can't stop people from having dual citizenships because people have had these citizenships for a long time. However, if your 2 or 3 passports are expired, you can renew them anytime; the government cannot stop you or question you for that. There are no limits on passport renewal. For example, if foreigners had lived in European or North American countries for a long time and had left those countries for a long time, they should still be able to come back to those countries and renew their expired passports anytime without causing problems. The government cannot cause complications for people or cancel people's citizenship and deport them just because they had left their countries for a long time. This treatment is not right, because it can cause violence and threats against the government, and we don't want that. Civilians can become angry with the government when they question people about their activities in a certain country: "Why have you left the country for a long time? What have you been doing outside of the country and how did you survive? How did you come back to the country and where is the stamp on your passport?" The government is not allowed to question people's personal lives, deport people out of the country, or cancel people's citizenships. These actions are against the law and can cause citizens to revolt with violence and threats. Foreigners that have lived for a long time in North America, Europe, Australia and New Zealand cannot be deported and lose their citizenships because it is against the law. Immigration has existed for long time; in fact, it has existed since Biblical times when God told Abraham that he could freely immigrate to any new land and nobody could remove him from that land. This Biblical imperative means that everybody should have the chance to go from one land to another land, so the government cannot stop and deport people or stop the immigration process. Nobody likes wrong laws, which cause people to become angry with the government. In the future, if your country has a problem, you should have the ability to move to another country to find a better life, property, and job. You don't want another country to cause complications and deport you. However, when people come to your country, you can't harass them, discriminate against them, and deport them. Since everybody likes to travel to other places, people are upset with the bad leaders of other countries that make wrong laws against immigrants or foreigners that have lived for a long time in Europe, North America, Australia, South Africa, and New Zealand. Most people want bad leaders to leave power and stop ruling the country. People still want good leaders rather than bad leaders in power because bad leaders always cause threats, violence, and especially police brutality.

The governments of UK, Netherlands, Belgium, Luxembourg, Germany, France, Switzerland, Austria, Italy, Spain, Portugal, Greece, Australia, New Zealand, US and Canada cannot deport immigrants, newcomers, foreigners, and refugees, especially black people because these actions are against the law and cause more violence and threats. Every three years, people living in a new country are accepted as permanent residents or citizens. However, the government should promise to give people permanent residency and citizenship without lying, cancelling people's permanent residency and citizenship, and questioning them, because these actions can cause more problems and threats when people become angry. Why do the governments put their own lives in danger? It doesn't make any sense. People should have permanent residency or citizenship when they have lived for a long time in North America, Europe, New Zealand, Australia and South Africa. These aspects are the government's responsibility. I still respect the government; I'm not against them and I don't want to criticize the government either. However, the public will become angry with the government. However, people still need to make sure that they respect the laws and rules without commit crime, theft, and terrorism. As long as people follow the rules, they will be fine and have the freedom to enjoy their life. The government should give people chances without complicating and controlling them. However, the immigration department performs many illegal actions by separating people from their families, friends, spouses, and partners. These actions make me, along with many other people, upset, especially when police officers at borders and airports commit illegal actions; the officers should be charged and lose their jobs because they shouldn't deport immigrants and refugees that are healthy and lack any disease, such as and HIV/AIDS and Ebola. Some police officers intentionally stop beautiful female immigrants and refugees who come into a country, so that they can illegally assault these women in public or rape them in a private place before deporting them; these actions are against the law. Policemen cannot perform these actions to the citizens of any country. These officers will eventually get caught and lose their jobs. Some Indian, Middle Eastern, African, Caribbean, Asian and Latina women are victimized many times by police officers of North America, Europe, Australia, New Zealand and South Africa and even in some countries of Latin America. These occurrences are totally wrong and against the law. This time, race wars, government domination, and especially police brutality should be gone because people are sick and tired of these abuses of power. These abuses are causing violence and threats, which are not good. Nobody can arrest or deport you and nobody can stop your rights for speaking the truth, especially if you're not a criminal or lawbreaker and you respect the government and police. I don't want to talk about politics, which aren't my business; I want only to speak the whole truth about things that happen and I have my opinions.

Some people think that the world is never going to change, but eventually, one day, the world is going to change. If God says the world will change, then it will change. God is almighty and we can't play games with God. All of the government domination will soon disappear because Jesus is coming back, but it's going to take a while to change. Let God forgive the government and police for the wrongs they are still doing because they don't know what they are doing. Before Jesus died, he asked forgiveness for the people that did wrong to him. I can also forgive people. I don't like violence, threats, or even criticism, and I don't want to say negative things or cause a war. God is my protection forever, so the government or police can't harm me because God will punish them for the rest of their whole lives. This will not be my fault because they will deserve their own fate. God is way better than these people. I don't want anyone to take offense because I don't want to make anyone upset. The problem starts with the government. People that work for the government may belong to government, but those people can make mistakes. However, they don't have weapons, so they don't abuse their power and they don't insult people. Consequently, not many people will complain about them and those people won't have a very bad reputation. A person who works for the police may not have power, but the police as a group have weapons and power; they are the only ones who abuse power to insult people and murder them. Murder is against the law and also the Bible; murderers won't get into the Kingdom of the Heavenly Father God. That's why many complaints will always occur about the police, causing them to get a bad reputation. When the civilians become angry with the police, it won't be the citizens' fault; rather, it will be the fault of the police who operated against the law by doing illegal actions and committing murder. It's total wrong ask good poops of today they will tell you the truth.

The biggest problem with the government involves citizenship issues. If people have a single, dual, or multiple citizenships, you automatically pay taxes to all of the countries that you have citizenships. Europe, Canada, US, Australia, New Zealand, China, Japan, and Israeli passports don't require work permits, study permit, student visas, or work visas. People holding these passports can travel, study, or work anytime in any country. These people can come from one country to go to any another country at any time. People can apply for an application for travel, work, or study, but they don't have to because there are no limits for that. You can travel and go to any other country at any time. The government cannot make laws that stop people from travelling. These laws would be wrong and make many people angry. People from Europe or another place in the world can stay in North America, Australia, or New Zealand anytime without limitations and come back to Europe or another place. Even the North Americans, Australians, New Zealanders, or people from other place can stay in Europe or in Caribbean countries any time and come back to North America, Australia, New Zealand, or other any place at any time. People shouldn't be restricted to staying in a country for only 6 months; people should have the ability to stay in a country for 10 months or even for 7 or 10 years without limitations because some people built their business and houses and some people made large purchases. People should be able to go back to their original country anytime without any problems. You can stay or live in any other country at any time as long as you are not a criminal, a terrorist, or lawbreaker in any country. The government should automatically know that you are in a certain country without bothering you and controlling you as long as you follow the rules and respect the law. The government is not allowed to ask you personal questions, such as the following: "How long are you going to stay in the country and when will you leave the country?" "What are you going to do in the country and what did you do and how do you survive?" These questions are not government business because they involve people's personal private lives. The government can't kick people out of the country because they spent too much time in the country during their vacation. The government cannot treat people like that and make those laws; it doesn't make any sense because people like to travel and have like to travel for a long time. The government cannot stop people for travelling and put limits on people during their vacation so that people can stay in country for only 6 or 7 months. People that have Canadian, European or American citizenship cannot spend very much time in another country because they aren't citizens of those places. It doesn't make any sense. The government shouldn't make these laws and treat people like that. If a Canadian or European citizen wants to spend time in the United States, they should be able to stay in the USA and leave anytime, even during vacation. However if an American citizen wants to live or stay in Europe or in Canada, they should be able to stay there without any time limitations. People can apply for permanent residency and citizenship in any country, and the government should give people these statuses without complications or refusals and without asking any irrelevant personal questions as long as the person is not a law breaker or criminal. There should be trust among the governments and citizens of various countries, including Europe, North America, Australia, New Zealand, and South Africa, especially during vacation. Even new immigrants and refugees who lived in North America, Europe, Australia, New Zealand, and South Africa for a long time should have permanent residency and citizenship for those countries; the government cannot refuse to give these statuses to immigrants and refugees without creating complications or asking them questions and without discriminating against them, especially when the government makes promises. I'm not against the government and I'm not talking about politics; I only speak the truth and fight for people's human rights. It was sad that one Somali man who lives in New York with an American permanent residency is not allowed to become an American citizen because he's black and a Muslim from Africa; this is an example of government discrimination. The government cannot discriminate against Muslims because Muslims are human beings. I become angry with the government because they can't make negative comments and stereotypes about Muslims, because not all Muslims are terrorists. The government should respect all Muslims and Christians because I have many Muslims and Christians friends that are good people. Why do the governments like to generalize people? In Canada, there was a similar issue with another Somalia man that couldn't get his Canadian permanent residency and become a Canadian citizen only because he is black and a Muslim despite the fact that he lived in Canada for 12 years. The government exercised discrimination and racism, which is wrong. He should get a permanent residency and citizenship in Canada.

Let me ask some questions to the government:

1. Why can we not live in peace and make friends with each other?

2. Why do we need to hate each other without living together and without enjoying our lives on Earth?
3. Why do humans have to kill other humans?
4. Why can't the government find positive ways to improve the economies of countries instead of making wars with other countries or creating and selling weapons internally and externally?
5. Why have the governments created crimes that involve discrimination and racism, especially American Republicans and Canadian Conservatives, all because of profit?
6. Why has the government created all kinds of diseases that can kill people, especially HIV/Aids and Ebola, throughout places in the whole world and then refuse to heal those diseases or and stop treatment even though they have lots money, lying that "we don't have money for that sorry" in order to retain their profits?
7. Why do we have false lawyers, criminal police officers, and bad armies that like to kill people because of their profits?
8. Why do doctors in hospitals and clinics refuse to heal people who are sick and make them more sick or kill them because of profit?
9. Why do the government, police officers and military become upset when people lie to them and yet they can lie to people, shoot people, and kill people for no reason?

None of these issues make any sense. There are many better ways to make profits and better solutions to avoid hurting people. The government shouldn't make profit in evil ways, such as creating and selling weapons or bombs, committing crimes, making war with other countries, killing people, creating diseases, like Ebola and Aids/HIV, that can kill people, using criminal police and armies for killing people, deporting people out of the country, separating people from their families, and exercising discrimination and racism. These problems will all be gone if the government stops committing these negative actions. We want positive change throughout the whole world. We don't want the government to cause any more problems, especially violence and threats; these issues will disappear if the government can solve their problems. Why does the government not want to make positive change? In North America, people should never again vote for Conservatives and Republicans, so these parties never come back in power because they don't treat people very well. I still respect the Conservatives and Republicans; I'm not against them but I don't support them either. I just want to continue speaking the truth and fighting for people's human rights so we can live in complete freedom again. I want to emphasize that my intention is not to discuss politics; this is not my business. I still respect politicians and I still respect the government and the laws of all countries in the world. Mr. Donald Trump needs to stop discrimination against Latinos in the United States and he needs to stop to deporting Latinos from the United States to Latin America. He can't just deport Latinos who have lived for a long time in the United States. Mr. Trump makes people very angry; he should respect Latinos and respect the rest of the other immigrants in America. He needs to stop calling people illegal immigrants. The term "illegal Immigrants" makes me and other people angry because it involves discrimination. The Latinos and the rest of the other immigrants in the United

States and in Canada are human beings. I'm not against Mr. Donald Trump; let God forgive him for his bad actions.

Eventually Jesus Christ will come back, which we know for sure. Before He returns, we need to stop our sins and the bad things that we have done on this Earth. We need to repent all of our sins and prepare for ourselves for Jesus Christ's return. We don't know the date that he's coming back. The Bible said that Jesus Christ is a good person but that he will come as a thief so that all of us will get to judge what we have done on this Earth. Jesus will find the people who were honest with him and obeyed him. All of the domination that we see on this Earth will eventually disappear, but it will take a long process before it gets done and victory happens. In particular, we will see the war between Israel and Palestine end. Once the war is done in Israel and Palestine, the real Jesus Christ will return. I'm asking forgiveness for myself from the Heavenly Father and Jesus Christ if I had sinned, lied, or committed a wrong action without knowing because I'm not perfect; I'm not better than the Heavenly Father and I'm not better than Jesus Christ. That's why I'm asking the Heavenly Father and Jesus Christ for forgiveness; I'm sorry that I was wrong and I was a sinner. I really want to get close to the Heavenly Father and I want see my brother Jesus Christ. God received Jesus as my savior. He's my God and he's a good person. I believe in Christ and I hope that I can have eternal life. I don't want to be a sinner anymore and become guilty again. I want all of my all sins to be washed away. This is also a chance for everybody to receive Jesus Christ in their lives; it's very important. Without Jesus Christ, I won't be important; but with Jesus Christ, I'm important. Jesus Christ is great for us. He loves us, and we should love him too. The Bible said that bad leaders, and especially murdering police officers, would not receive the kingdom of the Heavenly Father, which is only for good people. Personally, I don't like to judge or insult anyone. Most of the things that happen in the world are not my business or my problem. Only the Heavenly Father can take care and judge people. The Heavenly Father loves us, and we should love him too. I'm not trying to sell God's word because it is free. Some other churches sell God's word for profit, but I'm not going to judge them. I don't want people going to burn in hell. I want people to receive Jesus Christ, and I want people to obey God in the same way that I received Jesus Christ in my life and I still obey my Heavenly Father God. I want people to go to heaven and have eternal life. I really like to help people, and I want the blessing of God. I don't want my glory; I want the glory of God, which is much higher than personal glory. I want people to follow God; I don't want people to follow me. I want to gain the respect of people like everybody else. Thank you Jesus Christ for being forever with me. I will never leave Jesus Christ; I love him so much and he loves and everybody else. He won't ever leave us as long we will continue put our faith forever in him.

New Ideas, Dialogue, and Technology

I'm going to give more examples that police brutality continues to exist despite its illegal status.

- On June 8, 2015 in Dallas, TX, USA, there were problems between black and white teenagers that were having a pool party. I don't know the exact nature of the problem. However, people were complaining and someone called the police about bikini-clad wrestling. I don't understand why the people didn't tell those teenagers about the problem without calling the police. They could have warned these teenagers so that the next time, they can make sure it doesn't happen and avoid problems. The teenagers didn't understand that they were in a private place. Once police showed up, they asked, "who did this?" The white teenagers claimed that the black teenagers had caused the problem, and the police believed the teenagers without any investigation or proof. The police didn't know that their actions were filmed by camera and that someone was filming them in silence. Once the police accused the black teenagers, a policeman grabbed a black teenage girl, threw her on the ground aggressively, and put handcuffs on her arms. After the police had arrested her illegally, two black teenage guys told the officer, "leave her alone; she has done nothing wrong," while she screamed for help. In response, the policeman threatened the black teenagers; he pulled his gun and pointed his gun at these black teenager boys. This action of pulling a gun and pointing it at a person is illegal; the officer shouldn't have done this because as a policeman, he can be charged and lose his job. These black boys had no guns or other weapons, and they didn't threaten this policeman. After the officer pointed a gun at the boys, the other two policemen ran aggressively towards the boys and arrested them. The policeman who arrested the black teenage girl also threatened the boys and cursed at them. This action was illegal and inappropriate in public. In total, three policemen were caught on camera and charged for their criminal assault and illegal actions. With video evidence, the policemen could not deny or lie about their actions. People should film police officers because some officers aren't trustworthy and continue to commit crimes. Police brutality cannot continue exist all of the time because it could cause legal violations and threats. This time, the government should work towards stopping police brutality. The three officers should lose their jobs because the public was already upset and threatened police officers that put themselves at risk for mistreating citizens. The black teenage boys and girls were innocent and hadn't done anything wrong. Why did the police arrest only black teenagers and not white teenagers? This action truly shows the racism of the police.

- In the United States, one driver did not obey the police when an officer asked 6 times for ID. The driver overreacted; however, the driver's reaction was only a minor problem in comparison to the officer's reaction. After the driver refused to give ID, the policeman continually harassed the driver and stopped him. The policeman was caught on camera and charged because he yelled at the man, grabbed his stick, and smashed his car window. Then, the officer threw the man on the ground and arrested him. The man sustained an injury due to the policeman's actions.

- One day, my brother was driving to pick up his friend. When my brother stopped his car, he texted my friend to come outside. A policeman aggressively approached my brother and started accusing of him of texting while driving. However, the police had no proof, because my brother hadn't texted while the car was in motion. My brother tried to respectfully explain to the officer that he had not texted while driving, but the officer refused to listen to him. The police then asked him to show his ID and driver's license. My brother obeyed the officer and gave him the requested identification. However, the officer became aggressive and threatened my brother. He warned my brother to come out of the car and threatened to throw him on the ground if he refused. In response, my brother told the officer: "you aren't going do that to me because I respect you and you should respect me too; I haven't done anything wrong to you." The officer continued to threaten my brother and yelled at him. Then, my brother's friend showed up and asked: "what's going on?" At this point, the policeman became reserved and denied his actions without being aware that his actions may be filmed on someone else's cellphone. If something happened to my brother, I would have been upset and reacted badly against the officer because I'm not scared of the police. I could report the policeman and have him lose his job, which would be his fault rather than mine. I don't like to fight, threaten or resist an officer because I still respect police officers. I don't have any problem with police officers, but their behavior sometimes makes me upset and hurts my feelings as well as those of others feelings. There are other people who also become upset with police behavior. In Edmonton, AB in 2015, an officer gave my friend an illegal ticket for $500. My friend is a student and doesn't have a good job. My mother and my sister have also been threatened and harassed by a male EPS officer. Someone had hit my mother's car without my mother or sister being aware of the incident. The male police officer wasn't an honest person. While my mother and sister explained the situation to the policeman, the officer didn't believe them; he kept harassing and threatening them. I was more upset with the male police officer. He sent people to conduct an investigation, but the investigation was conducted in a false manner. The officer asked my mother and my sister to obtain witnesses before the officer returned. When the officer came back, my sister had nearly found a witness. However, the officer refused to listen to her and twisted the story. He kept accusing her of lying, stating that she or my mother had hit the car. My sister didn't hit my mother's car, and my mother didn't hit the car. The police can't arrest them in this situation; that is illegal and a type of discrimination. Some EPS officers are racist against blacks and perform illegal actions that show their racism. The young policeman harassed my mother and sister and intimidated them rather than conducting a proper investigation. Why couldn't the police officer make an appropriate investigation and charge the suspect who hit my mother's car and arrest that suspect?

- One black female from Trinidad, whose father lives in the Netherlands, is a Canadian Permanent Resident and Dutch Citizen. She has lived in Canada for 7 years and left the Netherlands 10 years ago, so her Dutch passport had expired. Normally, she should go to the Netherlands Ambassador to renew her Dutch passport in order to avoid problems. There have been many rule changes over the last few years, and she didn't know about these changes. Nobody told her that there is Dutch ambassador here in Canada. Her passport had expired for 10 years. She missed her family, and her parents had died from cancer a long time ago. When she came back to Holland in 2014, the Dutch government should have given her a chance or warning without causing complications or discriminating against her. The Dutch employees at the airport took her passport and citizenship away from her. This female shouldn't have lost her citizenship and been deported from Holland to Trinidad because she had been away from Holland for a long time. She had never committed any crime in the Netherlands or in Canada. She shouldn't have had the government take her citizenship away and deport her. These actions were illegal and considered discrimination simply because she left a country a long time ago; it doesn't make any sense. Although she was upset with the airport staff, she wasn't aggressive or threatening and she didn't have any weapon. Why couldn't the airport solve the problem instead of complicating her situation and calling police when she was upset? Her father knew that she had come to visit him and he was on his way to the airport. Although it took him a while before he came to pick up her from the Dutch National Airport, the staff kept harassing her while she politely explained the situation to them; however, they still didn't listen to her simply because she was black. When the police showed up, they didn't ask about the problem. Because she was black and she didn't have citizenship in Holland, the police brutally pushed her on the floor and shot her 36 times, killing her. Five policemen and one policewoman were charged and lost their jobs because their actions constituted racism, a criminal offense. Although the Dutch government and airport employees were found guilty, the six police officers were guiltier in the death of a 36 year-old black female. Her father was very upset because the government had deported her and took away her citizenship; these actions were immoral, discriminatory, and against the law. She had never committed any crime and had no criminal records in the Netherlands or in Canada. In the UK, a black male had the same issue with discrimination when he came from Canada to UK. Many people were upset with the government and police brutality. That black lady should have had a chance to renew her Dutch citizenship at any time without any offenses being committed against her. Finally, the police were caught on camera, charged, and lost their jobs.

- I still respect Canada's law concerning the new dual citizenship, which applies to not only people born in Canada but also to people with one Canadian parent or spouse. My opposition to any law does not mean that I'm against the law or disagree with the government. For example, if someone has European or Asian citizenship along with Canadian citizenship, they should be able to keep their dual citizenship without having to choose one and lose the other citizenship. The government can't force people to give up one of their citizenships. This action constitutes discrimination that will violate the law and cause more threats and crime, which will occur when civilians become very upset. We don't want unrest among the citizens because of a bad law. Sometimes the government doesn't realize that their laws are ineffective; however, there are consequences for bad laws. People that break the law put themselves at risk and have no one to blame but themselves. It doesn't matter if you were born Canadian or not, it doesn't matter if you are half-Canadian or not, it doesn't matter if you have a Canadian spouse or Canadian citizenship and it doesn't matter where you are from. You should still be able to keep both of your 2 or 3 dual citizenships as long you are not a criminal or lawbreaker. You should make sure that you follow the law without causing problems. Many good immigrants are important in this country, and they shouldn't be deported from Canada because deportation without reason is discrimination. Deportation should only apply for people who have broken the law and committed very serious crimes but never for innocent immigrants. The government should treat people with respect if people obey the law and avoid problems. I'm not talking about politics because they are not my business. I still respect the government and I don't have a problem with the government; I just speak the full truth. The government and police should stop calling people Illegal Immigrants; people don't want hear that term because it insults them and makes people angry.

- Simon, a Congolese guy, was detained by the police in Belgium National Airport because he had $10,000 cash in his hand. Simon wasn't a criminal and had no weapon with him. He hadn't done anything wrong nor was he aggressive. He tried to respectfully tell the police about the situation three times, but the police still did not understand and continued harassing him. The police stereotyped Simon by claiming that, "he's trying to claim to be a refuge or immigrant in Belgium;" however, it wasn't true. Simon came to Belgium as a tourist like most people from another any country. Simon had come to visit his family and shop before going back to his country; he spent only two months in Brussels. Why did the police continue to harass him simply because he was black? The police's actions constituted discrimination and racism. Simon tried to obtain help from a lawyer who could defend him against his deportation from Belgium to Congo. Although he spent money, the lawyer didn't do anything and refused to help without giving him his money back. The police and government illegally forced him to deport him from Belgium; basically, the lawyer just wanted his money without helping him, which was also illegal. The government, police, and lawyer were all wrong and against him. They shouldn't kick him out of the country. Simon became very upset that he had been arrested illegally. After his deportation, he became sick and died because the police were racist against him. They had poisoned him before his deportation in June 2015. Later, the police were caught on camera and charged afterwards. The policemen and policewomen involved in the incident lost their jobs and were sentenced to life in prison. The other immigrants were upset and protested against the police, government and lawyers for mistreating people, especially in the case of immigrants being deported and killed. Some people had threatened the police, while other people had attacked the police, killed them silently, and vandalized their offices. The lawyers, governments, and police are very corrupt, which explains why people become angry with them. Although the civilians committed illegal actions, the government and police are guilty of Simon's death. The lawyer was an accomplice together with police and government in his death.

- In Vancouver International Airport in October 2007, a Polish man named Robert Dziekanski was victimized by police brutality. Before Robert came to Canada, his mother advised him to go to the Canadian embassy in Poland. Robert wanted to come to Canada for visiting his mother as well as for studying and building his life in Canada. The embassy approved Robert and deemed him acceptable to come to Canada. When Robert arrived in Canada, the airport employees started to question him and detained him as if he had arrived illegally in Canada although he had only come to visit his mother. The airport staff should have gotten him an interpreter who could speak Polish, since Robert couldn't speak or understand English. They tried to deport him from Canada to Poland, but they shouldn't have done that because deportation of innocent immigrants is a type of discrimination and against the law. The airport employee could have solved the problem himself; however, he chose to call the police instead. Robert was not mentally unstable, aggressive, or criminal, nor did he possess any weapon. He didn't grab the TV or table to throw at the window, which the reports claimed. Robert Dziekanski wasn't at fault while the employees of the Vancouver Airport made him angry. Someone had called the police, and when the police showed up at the Vancouver Airport, they didn't deal with the problem properly or ask Robert about the situation. The police thought that Tasers couldn't kill him, but Tasers do kill people. Once the black office grabbed his Taser and used it on Robert, three other officers tried to arrest him. Another Hispanic officer jumped on Robert and broke his neck. The black officer kept Tasering until Robert died from a heart attack. There were 4 RCMP that were responsible for killing Robert. They provided a false testimony and lied; one young guy was a good witness who saw everything and filmed the incident in silence. The Polish community were upset with the 4 officers because they arrested him illegally and murdered him although he was innocent. His mother felt sad and extremely angry with the RMCP. Later, four policemen were charged, lost their jobs, and went to prison. The four policemen are 100% guilty; they were caught on camera. Even though this incident is over, more police officers will commit illegal actions and murder innocent citizens; however, every police officer will still be caught on camera and lose his/her job. I don't want to make generalizations about the police; some officers are good, but many officers are bad police. Black police officers named Kwesi Millington, Benjamin (Monty) Robinson, Bill Bentley, and Gerry Rundel were the officers that committed crime against Robert. The police should use Tasers correctly: for subduing rather than killing people. Officers that use Tasers for harming people will lose their jobs because it is illegal. In the UK, someone called the police about a black man that had a gun. However, the black man did not have a gun; he only had a toy that he bought for his son. When the police arrived in the train, the police asked the black man to show him the toy. The black man obeyed the officer; even the police weren't entirely sure if they could check if it was a real gun or not for public safety and their own safety. The black guy wasn't aggressive and he didn't threaten officer. However, the officers pointed a gun at him, and one officer had grabbed a Taser and Tasered the black man nine times until he died from a heart attack. This action was wrong; the people were upset. Later, the police officer was caught on camera and lost his job because his actions were racist act and he shouldn't kill a black male in a train. A bad officer had just killed him for fun. After, there was a protest against the police in the UK. This incident had occurred in a train from London to Liverpool in 2009. In the U.S., another policeman grabbed a gun and shot a black guy who had defend himself during a fight against the police, who had started the fight and harassed the black man. The young, racist policeman was caught and lost his job for murdering an innocent young black man with a gun by shooting him 7 times in Alabama.

- In Poland, two police officers stopped a mentally unstable man on the street that had not started harassing or fighting with police but had shown respect to the police. That man had no real weapon and was only holding a stick. However, a male and female police officers pulled out their guns and started to shoot him. Two seconds later, the man ran from the police officers, who chased him, stopped him, and beat him with their sticks. Rather than arresting the man, they continued to shoot at him and nearly killed him. I can understand why the police would pull a gun out if the homeless man had a gun. However, he didn't have a gun, so the police did not need to pull out their guns and shoot the man. Their behaviour was wrong; they shouldn't continually shoot the man. The officers' behaviour was against the law. They were caught on camera, which led to them getting in trouble and facing charges. If the homeless man had died, the police officers would face more serious consequences and go to prison forever. Although the man is still alive, he has lost the use of his legs. Both the two officers and the homeless man are at fault.

Why are people angry at the government?

Civilians can become upset if the government makes bad laws. Here is a list of some laws and actions that can make citizens upset:

- Discriminating against people
- Mistreating innocent citizens
- Taking people's human rights away
- Preventing people from getting dual citizenships and taking them away
- Deporting innocent immigrants from one country to another
- Detaining people
- Repressing innocent immigrants

These laws make citizens angry, which causes them to protest and rebel against the government, leading to violations, threats, vandalism, murder, and criminal activity. By making bad laws, the government puts themselves at risk. Since we don't want increased crime, the government should avoid making bad laws, such as deporting immigrants, which shows discrimination and is against the law. Even if people break the law and receive forgiveness, they should learn their lesson and never break the law again. If one civilian breaks the law, it will affect many other innocent civilians. The government needs to warn people, change laws, or solve miscommunication problems. For these reasons, many civilians become angry with the government. The government can't generalize people; they need to focus on the specific person who broke the law rather than stereotyping against innocent people. People should always follow and respect the law in order to avoid causing problems for themselves and other innocent people. That's why I warn people to never break the law because it leads to problems for many people.

Why are people angry at the police?

In addition to the government, the police also make civilians angry. While most police officers are good people, some of them are bad. Many police are wrong because they refuse to stop mistreating civilians. The police mistreat people in the following ways:

- Abuse their power
- Act aggressively and brutal towards people
- Shoot and kill people all the time
- Use dangerous Tasers to kills people
- Provoke people into fights
- Assault or beat people

- Rape, assault, and beat women
- Engage in sexual encounters and statutory rape with minors
- Steal people's wives and cheat on their own spouses
- Yell at people
- Exercise discrimination and racism against people
- Cover their face with masks and use gloves to commit crimes against civilians

For these reasons, civilians become angry with the police, especially when they act inappropriately and abuse their power. When the police break the law, they will lose their jobs without suspended pay. If the police continue their behaviour, they put themselves at risk, because many other people will want to kill them. Those people may be bigger and stronger than the police officers, so the police will experience more difficulty in attacking, shooting or killing them. For the police, it is easier to use force against the other people, but this behaviour represents an abuse of their power. Some stronger men may revenge, use threats, or commit violation against the police, and some people will even shoot or kill the police secretly. In some cases, the police may not have proof for the murders against them. Because they will find no evidence, they will have more difficulty in justifying laying charges because many police still mistreat people as well as shoot and kill innocent people. That will be the police's fault rather than the fault of the civilians. Police officers are always in the news for performing illegal actions, mistreating people, attacking people, or killing innocent civilians. Sometimes, an entire group of police officers help their co-worker by conspiring with one another for committing illegal actions or killing someone. However, conspiracy is still against the law and people still become angry with the police for these actions. Bad police officers cause members of society to create negative generalizations and stereotypes against the police. In turn, these stereotypes affect innocent police officers, because protesters will not discriminate against good police and bad police. Civilians will become confused about the difference between normal and abnormal police behaviour, and many people will treat the good police officers in a negative way. While many police deserve negative things to happen to them, they shouldn't put themselves at risk by their illegal actions of mistreating and killing people, making civilians upset and motivating them to protest. For these reasons, civilians get upset and want to avenge the police. Many police don't consider the possibility of civilians seeking revenge because they are blinded by their power or authority. When the civilians attack the police, the police can't entirely blame the civilians for their protest.

Many police don't know how to solve problems or calm down and take it easy. They don't want to listen to citizens' explanation of situations; they have little patience and control. Sometimes, I get very upset with the police. The police make false statements because they believe that people lack the intelligence to challenge their authority. Some police believe that by treating people with respect, they aren't doing their job properly. However, police should treat people with respect because people will treat them back with respect. By treating people with respect, the police are doing their job by earning respect from citizens, which, in turn, encourages citizens to follow the law. When police mistreat and murder people, they are doing a poor job. Most people won't trust bad police because they have forever lost the respect of the civilians. I do not have any membership in a gang, and I don't send people to attack or kill officers nor have I planned for the death of any police. Although some officers deserve their own death, I have nothing to do with police deaths. In fact, I often become very upset when innocent police officers die. I'm not a criminal; I have never had a problem with the police. I still respect the police because I don't want to hurt their feelings or make them upset. I am not against any particular officer and I have no problem with them. They can't hold anything against me because they don't have a proof or evidence. I'm not a criminal person, so I can't be treated as if I am a criminal. Police that abuse citizens will put themselves at risk as an officer when try to attack innocent people. If a police officer attacked me for no reason, I will use my own force to defend myself and other people will become angry with the officer. In fact, some people may secretly attack the officer because they put themselves at risk by abusing innocent citizens. If an officer gets attacked by the public for mistreating citizens, they have no one to blame or accuse except for themselves. I speak full the truth, and people can't hide the truth forever. Jesus Christ was hated by people because he spoke the full truth; similarly, some people may hate me because I am speaking the truth. That's why I am a discipline of Jesus Christ although I'm Protestant. So I can't threaten or violate or make negative comments against the police. I try not to make generalizations about police officers. My only question is why do some people murder innocent officers rather than avenging the specific officer who did something wrong?

How do people apply for and become a police officer?

Before you can become a police officer, you need your high school diploma as well as a college or university degree. In addition, you need to become a citizen of the country in which you wish to work and you need a criminal record check. If you have a criminal record, you can't become an officer. The police chief hires only people who have no criminal record. If a criminal person became a police officer, people will fear that the person may commit more crimes and even murder or kill innocent people. In turn, this will cause people to generalize other innocent police officers, leading protesters to kill innocent police officers. This rebellion may cause a war because of a criminal who became a police officer. The police chief can't hire a criminal person because it will pose a major danger to society.

Regular citizens who have no criminal record may want to work with the government because they want to preserve their own chance for the future. These people apply and get a better job, especially with the government or police force. Some people who have a good education, a good job, and no criminal record usually receive respect from other people. Many of these people apply for a police job and they will get the job ahead of people who have worked for 6, 7 or even 10 years. Once people get hired for a police job, they start to take advantage of the fact that police officers have a lot of power and authority. A lot of people in police jobs exploit the power and authority just to insult other people, to commit a criminal activity, or to kill other people, especially innocent people. Some innocent people fail to receive their due justice while the new employees of police departments continue to commit more criminal activities and more murder. These actions are against the law; these officers should get caught on camera and lose their jobs because their abuse of power is not fair to other people. For these reasons, citizens become angry and revenge them as well as generalize against the police. Threats against the police also affect innocent officers.

Innocent police can die because other citizens may kill them as a result of generalizing against all police. Citizens should revenge and kill bad police because these officers deserve their own death and put themselves at risk by mistreating and kill innocent citizens, which is illegal. The citizens shouldn't kill the innocent police officers if these officers have never committed crimes or killed people. Citizens, please do not kill the police or others citizens because this behaviour is illegal and makes people upset. Even if some police officers experience stress, they can't blame, mistreat, or murder citizens because police will lose their jobs while making citizens angry and prone to revenge. There is zero tolerance for this police behaviour. Some police form gangs similar to civilians, encouraging citizens to make negative generalizations about the police, which ultimately affect society and innocent officers. The American police seem to be the most brutal police in the world, as there are always negative news stories about these officers via the Internet, TV, and radio. I don't understand why Canadian Police want to imiate American police in terms of their brutality.

What is the best that we can do to stop police brutality, and how can we do that in order to achieve a better solution in society?

If you see the police committing a wrong action, you can film them without their knowledge. You need to ensure that they can't see you or know that you are filming them in order to avoid problems. Regardless of where you live in the world, make sure that your cellphone camera works properly so that you can film someone. Before you film the police, you have to adjust your camera cellphone and practice filming so that you avoid mistakes. You need to make sure that you can film someone properly and get a clear image of that person. When you film any person, suspect, terrorist, criminal, drug dealer, mafia, governor, military person, murderer, gang member, and police officer, you need to make sure that you don't get caught. People should continue film them because we don't trust them anymore. By catching criminals and police on camera, people will have proof, which will cause the police to lose their jobs and go to prison for life. Regardless of whether police officers are committing crimes in public or undercover, the police officers will eventually get caught for performing for their illegal actions and they will still lose their jobs. Many of the police can't be trusted except for good police. That's why we need to film suspects, terrorists, criminals, drug dealers, mafia members, governors, military people, murderers, gang members, and brutal police without their awareness. They won't be able to stop their illegal actions and they will deny and give false claims of self-defence in order to continue committing their crimes and murdering innocent people. That's why we will never stop filming them, because the public can't trust them anymore and the public feels unsafe and threatened with violations by these people. Although it is a democratic country, people fear for their lives. However, if people film the police and other criminals, they will get caught, lose their jobs, and spend life in prison.

In order to allow people to film the police, we need technology to be cheaper, so that everyone can afford it. That way, everybody can purchase cheaper silent small web cameras that can film the whole house and can connect to the computer, so that people can open and close their computer and still film. Then, people can keep the image so that other people can see the film. By being able to capture and film the whole house, people can protect themselves against any criminal, terrorist, thief, drug dealer, mafia, governor, military person, murderer, gang member and brutal police brutal officer. All of these criminals will get caught and charged if they have done something wrong to you, especially since it's illegal to break and enter into someone's house. Police officers or civilians aren't allowed to violate, threaten, and use brutality or force to enter someone's house even if your refuse to allow them to enter. You can't trust people because they can hurt your or even murder you when they are in your house. You are right to refuse their entry and to speak the truth about this type of situation. It's worse when the police think that they can stop you from permitting their entry into your house. It doesn't matter what the police do, but they will still get caught and charged, and the public will become upset with the police. In addition, the police cannot force you to keep secrets or tell the truth. For this reason, if we all silently film them, we can publish more videos on the Internet and YouTube as well as national and international TV channels like BBC and Global News. That's how the police will get caught on camera, lose their jobs, and go to prison for life. These consequences will their own fault, which is why we need to stop police brutality. Like others, we can film police brutality and publish videos on the Internet and YouTube as well as on BBC and Global News. Since we have seen these videos before, we plan to film police brutality and publish more videos on public media in order to permanently stop police brutality.

- In Vancouver, BC, on June 21, 2015, Raymond, a black guy, had a nice house and car. He was a very nice guy and he had his own construction business. He had never committed any crime in

Canada. Raymond had a very beautiful wife from Venezuela and two young daughters, but the two daughters lived with their grandmother from their father's side. Raymond was alone with his wife when the city police of Vancouver came to his door and knocked. Raymond opened the door and responded very nicely and respectfully to the police. Within two minutes, the officer asked him, "Can I come in your place please?" Raymond responded, "Yes, come in." When the officer stepped inside, he closed the door. He wondered what was going on, but the police didn't want tell specific details or inform Raymond about the problem. The neighbours were witnesses and heard everything that the police said and did that night. Raymond was with his wife when the police started to change the story and lied in order to detain him for suspicion of theft. Five seconds later, the police started to brutalize him. The police were jealous of him because had a nice house and beautiful Spanish wife. They claimed that he stole a car and house; however, he showed the police his receipt from the car purchase and the mortgage papers from his house. The police still did not believe him even when his wife was trying to explain that he bought the car and house. The police officer still continued to harass and brutalize him. The policeman grabbed a gun and shot Raymond 5 times and Tasered him twice. As a result, he died in front of his wife. Then, a policeman named Dave Collins grab Raymond's wife and sexually assaulted her. The officer stripped her naked and raped her because she was a very attractive woman. As a result, he made her pregnant. The city of Vancouver was so mad at the police officer. Two weeks later, Dave Collins was charged and lost his job. Now he's in prison and will have a life sentence life because he was a real racist, that committed a criminal offense.

In Louisiana USA, a young girl filmed a policeman in United Station. The policeman had no clue that the young lady behind him was filming him and publishing the video on public media. The policeman was caught and lost his job for his illegal action in public. In this case, because called the police about a homeless man and told the officer that the homeless man had done something wrong; however, the homeless man was innocent. The policeman, named Carlos Pedro Perez, showed up to the station, which was right. However, rather than trying to solve the problem, the police officer had shown brutality by beating and arresting the homeless man. Carlos claimed that he heard the homeless man was brutal, aggressive, or crazy; however, the officer had no proof or evidence. Police officers can't use aggression unless the civilian starts to show aggression towards them. In this case, the older, white homeless man didn't even touch, hit or attack Carlos. Why did the officer have to act like that towards against him, grabbing him, pushing him, throwing him on the floor, and starting to hit and kick him? Then, the officer arrested him for unreasonable behaviour. Carlos lied, claiming that the homeless man swore at him and touched him; however, this was not true. Rather, the officer started to swear, hit him, and ask stupid questions to the homeless man. Two weeks later, Carlos was charged and suspended. After his suspension, he repeated the same problem with another person and received a warning and one more chance, but the police officer didn't listen and didn't care. When he repeated his brutality again, he was caught on camera for his illegal action in public, and two weeks later, he lost his job. When police officers get caught on camera, they can't deny, lie, or give false claim about self-defence. So the officer can't be right!

How can you educate citizens how to obey and respect authorities?

I can tell the citizens to avoid overreacting with the police in the case of minor problems. This way, people can avoid problems with the police officers. Some of the behaviours to avoid include the following:

- Arguing with or resisting the police officer
- Screaming or using swear words with the police officer
- Touching or hitting police officers
- Displaying rudeness or refusing the answer their question
- Closing the window or door of your car or your house if they ask you.

In most cases, it depends on the individual officer. Some police may react very badly to civilian rudeness. For example, they may hurt, beat, attack or even murder you. This reaction is against the law; the officer can get charged, lose their jobs and go to prison for a life sentence. In this case, they could have just arrested you or used their Taser to calm you down. Some of these incidents are our fault rather than that of the police. Some police officers try to perform their job properly, and in some cases they don't mean to insult us. However, it's better for people to obey the police officers as authorities if people don't want problems because you shouldn't put your own life at risk. You should never use weapons in front of the police because you will become guiltier. So don't be silly and act this way.

What do you want from people?

- I want you to respect the police officers and obey them
- I want the police to respect the citizens if the citizens respect them
- I want you to answer the police officer's questions only if they ask you. If you don't know how to answer the question, then you should be OK as long as you aren't a criminal
- I want you to show the police your ID, permit status, or driver's license if they ask you. However, don't show them your ID if they didn't ask for it.
- You ask the police questions only when you don't understand something so they can explain to you. Then, you should listen carefully and pay attention
- Be very polite and respectful with police and talk nicely to them in order to avoid problems and don't put yourself at risk. I guarantee that police brutality won't continue to exist in the future anymore and will never return.
- Because police brutality can ruin their reputation forever and give them criminal records, we need to work on how to stop police brutality and change citizens' behavior with the police

I tried to work on reducing police brutality as well as other ways to change the world. However, I'm not the only one who's working on these issues. I don't have real power to change the world, and these issues aren't necessarily my business; I just speak the full truth. I don't want to criticize the government or politics because those issues aren't my business. I don't have a problem with the government or the police. I still respect both of these authority figures because I'm not going to put my life at risk. All I want is for people to respect the police and the government as well as obey the law. I'm still working on to put peace and more new dialogs and new technologies. Nobody has the right to stop someone from speaking the truth, but I have limits for speaking the truth in order to avoid problems. The full truth that I speak focuses only on solving major problems rather than minor problems, so I don't need to speak the full truth for those problems. People that know me realize that I'm a very nice guy and I don't want to hurt anybody feelings. God sent me to help you guys and solve your problems.

Before June 15, 2015, I had to write all of my all exams, and I passed my CST for demolition construction. This course explains me everything about demolition construction. Of course, I have to work efficiently without being lazy or working too slowly; however, I can't rush because if I get into an accident at a regular construction or demolition site, nobody, including the government or even my employer, will pay for my accident. That's why I avoid problems and accidents. Safety and protection is the most important for your body and your health. People can't get hurt or have back pain because they have to work safety and properly instead of rushing. People should ask others to help them or they can use temporary employees for help, so the job can be done as quickly as possible without anyone getting injured. While some employers are good, other employers are bad. Many of the employers perform illegal actions against their employees by not teaching employees about proper safety protection. People can hold the employee responsible for accidents, but employers have a greater responsibility because they can't make excuses for unreasonably firing people unreasonable unless the employee committed real offense or someone disobeyed the rules of the company. When I started work at my new job with the temp agency, it was on June 15, 2015. The company knew that I was a hard worker like everybody else; I was punctual and I respected the rules and always showed up on time without making excuses. If I had an issue, I would tell the supervisor; however, I had no issues with the job and everything was good. I worked for one week, and then the office called to let me know that the company didn't need me anymore. I asked, "Why? What's going on? Did the supervisor or someone complain about me? There must be some issue." The following Monday, I found out that the supervisor had a problem with me but he didn't want to tell me the truth. I didn't resist or argue with him because I didn't want a problem. I didn't want to ruin my reputation; otherwise, the agency wouldn't give me any more jobs. I was disappointed that I lost my job, as my contract was initially for one year. I didn't want to make an issue at all or complain. I forgot about this problem and let it go because I realized that this is not my problem anymore and now I'm fine. I later found out that I wasn't the only person replaced, as 4 or 5 of co-workers were also let go. I found out that the company discriminates against black people, as they fire only black people rather than white people. I'm not going to make an issue about this problem; I will let God forgive them despite the fact that this discrimination wasn't right. This country has a lot of discrimination and some people get upset about it. When 3 Ethiopian guys replaced us a week after, they also lost their jobs, and white, Hispanic, and Arab guys were hired. I'm not jealous or complaining about that; it's their good luck and blessing. My faith in God will allow me to get a better future job than work in a Demolition Construction Company. This not my first time working in construction, demolition construction, landscaping, or warehouse companies, because I have experience in these jobs. I have performed this type of work before with other temp agencies. There is a lot of dust in Demolition Construction, so you have care for and change masks to keep your breath clean and healthy in order to avoid diseases and death because the air has lots of dangerous chemicals with toxins. It's very important to know these things for your safety and security. Even if you wear a mask all day but you still can't breathe properly, you need to get a permanent mask rather than a temporary mask.

A man named Dylann Roof entered a black church in an African American community and committed violations and threats against black people in the church. He shot 9 black members of the Emmanuel AME Church in Charleston, South Carolina and died. These events happened on his birthday when he had just turned 21 years old. I don't think he had any right to have protection or equal treatment. Why do white American citizens always make negative comments about black citizens and lie? The 9 black people in the congregation of the Emmanuel AME Church in Charleston were innocent. I don't think that Dylann he had a mental illness; he was just a racist and just killed the church members because of their skin color. People shouldn't say that a black organization tried to make him look guilty. No! Dylann Roof is 100% guilty and he deserves to go to prison. It seems to me that a white organization colluded with Dylann Roof to kill 9 black people because of the money. It still represents a racist action and makes people angrier. Why did the church members ask forgiveness for the murderer? They said: "let God forgive you to let you go and his mercy to you." It doesn't make any sense because Dylann should have a life sentence in prison for what he did. He knew he committed racism and murder; he was very wrong and broke the law because of his evil nature rather than a mental illness. God forgives everything but accepts that people knew it was wrong. So there's no excuse. Please don't play games with God because no one is better than God. God is better than all of us because he created everything in this earth. He respects us and we should respect him more. I try not to discriminate against or generalise white people; I just speak the truth about what bothers me and hurts my feelings, I have many white friends myself, so how can I be racist? I'm not a racist.

www.ingramcontent.com/pod-product-compliance
Lightning Source LLC
Chambersburg PA
CBHW07085812O626
46546CB00001B/52